P9-CRJ-875

# THE GOOD FIGHT

ALSO BY SENATOR HARRY REID

*Searchlight: The Camp That Didn't Fail*

# HARD LESSONS FROM
# SEARCHLIGHT TO WASHINGTON

# THE
# GOOD FIGHT

SENATOR HARRY REID
WITH MARK WARREN

G. P. PUTNAM'S SONS
*New York*

S

PUTNAM

G. P. PUTNAM'S SONS
*Publishers Since 1838*
Published by the Penguin Group
Penguin Group (USA) Inc., 375 Hudson Street, New York, New York 10014, USA  •  Penguin Group (Canada), 90 Eglinton Avenue East, Suite 700, Toronto, Ontario M4P 2Y3, Canada (a division of Pearson Canada Inc.)  •  Penguin Books Ltd, 80 Strand, London WC2R 0RL, England  •  Penguin Ireland, 25 St Stephen's Green, Dublin 2, Ireland (a division of Penguin Books Ltd)  •  Penguin Group (Australia), 250 Camberwell Road, Camberwell, Victoria 3124, Australia (a division of Pearson Australia Group Pty Ltd)  •  Penguin Books India Pvt Ltd, 11 Community Centre, Panchsheel Park, New Delhi—110 017, India  •  Penguin Group (NZ), 67 Apollo Drive, Rosedale, North Shore 0632, New Zealand (a division of Pearson New Zealand Ltd)  •  Penguin Books (South Africa) (Pty) Ltd, 24 Sturdee Avenue, Rosebank, Johannesburg 2196, South Africa

Penguin Books Ltd, Registered Offices: 80 Strand, London WC2R 0RL, England

Library of Congress Cataloging-in-Publication Data

Reid, Harry, 1939–
    The good fight : hard lessons from Searchlight to Washington / Senator Harry Reid ; with Mark Warren.
        p.        cm.
    ISBN 978-0-399-15499-7
    1. Reid, Harry, 1939–    2. Legislators—United States—Biography.    3. United States. Congress. Senate.—Biography.    4. United States—Politics and government—2001–    5. United States—Politics and government—20th century.    6. Searchlight (Nev.)—History.    7. Searchlight (Nev.)—Biography.    I. Warren, Mark (Mark E.)    II. Title.
    E840.8.R447A3        2008                    2008007924
    328.73092—dc22
    [B]

Printed in the United States of America
10   9   8   7   6   5   4   3   2   1

BOOK DESIGN BY MARYSARAH QUINN

I dedicate this book to Marine Private O'Callaghan . . . Air Force Sergeant O'Callaghan . . . Army Sergeant O'Callaghan . . . Governor O'Callaghan, and to my friend, Mike, an inspiration to me in his life's example, and still an inspiration in death.

And to Susan McCue, a talented and dedicated young woman on whom I've relied for two decades, and from whom the idea for this book came.

# CONTENTS

*Preface*  xi

1.  A MEETING AT THE WHITE HOUSE  *1*

2.  SEARCHLIGHT  *23*

3.  THE MINORITY  *57*

4.  THE OUTSIDE WORLD  *99*

5.  SOCIAL INSECURITY  *135*

6.  THE CASES NOBODY WOULD TAKE  *155*

7.  THE NUCLEAR OPTION  *195*

8.  THE BEST DAY, THE WORST DAY, AND THE MOB  *219*

9.  THE PAST MEETS THE PRESENT  *273*

10.  THE FUTURE  *287*

*Acknowledgments*  *292*

# PREFACE

THIS STORY begins at the end.

It begins at the end of a presidency that has tested our values, compromised our Constitution, and usurped our rights as Americans.

At the end of an era of crippling partisan rancor, during which the President's political opponents were branded as insufficiently patriotic.

At the end of a time in which we suffered a vicious and unprovoked attack on our soil and responded with force, sometimes in a focused and just way, sometimes not.

At the end of a period in our history in which diplomacy was allowed to fail as a first resort in deference to military action, and our intelligence-gathering was politicized to a stunning degree, as was war itself.

At the end of an era in which the White House looked on haplessly as Americans in a great American city cried for help from rooftops and their cries went seemingly unheard and the White House seemed not to understand what to do.

At the end of a period of profligate government spending in a budget of misplaced priorities by a White House that once billed itself as conservative with the people's money.

This story begins at the end of all of these things. And this list could go on.

My purpose in this book is to tell you something of who I am, and how I came to be the Senate Majority Leader at such a time in our history. My path to the present was as circuitous and turbulent and unique as it was unlikely. I come from a flyspeck on the map called Searchlight in remote southern Nevada, grew up during the war, and I don't mean this as a boast, but people who come from where I come from generally do not end up in the United States Senate. And in truth, where I've ended up was the furthest thing from my mind as I was getting started.

The saying goes that to look forward, you must look back. As you read, you'll find that the chapters alternate between the past and the present, because I believe that the two can be mutually illuminating. I am immensely proud of my hometown and of my home state. And I am equally proud of the work I've had the pleasure and privilege of doing in Washington, D.C., for the past twenty-five years. If I can do nothing more here than explain those two places—Searchlight and Washington—to each other just a little bit, then I will have done something.

Looking back is something I've not often done, and it doesn't come very naturally or easily to me. Not all is sweetness and light in my past, and there have been more than a few scars, but I suppose that holds true for everyone.

H.R.
Searchlight, Nevada
February 2008

# ONE

# A MEETING AT
# THE WHITE HOUSE

I AM NOT A PACIFIST. War is bad in every instance, but sometimes reasonable people are left with no other choice. Such a time
came in early 1991, during the administration of George Herbert
Walker Bush, when Iraqi dictator Saddam Hussein invaded the
neighboring nation of Kuwait with his massive army and was poised
to threaten the entire Arabian peninsula and the largest oil reserves
in the world. President Bush had been deliberate in his response to
Hussein's aggression, properly working all the diplomatic angles,
masterfully assembling a vast coalition to oppose Hussein, including
the full array of his Middle East neighbors, and making it clear to all
that if Hussein did not withdraw his forces back to Iraq, the civilized
nations of the world would destroy his army and remove him from
Kuwait. Hundreds of thousands of soldiers and Marines and troops
from dozens of countries had been staging in Saudi Arabia for
months. U.S. Navy carriers steamed into the Persian Gulf, the Indian

Ocean, and the eastern Mediterranean. Hussein would not listen. War seemed inevitable.

On the afternoon of January 12, 1991, during my first term in the Senate, I was in the cloakroom, about to walk onto the Senate floor to give a speech about the coming war, when the phone rang and the clerk who answered it said, "Senator, it's the President. He wants to talk to you." He was calling to lobby me to support the impending military action. I got on the phone and said, "Mr. President, you don't need to waste any time with me. I'm about to become the first Democrat to endorse this in the Senate, but you've got to give me your word that you're going to do it. Tell me that you're not going to spend weeks making up your mind."

"No, I won't do that," the President said. "I'm going to do something quickly."

So I went to the floor and gave my speech supporting the President. Not many Democrats took this position, but after I spoke, a number did follow suit—Richard Bryan, my colleague from Nevada, Al Gore of Tennessee, Bob Graham from Florida—and there were enough of us to give the President majority support in the Senate. The resolution passed 52 to 47. And President Bush was as good as his word. Three days after he signed the resolution, I was in my car on the way home when the bombing started. It was on the radio.

My point in telling this story is not to adjudicate whether or not the first Gulf War was worthwhile—I believe it was—but rather to establish that I have no natural animus to Presidents named George Bush. I admire the current President's father deeply, and believe that he is a very decent man who has lived his life for his country.

I came to the Senate two years before he was elected President. My first briefing on the first President Bush came in the fall of 1988, just after the election. Senator Lloyd Bentsen, who had been the

Democratic Vice Presidential nominee that year—on the ticket, with Massachusetts governor Michael Dukakis, that had just lost to Bush—nonetheless pulled me aside one day to reassure me that Bush was a great man and would make a good President. "You'll love him," Bentsen told me. "He's the nicest guy, very pragmatic. No one's been better prepared to be President than him. He's been a member of Congress, head of the Republican National Committee, head of the CIA, ambassador to the United Nations, ambassador to China, Vice President." Bentsen went on and on effusively about what a quality man President-elect Bush was. Then he paused and said, "But watch out for his wife; she's a bitch."

I have never had anything against Mrs. Bush, but guided by Bentsen's crude advice, I've always said that our forty-third President is more his mother than his dad. I have made no secret of my antipathy toward the second President Bush, nor have I hidden my opinion of the job he has done. I believe that the current President is an ideologue who has done incalculable damage to the government, reputation, and moral standing of the United States of America. His vaunted "CEO presidency" has instead been incompetent in the face of grave challenge at home and abroad, when we can least afford incompetence.

It is only fair, I suppose, to say that the feelings may be mutual. That's almost a certainty if a meeting at the White House in the spring of 2007 is any indication.

There's an old expression among lawyers that if you've got the law on your side, pound the law; if you've got the facts on your side, pound the facts; if you've got neither, pound the table. On this day, President Bush was pounding the table.

It was the afternoon of April 18, 2007. The mood in the Cabinet Room of the White House was somber, and the President seemed rather unhappy. His face was red, and on it he wore an expression that made him look impatient and spoiled. The room was quiet save for his taut voice. "If you think this is about my personal legacy, you're *wrong,*" he told me sharply. "I strongly reject that. You don't know what motivates me." I sat to the President's left, Speaker Pelosi to his right. Directly across from him, his hands impassively folded on the table, Vice President Cheney slumped in his chair, silent. The delicate china teacups and sugar bowls with their little silver spoons that were spread out on the table seemed out of place, as if they had been left behind from a more pleasant occasion.

The Speaker and I had come to the White House to talk about bringing the war in Iraq to a responsible end. A few days earlier, the President had accepted our invitation to meet and discuss the collision course that the Congress and the White House were on over the President's war policy. This would be the first negotiating session that the White House had ever deigned to convene with Democrats, but I was not hopeful it would yield any meaningful results. Just the day before, the President had announced that while he had agreed to the meeting, he had no intention of negotiating. Given the President that I had come to know, this pronouncement was not surprising. The contempt that he and the Vice President have for the American system of checks and balances as enshrined in the Constitution was, by this afternoon at the White House, well known.

The House and Senate had each just passed a supplemental appropriations bill to finance the war efforts in Iraq and Afghanistan through September 2007. But this bill was different from any other defense appropriations bill passed since the war began. The Congress was now in Democratic hands, and unlike the unquestioning rubber stamp that President Bush had received from the Republican Congress for most of his presidency, the new Congress was asserting its responsibility as a coequal branch of the government for the first time this century. The war was not going well. Just a couple of months before, the bipartisan Iraq Study Group said that "the situation in Iraq is grave and deteriorating." In the words of Republican Senator John Warner of Virginia, Iraq was "drifting sideways," which was a polite way to describe what had become a strategic catastrophe for the United States. It was well past time for the President, as Commander in Chief, to do something about it. And if he wouldn't, then the Congress had to act. Or at least try like hell.

Ever since returning to Washington in the minority, Congressional Republicans had been trying to find a way to continue blocking debate on the war while at the same time evading responsibility for the President's surge, his plan to increase troop strength and escalate the conflict. This is a very interesting trick to attempt in public. In January and February, just after the President announced his new strategy, the focus in Congress had become centered on a nonbinding resolution that hailed the troops for their service while at the same time opposing the surge for not making any sense.

It seemed that several Republicans were inclined to support such a resolution, just so that the Senate might, four years on, finally have a chance to exercise its oversight obligations and debate the war. Chuck Hagel of Nebraska, who as a soldier in Vietnam heroically saved his own brother's life, was furious at the administration's incompetent handling of postinvasion Iraq, and his sense of betrayal at the White House's fraudulent pretexts for war was palpable. I like Hagel. We disagree on a lot of things, but I think he's a principled man who would make a much better President than those who actually ran on the Republican side this year. Hagel's courage in opposing the war would end his political career. I admired the courage that it took for him to break so completely with his President and party. His opposition to the war was real, and by that I mean that he certainly wasn't just assuming some sort of negotiating position. So the Republican leader in the Senate, Mitch McConnell, would quarantine him and try to hold the rest of his caucus together. Given that it takes 60 votes to bring up a contested bill in the Senate, and the Senate is evenly split, we were going to need more than one Republican. Several were publicly wavering. And some were consistently sending signals that they were with us, but when it came time to vote, they were not. Arlen Specter of Pennsylvania is always with us when we don't need him. Lisa Murkowski of Alaska would tell me later that not voting for a Democratic troop-rest bill was the biggest mistake she'd ever made, only to then make the same mistake several more times. Richard Lugar of Indiana would talk very tough about adopting a new course in Iraq, but when it came time to vote he was as obedient as ever.

During that time, I had been talking regularly to John Warner, whom I consider to be a good friend. No one is more respected on military matters in the Senate. I think it's safe to say that privately, Senator Warner's position on the Iraq War was closer to mine than it was to the President's, and if he were to publicly say so, it would produce shock waves throughout Washington and give cover to some of his colleagues who wanted to break ranks. Behind Warner was a group of about six Republicans who were poised to do just that. The cooperation of such a group was the only way that Congress would be able to force the President to change. The war was now viewed by most Americans as a colossal mistake. Several of these senators were facing reelection next year. Would they back up their tough words with some action?

Now, this may come as a shock, but legislators can't or don't always vote the way they want to on things. And sure enough, in early February we brought the resolution to the floor, and none of them voted for it.

"You can run but you can't hide," I told my Republican colleagues on the floor after the vote. "We *are* going to debate Iraq."

It turns out that they had been told by their leader, Senator McConnell, that he was working on a deal with me, and to hang tight in the meantime. But this was not true. Because we have to organize the Senate, McConnell and I talk almost every day. No such deal was under way.

Ben Nelson, Democrat of Nebraska, came to me and told me that Warner was embarrassed by the situation. The next day I ran into Senator Warner outside my office in the Capitol. "Are we still friends?" he said, a weak smile on his face. "You're not too mad at me, are you?"

"No, no," I said. "Just do the right thing next time."

We would never get the votes to bring up the resolution.

And then, in a bizarre move just before the President's Day recess, Senators Hagel and Olympia Snowe of Maine sent me a letter just as the Senate was preparing to leave Washington for a week: We will not vote to adjourn because we want a debate on Iraq, they wrote. The pressure on them had been building, and they needed to have a vote before recess to be clean on this thing. Senate Republicans just assumed that of course the majority would vote to adjourn and get out of town, and they would have their talking point: See? There's a war on and the Democrats don't want to debate.

In the Democratic caucus, it was unanimous, all around the room. There would be no adjournment. We'd work through the long weekend. We'd give the Republicans the debate that they only pretended to want. "To hell with them," I told my members. "Let's call their bluff."

Most United States senators have plenty of money and live comfortable lives. So time is the most valuable commodity most of us have. When the Democrats took over the Senate, I announced that unlike the last Senate, this Senate would work Mondays and Fridays. With this particular group of 100, there is perhaps no more effective tool for getting agreement on the floor than playing schedules out of National Airport. So the prospect of working on Saturday during what was supposed to be a recess was grim. But so, too, was the war in Iraq.

The United States Senate would be in session during President's Day weekend, 2007. And the Republicans would again vote as a bloc against consideration of the resolution, and against debating the President's Iraq policy.

But over the next two months, the sentiment in Congress and in the country shifted. And we went from not being able to pass meaningless resolutions to actually passing—by a significant majority in the House and by a 51–47 vote in the Senate—a bill to continue funding the war that also required the President to begin a strategic redeployment from Iraq.

Before the 2006 election, we might have gotten 30 votes on such a bill. Then 40 votes, then 42. Legislating is a process, a flurry of deals. What's impossible today is possible tomorrow, and sometimes you have to grind it out. Of course, a certain amount of politics and posturing is always involved. Because we did not have the 60 votes necessary to overcome a filibuster, the White House and the Senate Republicans could have prevented us from ever bringing the bill to the floor. Instead, they made a tactical decision that a dramatic gesture was called for, and a veto fight is always more dramatic than a filibuster. So the Republicans stood aside, we passed our bill, and we were able to demonstrate to the world that a majority of the Congress agreed with the vast majority of the American public that this war was a pestilence and needed to be brought to a responsible end.

The Congress had been very clear from the beginning of the war that we would make sure that our troops had everything they needed, and we had lived up to that commitment. Under the bill just passed, Congress would continue to fund the war effort, yes, but in exchange the President would by law have to begin bringing the troops home within 120 days. All combat troops would be redeployed by May 1, 2008. Troops trained in counterterrorism, forces training Iraqi soldiers and police, and enough of a force to protect those American assets, though, would remain in the country for some time to come. President Bush had vowed a veto, saying that Congress was insisting on a "surrender date." A couple of days before the meeting, in response to a reporter's question, I had said, "We are going to go to the White House on Wednesday with confidence that truth and justice will prevail and the President will listen to us. Maybe he's so protected in that White House that he really doesn't hear what's going on on the outside. Now he will hear it. We will express to him in no uncertain terms that he is wrong in his threats to Congress." And it's true, this President is isolated in the extreme—everybody who talks to him works for him—and so as rare as it is to get an opportunity to speak to the President directly and tell him how you really feel, it is even more rare for him to hear an unvarnished opinion.

I may have been premature with my notions of truth and justice, but we were here to talk nonetheless. And I had actually not come to the White House to antagonize the President, but sometimes people just have to be told things that they don't want to hear.

In any case, he had taken offense at something I said. I had not observed protocol. One simply does not say such things to George W. Bush, who is unaccustomed to dissent of any kind.

You should know that these sorts of meetings are typically a waste of time, part of the Kabuki theater of Washington, full of niceties and platitudes and not much else. *"Thank you* so much *for seeing us today, Mr. President."* That sort of thing. Senator Robert C. Byrd of West Virginia, the dean of the Senate and perhaps the greatest historian the Congress will ever produce, has expressed his contempt for such proceedings in strong language, especially those he has experienced during this presidency, calling them "shams," and likening the members of Congress invited to take part in them to "potted plants." What has so enraged Senator Byrd is the obvious contempt for Congress that began to emanate from the White House shortly after September 11, 2001, and has continued unabated ever since. On this point, Senator Byrd and I are in complete agreement. This meeting would be only one in a series of such meetings between the President and the leaders of Congress about the state of the Iraq War. The meetings would all in their way prove to be exercises in futility—that is, when they were not proving to be displays of outrageous behavior.

Fast-forward for a moment to another day and another meeting— September 11, 2007. I again sat next to the President in this same room. But on the sixth anniversary of the attacks that changed the course of history, the atmosphere in the Cabinet Room was not somber. In fact, on that solemn day, the President was anything but solemn. That day, he wore on his face a look of bravado that we've all come to know, and he said something that I will never have the words to adequately describe. But to understand what he said is to understand something profound about the problem at the heart of this administration. Speaking of the fact that the war was being used by radical Islamists for jihadi recruitment, Bush said, "Of course, al Qaeda needs new recruits, because we're *killin'* 'em." He then gave a smirk—that "Bring 'em on" smirk—that we've also come to know. *"We're killin' 'em all,"* he said.

A few days before, in Australia, the President had embarrassed America when he told the deputy prime minister, "We're kicking ass!" when asked how things were going in Iraq.

With Iraq flowing in blood, both ours and theirs, costing the American taxpayers $12 billion every month, and not getting any closer to resolution—with Osama bin Laden still at large and seemingly off Bush's radar—the President of the United States spoke of the situation from the White House as if it were some kind of sporting event or action movie. Sometimes it seems as if he really has no idea of the gravity of his words and decisions. This is no way for a President to talk, from either party, under any circumstances, much less about a terrible, misguided war that he started and has no idea how to stop. And his words aside, it calls into doubt his basic decision-making. And on September 11, no less.

One wants to believe the best about the President of the United States. One wants to believe that he has an open mind and acts in good faith. Our very system depends on it. But on the issue of the war, by that April afternoon in the Cabinet Room, it was impossible to believe this any longer. In this White House, cheap political calculations have superseded sound policy almost every time. And President Bush is incapable of conceding his faults, any faults. I think back to one of his press conferences in early 2004, in which he was asked what his greatest mistake had been during his first term, and he could think of nothing to say. Nothing came to mind. Not a single mistake. Well, I personally make mistakes all the time, and I know from experience that there is an enormous difference between resolve and intractability. President Bush does not seem to be aware of this difference. He has become vested in the mistake we call the Iraq War, and chooses to compound his mistake rather than correct it. To say that this trait is dangerous in a President is something of an understatement.

On this April day, the war in Iraq had been raging for four years and one month. The mission had changed utterly since the invasion of spring 2003, lurching from the initial urgency of removing the imminent threat posed to the United States by Saddam Hussein's weapons of mass destruction, which I had supported, to later democratizing the Middle East, to now, the President's last-ditch attempt to use the military at his disposal to quell a terrible religious war, a civil war, and give the feeble government in Baghdad a chance to take responsibility for its own affairs. This was the President's theory, anyway. And in spite of an unseemly degree of spin coming from the White House, it simply wasn't working. No amount of spin will ever make a falsehood the truth.

The truth is, by the spring of 2007, we were fighting a war in which our soldiers were little more than sitting ducks. More than 3,200 had been killed by then, tens of thousands more maimed or ruined for life. And our soldiers were being subjected to this fate in a cause that had by then become a strategic disaster for the United States. And whether we liked it or not, Iraq was breaking apart. Shiites were being cleansed from Sunni areas. Sunnis were being cleansed from Shiite areas. And serving bravely, the finest fighting force in the history of the world, the United States military, were pawns in this ancient blood feud. When we as a country should have been eliminating the terrorists that had perpetrated the cowardly attacks of September 11, 2001, we were instead pinned down in an Iraqi civil war, with no end in sight, no plausible definition of victory, and no strategy for making our country safer. And now Iraq was a breeding ground for terrorists. Finding a way to responsibly end this intractable war was the only way to stop this strategic stupidity.

The White House had taken us down this path with its power almost entirely unchecked. A Republican Congress that had convened 170 hours of hearings into whether President Clinton had misused the White House Christmas card list had held virtually no oversight hearings into this war, either its strategy or its cost. One of the longest wars in American history, and the United States Congress had utterly abdicated its Constitutional responsibilities out of partisan deference to the President. The White House had gone blind into Baghdad. And the Congress had gone mute. With our new Democratic majority, this silence would now stop.

With the slimmest possible margin in the Senate, the Democrats' chances for success in forcing the President to change his strategy in Iraq were small, and we may well fail, but the bowing and scraping subservience to this President was over. No longer would Congress turn a blind eye to the Bush administration's incompetence and dishonesty. This was not only the right thing to do, it was our Constitutional duty.

And now, before the President in the White House, Speaker Pelosi spoke first. Tough and respectful, she had come to negotiate in spite of the President's stated prohibition. She told the President that she was not yet willing to concede that he was going to veto the bill that Congress had passed, that it was a good bill, and needed his signature. And she was right. It was, in fact, excellent legislation. H.R. 1591, the U.S. Troop Readiness, Veterans' Health, and Iraq Accountability Act of 2007, gave the armed forces and returning veterans more than the President had requested, because their needs are far greater than the President understands. Among other things, the bill included a $1 billion increase for National Guard and Reserve equipment; $1.1 billion for military housing; $3 billion for mine-resistant ambush-protected vehicles ($1.1 billion more than the President asked for); and more than $5 billion for health care. The bill also required that the President begin a strategic redeployment of our troops from Iraq within four months.

Speaker Pelosi was still negotiating because she wanted to be able to say that we had brought the message of the election to the President and had spared no effort in trying to reason with him. Actually, she and I had agreed that we would go to the White House and each deliver essentially the same message. But the night before, I thought better of that. What would be the point? The President had already announced his intention to not listen to any such appeals. If the President doesn't want to negotiate, fine. I would take him at his word, and not even try. Instead, I would endeavor to speak to the historic moment. While the map may have been different, the situation we faced in Iraq was not new. Americans had faced bad wars and worse choices before.

And then the Speaker was finished and it was my turn. The President turned to me and said, "Senator Reid?"

"Mr. President, I will try to say this as respectfully as I can," I began. "You are the President, elected by the American people. I am in awe of your power, and recognize the majesty of your office. But Mr. President, I'm going to tell you honestly how I feel: We are in a crisis. I am reminded of the situation Lyndon Johnson faced in 1965 as he made the decision to surge in Vietnam, a war that by then he knew was lost. Mr. President, just as in Vietnam in 1965, this war cannot be won militarily."

Two days before, I had met in my office at the Capitol with two retired Army generals, Lieutenant General Robert Gard and Brigadier General John Johns, both of whom had Ph.D.s and both of whom had seen several tours in Vietnam, among other distinguished service, General Gard being one of the country's foremost experts in counterinsurgency. These two compact, intense men made a big im-

pression on me, and greatly helped to clarify my thinking in advance
of meeting with the President. Gard and Johns vividly took me back
in time to March 1965, as President Johnson was ordering his own
surge in Vietnam—20,000 ground troops and a campaign of bom-
bardment in the north. Operation Rolling Thunder began as an
eight-week mission to boost morale in Saigon and to persuade the
Vietcong to give up—to convince them that their insurgency was no
match for American military might. At times it seemed that the operation was succeeding, and there always seemed to be a light at the
end of the tunnel. But three years later, after having dropped more
tonnage on North Vietnam than was dropped on all of Europe during World War II, the operation was suspended, a terrible and costly
failure. We now know that President Johnson and Secretary of
Defense Robert McNamara realized that the strategy was doomed
from the start. On February 26, a week before the operation began,
the President told McNamara, "I don't think anything is going to be
as bad as losing, and I don't see any way of winning." Johnson, who
had a tremendous capacity for work and knew better than almost
anyone how to be President, nonetheless began to confide that he
doubted that he had the temperament to be Commander in Chief.
And so the most powerful men in the world pursued their strategy
out of fear and hubris, compounding a mistake, desperate to avoid
the stigma that would come with being "the first American President
to lose a war."

At the time of President Johnson's surge in early 1965, 24,000
Americans were dead. By the end of Johnson's escalation, another
34,000 soldiers would be lost.

The parallels to our own time were inescapable. "Mr. President,"
I said, "this war cannot be won militarily. It is wrong to continue to
send soldiers into a war that cannot be won militarily.

"It's not just Harry Reid saying that. It's a majority of the House and Senate, it's an overwhelming majority of the American people, it's our own military. It's not just me. We've got to find a way to leave with dignity, Mr. President, so that the valiant people who have fought and died there are not lost in vain. We've got to adopt a better strategy and figure out a way to claim victory."

In our meeting, General Gard had cited a recent ABC/USA Today poll that showed that 97 percent of the Iraqi Sunnis and 83 percent of the Shia opposed the presence of U.S. combat troops. The vast majority of the country. "I think the Iraqi people understand the situation there better than those who are advocating to continue the current course after we have lost the support of the Iraqi people," General Gard had told me. "You can't win without it."

"Not only has our effort in Iraq been misplaced and an inappropriate use of U.S. combat forces," General Johns said, "but it has eroded our moral standing throughout the world. You can listen to simplistic statements of the administration, appealing to emotion and fear, or you can take an analytical approach and see the reality of the world. I live in an entirely different world of reality than do President Bush, Vice President Cheney, and other members of the administration."

General Johns had spent the 1960s in counterinsurgency doctrine development, teaching at Fort Bragg, North Carolina, had served as adviser to the political warfare school in Vietnam, and then had spent four years on the Army staff writing papers that were distributed as policy guidance. "The only recommendation in my major studies that was rejected by the secretary of the Army was to not use U.S. ground combat forces," he said. "Ground forces in that setting are counterproductive. They will always eventually be seen as an occupying force and create resentment.

"Now we talk about the surge. And let me tell you why I'm against it. You're going to buy time by pressing down in Baghdad, and you may have some Shiites fade into the background and wait it out, and then when we leave they will move back in. This is not a difficult outcome to predict. Insurgencies are designed to last as long as the foreign army is there. And we are obviously a foreign army.

"The legislation being sent to the President does not cut off funds from executing the surge strategy. What the bill says is that the commitment is not going to be open-ended, as it has been the last four years, where the Congress, led by the Republicans, has given the President free rein to keep announcing benchmarks and not meeting them. Saying, 'We did that; it didn't work. But just give us a little more time. We see the light at the end of the tunnel.' And excuse me, I saw the light flashing at the end of the tunnel in the Pentagon in the mid-sixties at the time we were telling the American people what we were doing in Vietnam, and a confidential memo from John McNaughton, for whom General Gard worked, was saying 'The present U.S. objective in Vietnam is to avoid humiliation.' You can read it in the *Pentagon Papers*. The American people need to be told the truth."

General Gard told me that the situation we faced in the spring of 2007 was eerily reminiscent of the one he lived through in the spring of 1965. "Because the President didn't want to be tarred with losing a war, we continued on, for *five more years*," he said, "with an outcome we could have achieved without ever escalating."

These two outspoken generals were as persuasive as they were brave, and I was greatly affected by their experience and analysis. And it wasn't just Gard and Johns. In the months before our meeting, several recently retired generals had bravely spoken out against the President's war strategy. Some who were involved in this "revolt of the generals" retired just so that they might be able to speak out. Coming out against your Commander in Chief is never an easy thing to do, and is that much more difficult for men who have dedicated their entire lives to defending the United States of America. They were making themselves vulnerable to being tarred by White House surrogates as being part of the "cut and run" crowd. Just as one of the bravest men I've ever known, former Georgia senator and war hero Max Cleland, who left three of his limbs in Vietnam, had been slandered during his reelection campaign in 2002 for "breaking his oath to protect and defend the Constitution." Just as Senator John Kerry had his heroism savaged by liars during the Presidential campaign of 2004. Such is the politics of war in Washington today.

President Bush did not want to hear comparisons to Lyndon Johnson and surges past. "If you think this is about my personal legacy, you're *wrong*. I strongly reject that," the President said. "You don't know what motivates me. I believe that we need to do this thing. It is *necessary* to our success in the war against terror.

"I feel that this strategy—I know people can disagree about the surge, and that's fine, I understand—but I felt that a surge was necessary to give the government the breathing space for a political solution. This is the right thing to do. I couldn't hug a mother if I didn't believe this *can* succeed."

So a veto was coming. It was, of course, his prerogative, but a bad decision nonetheless. Tours were being extended in Iraq, our military was at the breaking point, and the President was just forestalling the inevitable.

Unspoken in the Cabinet Room, though, was the fact that a veto would actually serve both of our purposes. Congress proves that we can get a bill to the President that forces him to change. And he gets to prove that with the stroke of a pen, he is still the President.

But after the veto, what comes next? How would this end?

The $100 billion supplemental bill that we were debating was needed to pay for ongoing operations. If the meeting that day had resulted in a Presidential change of heart, and we as a country had decided to redeploy our troops from the middle of combat to Kuwait and Kurdistan the very next day, the Pentagon would still need that $100 billion. So abrupt defunding was not a realistic option, in my view.

The compromise would have to be somewhere between our timeline, which the President was on the verge of vetoing, and the clean funding bill with no accountability whatsoever that the President was demanding.

Politically, the challenge for the Democrats was that much of the focus was now centered on the money for the war, and not enough on the fatally flawed war policy that the President was pursuing. Democrats would be at their weakest when the White House could say, "You're cutting funds for the troops." We needed a policy debate separate from the money. We needed to make it hard for Republicans who stood to lose their elections—Susan Collins from Maine, Norm Coleman from Minnesota, John Sununu of New Hampshire—to continue to cover for the President. With the exception of Senator Joe Lieberman, who did not attend Democratic caucus meetings when we dealt with the subject of the war, the Democratic caucus was unified. (Lieberman, however, works in lockstep with the Democrats on everything else.) We have a very diverse caucus, so to describe this as a small miracle is no overstatement. No, the only way to make this work would be to peel off Republicans. This would not be easy, if it was even possible.

Out in the country, meanwhile, 70 percent of Americans wanted us to do something dramatic, and do it now. What's more, we were getting hammered by the Democratic base, which had always been against the war but now, emboldened by the election of 2006, was demanding action to end it and did not understand inaction.

"Mr. President," I said, "we could all race to the microphones and do our thirty-second spots, and it doesn't do us any good, and doesn't do the country any good. We want to pass the money for the troops. And at the same time we are determined to change the policy in Iraq."

With that, the meeting adjourned. Not much was said on the way out of the White House. Hands were not shaken.

Two days later, I publicly said that the war is lost. My statement was met with widespread condemnation, as if I were laying blame for this debacle at the doorstep of the enlisted man. Nothing could be further from the truth. The blame belongs at 1600 Pennsylvania Avenue. And it belongs at the Capitol, for through all these years of war, the Congress had been the President's silent partner.

Could I have couched my words more carefully? Maybe. But I said it, and I meant it, and I am not apologizing for it. It is just the truth. Remember, even the new commander in Baghdad, General David Petraeus, had said that this war could not be won militarily. And he still says this. But the President intends to keep our military in Iraq and in a state of war for years to come. Our men and women in uniform have performed magnificently, and long ago accomplished what they were sent there to accomplish. And we have pushed them up to and past the breaking point. Now it is time to bring them home. Iraq is not our country, and the victory to be won there is not ours, and never has been.

I speak bluntly. Sometimes I can be impulsive. I believe something to be right and I do it. And then I don't worry about it. This has not always necessarily served me well, but it is who I am. I can be no one else. Coming from where I come from, you quickly learn to accept that, and get on with it.

You see, I am from Searchlight.

# TWO

# SEARCHLIGHT

I COME FROM A MINING TOWN.

But by the time I came along—December 2, 1939—the leading industry in my hometown of Searchlight, Nevada, was no longer mining, it was prostitution. I don't exaggerate. There was a local law that said you could not have a house of prostitution or a place that served alcohol within so many feet of a school. Once, when it was determined that one of the clubs was in violation of this law, they moved the school.

As a boy, I learned to swim at a whorehouse. Nobody in town had ever seen such a fancy inground tiled pool in their lives as the pool at the El Rey. Or any pool at all, for that matter. At least nobody that we knew. The El Rey was the main bordello when I was growing up in Searchlight. Every Thursday afternoon, the whoremonger in town, a kindly bear of a man by the name of Willie Martello, would ask the girls who worked the El Rey to clear out, and he'd invite the children in town, usually no more than a dozen or so at a time, to swim in his pool. And we would live the life of Riley for a couple of hours, splashing in the azure blue of that whorehouse pool. This was a rare luxury in a hard town. When I was coming up, there were several other brothels in Searchlight—the Crystal Club, Searchlight Casino, Sandy's—thirteen in all, and no churches to be found.

In my home, we had no religion. None, zero. And when I say none, I don't mean 10 percent religious, I mean none. It wasn't that my parents were atheists or something, it was that religion just wasn't part of our lives. But Franklin Roosevelt was. In our little home, my mother had a navy-blue embroidered pillowcase with a little fringe on it, and she put it up on the wall. On it, in bright yellow stitching, it read, *"We can. We will. We must.* —Franklin Delano Roosevelt." And that was my religion.

Otherwise, my father's concerns were much more terrestrial, and he spent his time not gazing heavenward but downward, under the ground, looking for gold. Initially, that was the only reason anybody came to Searchlight.

Since the beginning, man has scratched the earth with simple tools to get at the richness that lies beneath. Four thousand years before Christ, the Neanderthals mined flint to make weapons, and ever since then, when something of value has been found in the ground, men have come running.

The strike that created my hometown happened in 1897, when a man named George Frederick Colton found gold at what would become the Duplex Mine in the middle of town. By the turn of the century Searchlight was booming. But reversals come quick. Within a decade, the town was in a serious decline. In all, more than 250,000 ounces of gold have been pulled from the ground at Searchlight, half of that before 1909. Thirty years later, with the boom a distant memory, I was born in my grandmother's house, a two-room shack, delivered by a doctor by the name of Fenlon who would himself soon leave town for someplace more prosperous.

It's an interesting man who makes his way to the middle of nowhere seeking his life and fortune. That's what my grandfather, John Reid, did, when he was drawn to Searchlight from California just after the turn of the century. And that, of course, is also the story of our country—a certain vagabond spirit, in the best sense of that word. The middle of nowhere is a hard place to live. So many of our fathers were drunks, and some of our mothers were as well.

When I was a kid I didn't realize Searchlight was the middle of nowhere. I figured everybody on earth lived like we did, and I thought my town was the center of the known universe. The landscape, scarred with hundreds of claims, some active, many abandoned, was so interesting to a boy looking for adventure. All manner of treasure was to be found down those holes, if not actually much gold. Over time, the gold in the ore became harder and harder to find and more expensive to produce. Some of the mining outfits would dig a hole, find nothing there, and immediately dig another hole. And so there are hundreds of holes in the ground in Searchlight. Hundreds. Anyplace you look there are holes. When I was coming up, people always said, "Better be careful of the holes—better fence some of them." And my dad would say, "Anybody's dumb enough to fall down a hole, they should fall down a hole."

During the boom, if a modern convenience existed, it could be found in Searchlight—telephone, telegraph, a doctor, a dentist, a railroad, and electricity, which is astounding considering that much of rural America wouldn't be electrified for decades. Back then, Searchlight was bigger than Las Vegas. When I was a boy, it was barely hanging on. And we knew none of the luxuries that those who came before us had enjoyed on the same spot. Searchlight never became a ghost town, but it sure tried.

By the 1940s, the town's regression was almost complete. There wasn't a single telephone in the town. No television set, no telegraph.

Nothing other than the mail to communicate with the outside world. Unreliable electricity. No doctor, no dentist. You didn't go to the doctor unless you were on your deathbed. And even then, who's going to print the money for you to pay the bill?

The isolation and the dwindling prospects could put a dent in your pioneer spirit and take a toll on your family. Put the lens a little closer, on the Reid house. At the time I thought our house was really nice, but as I look back, I guess it wasn't.

First, it is made of railroad ties. And railroad ties are soaked in creosote—oil—to keep the termites out. So this house of ours is as flammable as a house can be. My dad put chicken wire up and added a coat of plaster to make a rough stucco exterior. We had a little tree in our yard for a while. It died. The yard is just rocks—things don't grow.

My brother and I always go in the back door. There is a kitchen, and the kitchen has a woodstove when you come in, right next to the sink. And an electric stove, not a fancy one, but a stove, and a refrigerator. And then there is a little room with no door on it. It's where a bathroom should be, but it isn't a bathroom. We use an outhouse instead. But my mother stores stuff in this little room. She takes in laundry from the card dealers at the casinos and from the brothels, and this is where she keeps her clothes wringer and her wash soap. Continue the tour into what is called the front room. It's the biggest room in the house, and it's where the radio is, but otherwise we barely use it because it gets so cold there. The floors are linoleum. But don't leave the room until you look up and see the star on the ceiling, made of rough-cut pieces of wood arranged around the light fixture. It's the handiwork of a guy named Pop Payne, and it's real nice to look at. It really makes the house special. And then come back around to the two tiny bedrooms, and that's it.

Now, the back bedroom of our palace, measuring out at eight feet by eleven feet, is the room I share with my little brother Larry, who came along a couple of years after me. Larry lives like a king, because as the youngest he gets the five-gallon bucket. Me, I have to go to the outhouse, which at night in the wintertime seems like it's a mile away. The linoleum floor is like ice.

Look closer, and you'll see my parents, Harry and Inez Reid. My father is a powerful man, a very good miner, and is very quiet. Brooding. He doesn't much like to be around people. Larry and I are quiet like him. Larry is especially quiet, and my father has a special feeling for him.

Pop always works, but because of unreliable and unscrupulous bosses, he often doesn't get paid. The checks bounce all the time, but that doesn't seem to bother him too much. I can see him always reading a book, some technical manual or, more likely, some dime novel. Never books written by women, that's his prejudice. Only books by men. I wake up in the morning and walk into the kitchen and Pop's sitting at the table, drinking strong coffee and escaping into some book, which some people might not expect, since he didn't even finish eighth grade.

But don't let his lack of education fool you, he can do anything. He just prefers to work alone, that's all. He's a carpenter, he can do finishing work, he is a blacksmith, he can sharpen steel and picks and saws, he can overhaul the engine of a car, he's a welder. He can walk around a pile of rocks or dirt, observe its height and slope, and calculate its volume in his head. This drives the engineers crazy, because they can't figure out how somebody like him can do something like that. He can do anything. But mostly, he's a miner. And he can go down in a mine, take a compass, and do underground mapping. That's something the college boys can't figure out either. And Pop just smiles.

Like I said, he keeps to himself. We live up on a hill, and if Pop sees somebody coming, he tells us to stay quiet. At nighttime, people come by and call out, "Harry, Harry!" but my dad won't let us answer the door. Part of it is that all his friends like to drink, and a lot of times he doesn't have any money, and they're already way ahead of him anyway, already loaded. My brother Don is the same way. His friends come by and he says, "Tell 'em I'm not here." I ask him why he does that, and he says because they're just going down for the girls. "I have nothing for the whores. What is there down there for me?" he says.

If quiet is a heritable trait, and we got quiet from my father, then we got confidence from my mother. Mom, now, she's not quiet. She loves being around people, and is more social and optimistic than my dad. She always just knows that things are going to work out. Loves going to all my ball games. Sometimes she embarrasses me with her yelling, but I'm glad she's there. She's a reader, too, when she has the time. Zane Grey is her absolute favorite. She has her eccentricities, too. She has a rule for me and my brothers: Don't you eat at anybody's house, don't you accept anything from them. I guess she doesn't want anybody coming to our place, because she doesn't have anything to give them. But Mother breaks her back to make sure that with our limited money we always have everything we need. And we do. She makes sure we have clothes that are as good as the other kids' clothes. And they are.

They both drink too much. My father'll drink until he runs out of money. Sometimes they get loaded and whoop it up. Once or twice, Pop has run afoul of the law. One night after his shift, my dad and his brother Rob get in a fight down in the bars and when they come out the cops are waiting for them. They beat Pop on the head with a sap, a hard leather pouch filled with BBs, and then haul him to jail in Las Vegas. My dad has a nice new scar on his head to show for his night out.

Every now and then, he'll be too drunk to go to work. And sometimes Mom and Pop fight with each other, physically, in front of us children. My father can be mean to my mother. After Don and Dale are off at high school, Larry and I sit, wide-eyed, listening to what goes on on the other side of the closed door.

I am not confessional by nature, so some of these things are surpassing hard for me to say. I loved my parents very much. They gave life everything they had. But no child should be raised the way I was raised.

The foundation of our house is still there. It would eventually burn down.

And that's life in a boomtown gone bust.


IT ONLY FOLLOWS, in a town where the number-one business was prostitution, that the leading citizen would be a whoremonger. Not only would Willie Martello let us swim in his pool, but he would hand out five-dollar bills to the kids at Christmastime. My dad used to make fun of him for doing this, because five bucks is how much it cost to go with one of Willie's girls. "That's *so* generous," my dad would say. I didn't get my father's sarcasm, and so I thought, "Yeah, it *is* generous," because a fiver was the most money I'd ever seen in my life.

Business was good for Willie. And when military payday came, a couple times a month, it seemed like Searchlight would double in size. There'd be men from all over.

The clubs catered to nearby Nellis Gunnery School, later to become Nellis Air Force Base, and they catered to Camp Ibis in California, where Patton trained his tank corps, and Camp Desert Rock, and Indian Springs Air Force Base. And they catered to the miners, without whom Searchlight wouldn't have ever existed.

In fact, but for the discovery of gold in those waning years of the nineteenth century, my hometown, the town where I live today, would likely still be a patch of pristine desert. Situated on a rocky, windy, and arid rise without artesian wells or surface water of any kind, the place where Searchlight came to be was not a gathering spot for Indian or animal. There was nothing there. Nothing.

Fifty-five miles south of Las Vegas, the town is nestled in the southern tip of Nevada. Twenty miles west along an empty road lined densely with Joshua tree forests is Nipton, California. Fourteen miles east is Arizona. My father's father came to Searchlight from California to work the mines in about 1902. He had run a confectionery and had been a forest ranger and an itinerant laborer, and the gold strike in southern Nevada must have looked promising to him, if not to everyone else. It is said that the mining camp that became the town of Searchlight got its name when Fred Colton, in describing what he and a couple of other prospectors had found, said, "I think I've got something here." And they looked at it harder and said, "There is gold there all right, but it would take a searchlight to find it."

Mark Twain wrote of his own similar strike in *Roughing It*, the chronicle of his travels to the Nevada Territory:

> After a great deal of effort we managed to discern some little fine yellow specks, and judged that a couple of tons of them massed together might make a gold dollar, possibly. We were not jubilant, but Mr. Ballou said there were worse ledges in the world than that. He saved what he called the "richest" piece of the rock, in

order to determine its value by the process called the "fire assay."
Then we named the mine "Monarch of the Mountains" (modesty
of nomenclature is not a prominent feature in the mines).

And so it was in Searchlight, too, that men in the first decade of
the twentieth century made big boasts and audacious claims. Some
got rich, and many left poor. And like Twain's mine, the hundreds of
shafts sunk into the ground around Searchlight came with names
wonderful and weird, names that reflected the characters who would
pick up and come to this place.

The Chief of the Hills, the Golden Garter, the Silk Stocking, the
Red Bird, the Blue Bird, the Philadelphia, the New York, the
Spokane, the Dubuque, the June Bug, the Little Bug, and the Carrie
Nation are only a few of the mines that sprang up in the Searchlight
Mining District almost overnight upon Colton's discovery. And the
wheeling and dealing and speculation commenced, usually, at the
saloon.

One claim that would become the greatest mine in Searchlight
was sold for $1,500, a team of mules, a buckboard, and a double-
barreled shotgun. Another that produced at least $150,000 in gold
changed hands for a pint of Cyrus Noble whiskey. Ten days before the
assessment work on the mine was due, the owner walked into a
Searchlight bar and shouted, "What am I offered for my claim?"

"I'll give a cigar," came a reply. The offer was accepted. Immediately,
the new owner rolled over his new stake. "What am I offered for my
claim?" he shouted.

Another miner at the bar responded, "I'll give you this bottle of
Cyrus Noble."

"Sold!" And the Cyrus Noble mine got its name.

Searchlight was a rough-and-tumble mining camp, the work was dangerous, and plenty of men died underground. But the pioneers also made time for entertainment. The Nevada guide published by the WPA Writer's Project the year after I was born records a special day in town:

> On July 4, 1902, for instance, there was a burro fight. Two jack burros, noted for their courage, were brought in. Thousands of dollars and various mining claims were wagered on the outcome of their scrap. One of the burros, the property of a desert rat, was named Thunder, the other, a lean, lanky beast, was called Hornet. The two burros squared off on a level area below the camp and raised a dust cloud visible for miles. Thunder had the best of it in the early going, but after Hornet got his second wind he plied his heels and teeth so well that he drove Thunder into the desert. Thereupon the men collected their wagers and went to the saloon for the usual celebration.

At one point during the boom, lodging ran out and tent hotels began springing up. The local newspaper said, "In answer to the urgent demand for accommodations a number of tent lodging houses are going to be replaced as quickly as possible by wooden structures. It is a long time since there was a tent hotel in Searchlight. A month ago no one would have patronized such a place. . . . Wooden buildings can't be put up fast enough."

In the first decade of the twentieth century, the mines swelled the peak population of Searchlight to three thousand. There were some decent mines, but alone among them the mighty Quartette was actually a world-class operation and really put the town on the map. For a time during the boom, the Quartette ran twenty-four-hour operations. The mine would easily yield half the gold that came out of the ground in Searchlight.

Initially, things must not have worked out for my grandfather, because he left Searchlight in 1910 and went back to California, where my father was born at Cajon Pass in 1913. But then the Reids headed back in 1927, and this time they didn't leave. My father met my mother, whose people were from Sandy, Utah. I learned much later in life that in the distant past, she had been a Mormon. Mom had two sons from another man, whom my father would raise as his own. And then, as the next world war got started, came me and my little brother, Larry.

Dr. Robert Fenlon was there when I was born, he signed the birth certificate, and a few years later he took off for Boulder City, Nevada, which, unlike Searchlight, had a population on the rise. Kids back then were bigger than they are now, because there was no such thing as induced labor. And I was a big baby. What my grandmother used to tell me is that I was so big at birth, ten pounds, that my head was misshapen. She said she worked on my head after I came out like it was modeling clay so that it might be a normal shape.

It's funny, as you get older, there are lots of people in town who say they were there when you were born. There must be a hundred people who attended my birth.

My father almost didn't live to be one of them. Less than a week before I was born, he was working with his friend Carl Myers, sinking a vertical shaft owned by the Bi-Metals Mining Company outside of Kingman, Arizona. These shafts were often hundreds of feet deep, driving straight into the ground, or on an incline, depending on the vein. Miners would use explosives to push deeper and deeper into the ground. You'd blast at the end of a shift so that by the next day the air would have cleared, and then you'd muck—or shovel—the ore. Blast and muck, blast and muck. Different mines had different setups, but generally there were two buckets. You'd fill one bucket while the hoist man up top was emptying the other and sending it back down.

Planting dynamite is something of an art and a science. To be productive, each explosion required ten or twelve sticks of dynamite. Say there's an outcropping that shows some promise and you want to investigate, figure out which way the vein goes, if it gets bigger or peters out. Or if you need air, you'd have to blast a ventilation shaft so you'd have circulation. Otherwise, the air got real bad down there. The miners would do all of this on their own, without engineers. All on educated guesses. You drilled holes and put the sticks in place, and the depth and direction of the blast depended on the angle at which you drilled. And here's the main trick: You had to have a dozen different lengths of fuse so that you could stagger and then count the separate explosions, because if there was only one big explosion, it was impossible to tell if all the charges had gone off before you went back down the hole. So the charges would go off in sequence. A miner had to light the fuses and get far enough up the hole to safety before the blasts started.

To move up and down the shaft, a miner would use what was called a sinking ladder. You couldn't leave the ladder at the bottom of the mine, because it would get blown to bits when the explosives went off, so miners would carry it with them as they climbed up to escape the blast they set. Myers and my father were down in the shaft setting charges of dynamite when the accident happened. An article in the *Tribune Intermountain News* from December 1939 tells the rest of the story:

> Reid had planted eleven charges of powder at the bottom of the eighty-three-foot shaft, and lighted all fuses, with time enough to allow him to join his partner, Myers, at the station twenty-five feet above.

A runner set off one of those charges prematurely just as Reid started to ascend the ladder, injuring him severely. A doctor said later Reid had approximately 300 rock splinters in his left leg and thigh as a result of the blast.

After the first blast, Myers called down to his partner, and when he received no answer descended the ladder. Every second was precious. Myers knew there were 10 more charges, which might explode at any instant, blowing both men to bits.

Myers loaded the inert Reid on his back and climbed back up the rickety ladder to the station finding safety behind a muck pile at almost the instant the 10 remaining charges exploded.

Myers then carried his companion out of the shaft and took him to a hospital, where physicians said he would recover.

When the story got around Searchlight, somebody said that Carl should get a medal for his bravery. He replied, "To hell with the medal. Harry's alive, isn't he?" A few months later Carl Myers did receive the Carnegie Medal for his bravery. He was always a hero to my family. He didn't get up that morning and say, "I think I'll be a hero today." But because of what he did that day, my mother didn't become a widow with a newborn, as happened to so many who worked in the mines with my father.

For years after my father's near-miss, my mother would dig the rocks out of his back.

A few years before I was born, my father's brother Mason was killed with another miner in an almost identical explosion. My Uncle Mason was very handsome and is said to have been the nicest of all the Reid brothers. Mason and the other man, Smokey Pridgeon, were killed at the Black Mountain Mine in 1935 when the holes in the tunnel they were working went off prematurely. A teetotaling man is said to have gotten drunk when he was asked to bring the two bodies out of the tunnel. "I had to drink," he said. "Those two boys were in pieces."

A friend of my father's named Bill Hudgens was killed in a blast in 1940 when a rock fell on his head. Had he not been working alone he probably would have survived. But after the rock hit him he tried to climb out of the mine and fell while climbing a ladder. My dad brought him out of the hole. Hudgens left two little children and a pregnant wife.

Even with the physical risk, and the toll on his body, my dad loved being a miner. He loved it because he was good at it, and because he was more content battling the earth than being around people. Underground, there was no one to avoid. Underground, Pop was consummate and assured. Physically, he was an imposing man, a much bigger man than I am, and it was almost a miracle that Carl Myers could even carry him out of that mine, as my dad outweighed Carl by a lot.

Most men down in the mine would use a jackleg to brace their jackhammers against a rock facing. My dad thought jacklegs were for weaklings. He'd just pick up the jackhammer and go straight into the rock on his own strength. He was also widely known as one of the quickest muckers and one of the few people in the area who could square-set timber.

It just didn't matter that any day he might not come home. It didn't matter that the work was sporadic and the pay was miserable. It didn't matter that my father had the hardest job of any man I've ever known. My father was born to mine, and it was the only thing he wanted to do. It made him happy. And I truly believe that it was one of the few places he was comfortable in this world.

At the outbreak of World War II, the mines closed for a time. Gold just wasn't worth mining. And so my dad moved the family and went to work 45 miles north at the plants in Henderson, where they made magnesium for the bombs. The place was called Basic Magnesium, and it was considered a defense installation, so the men working there were exempt from serving in the military.

We lived in a little house at 14 East Texas Street. Over the years, Pop became a member of the Laborers, Machinists, and Operators unions. He worked regular eight-hour shifts, had two days off each week, and dressed decently, and a check that didn't bounce came in on a regular basis. We were so happy.

One of the other benefits of living in Henderson was that we got to see my brothers Don and Dale, who were in high school there, since there wasn't a high school anywhere around Searchlight. As Henderson was a company town, they went to Basic High School, where Don was on the basketball team. One of my earliest memories is of bugging him to take me to practice with him. He agreed, but he told me that I couldn't get in anyone's way, and I couldn't say a word. Not a word. I wasn't older than four or five, and I was so excited. I sat there with a big smile on my face the whole time. The practice ended, the team cleared the court, the gym lights went out, and I just sat there. My brother was home before he realized that he had left me there in the pitch darkness of the gym. I don't remember being afraid. But my brother told me not to say anything, so I didn't.

Don, who was twelve years older than me, would go away to school and then enlist in the Marines, and would come back kind of sophisticated. And with his newfound sophistication, he would teach me things I might not have learned otherwise. It was Don who taught me not to spit. That's crude, he'd say. And it was Don who taught me not to smoke.

I was out driving with him on the old railroad grade, looking for rabbits, and he was smoking. He had quite a habit by then. I was a young boy, a little older than at basketball practice, but not much older. Well, he was smoking his Kools, and I was desperate for a puff. "Don, give me a puff, give me a puff, *give me a puff.*" I wouldn't leave it alone, just kept bothering him. "Give me *a puff!*" Finally, he said okay. He took his cigarette and handed it to me. "Here's what you do," he said. "You take this thing and you suck in just as hard as you can. Okay? As hard as you can." Well, I did and it hurt so bad I can still feel it. He cured me of cigarettes. I never smoked another.

Things didn't last for us in Henderson. As soon as the mines opened back up in Searchlight, my dad got out of town. He just wasn't happy there. It seemed as if he just couldn't be satisfied working above ground in a structured environment. That's just who he was. He quit the job with regular hours and regular pay to go back to the mines of Searchlight, and he took us with him. As kids, we did not understand this, and we were not at all happy about it. But I now know that that's what some people do in life. They get good at something and feel comfortable doing it, and even though there may be something out there that's better for them and their family, they're not going to do it, because it's not who they are. That was my pop, anyway. He simply had no choice.

When I was eleven I started helping my father out in the mines. Like many of the miners in town, he would either lease space or work for someone and get a rate of so much per foot. If he found any gold, the owner would get a percentage on the lease. Most often he would work alone, even though that was against the law. The mining inspectors rarely came to Searchlight. So he would ask me to keep him company and I would. I had my own carbide light and my own helmet. My mother would pack us a sandwich. He and I would be down there in the dark and not say much. I panned for gold, and I got pretty good at mucking, and I would watch him work. I was amazed at how quickly he would pound through this impenetrable rock. And man, whatever you did, just stay out of his way down there. I spent a lot of time in the mines with him, and the older I got, the more I was able to do. Never got paid for it in anything other than memories.

While I loved spending time with my father, I also knew that mining would not be the love of my life.

After a day's work underground, he and I would both go home filthy. We'd haul our lunch buckets and our gear and climb into the family jalopy. Sometimes I'd get to drive, and my dad would say, "Home, James," like he was a fancy man and I was his chauffeur.

IT WAS THE RADIO that opened the world to us in Searchlight. My brother and I would huddle in front of our old console. Often the reception was lousy, and if the weather wasn't just right you were out of luck, but we became devoted to *The Shadow, Gunsmoke,* and *Dragnet.* We'd listen to Ronald Reagan and Red Foley, too. And there'd be music. Ernest Tubb, Hank Snow. And in the evenings, when we couldn't pick up anything else, we would listen to a Mexican station, XERL, that offered real cowboy music and all manner of magic rings and magic worms for sale. I loved that station, and got ripped off by them many times. But without question the main event on the radio was the major-league baseball Game of the Day. Day after day in the summertime, I'd sit riveted by the play-by-play in exotic Pittsburgh, Detroit, and Cleveland. And when the game would be a rainout in some far-off city, no one in America would be more disappointed than a kid out in the Nevada desert.

The Indians became my team, and I can still easily remember

the World Championship lineup from 1948. I also followed the Cardinals, because Dizzy Dean was the announcer for Game of the Day and Dizzy was a Cardinal.

But the big news of the whole era was happening at Ebbets Field in Brooklyn, New York. Wherever that was. I can't remember ever seeing a black person in Searchlight. I'm not sure I caught the importance of the event when Jackie Robinson broke the color barrier in baseball. And radio being radio, I'm not sure I even knew that Robinson was black. I can't remember ever seeing a black person in Searchlight. All I cared about was that in 1947, Robinson started in 151 games, batted .297, led the National League in stolen bases, and won Rookie of the Year. And that meant he was great in my book.

It wasn't until a couple of years later that I began to realize just what Jackie Robinson had done, and I also learned the hell he had been put through doing it—cursed as a "nigger" from coast to coast, boycotted by opposing teams, threatened—taking unbelievable abuse, until finally Dodger manager Leo Durocher told his team, "I don't care if the guy is yellow or black, or if he has stripes like a fucking zebra. I'm the manager of this team, and I say he plays. What's more, I say he can make us all rich. And if any of you can't use the money, I'll see that you are all traded."

By this time, baseball had become a big part of me, and was an important window onto the big world for me, and I genuinely didn't understand. The guy was a great ballplayer, so why all the name-calling? How come he had to work twice as hard as everybody *and* put up with that crap? Obviously I didn't yet know much about the world. But I was starting to learn. And I did know that we did our fair share of name-calling in Searchlight.

In fact, we could compete at an Olympic level in name-calling. Pete Domitrovich had a big nose, so the whole town—every single person in Searchlight—called him "Big Nose Pete." The disabled man was "Cripple Jack." And I became known as Pinky.

My mother would have nothing to do with this name-calling. I remember one day walking down in front of our house was an old man known to everyone in town as "Old Man Roe." As he walked by the house I yelled, "Hey, Old Man Roe." My mother came running out of the house with an angry look on her face. "You can't call him Old Man Roe. That's not his name." After that, I'd still call people names, just not in front of my mother.

Searchlight in the late 1940s and 1950s was about as far as you could get from Brooklyn and the base paths of Ebbets Field.

But along with giving me something to dream about on summer afternoons, Jackie Robinson brought to my hometown awareness of a huge struggle that was beginning in America—not with speeches or demonstrations—but with RBIs. In Searchlight, I could listen to the radio and hear about the very beginning of the civil rights movement, and it seemed a million miles away. But I lived for baseball, and while he may have been playing second base 2,500 miles away in Brooklyn, Jackie Robinson was reaching into my town and opening my mind. It wasn't until I got older that I understood what a lesson that was.

ONE TIME A KID moved in from out of town, which was unheard of. Nice kid, so the first thing I did was pick a fight with him. He was new, and I was jealous of him. He probably dressed decently, was probably well spoken. He was just different. The typical things that threaten people. Big mistake. The kid could fight. Let's just say that nobody won the fight, and that was the last time I picked a fight with somebody I didn't know. I can still see his face, but I can't remember his name.

Later I'd learn to box so that I could channel my brawling instincts into something more respectable. But in the meantime, I got myself into more fights. When I was in eighth grade, there was a kid I didn't like very much at all. Compounding this basic problem, his mother also happened to be the teacher. In Searchlight, our schoolhouse was only one room, with first through eighth grade crammed together. So if you didn't like somebody in class, there was no way to avoid him. This made for an uncomfortable situation.

The teacher's son knew he had a position of dominance over the rest of us. He knew his mother would always treat him differently, and this delighted him to no end. One day I'd had enough. I had reached my limit of annoyance with this particular boy and decided to take action.

So right there in the classroom, I beat the crap out of the kid, in front of all the other students and his own mother. I did such a good job beating him up that I broke my hand on his hard head. After the fight I went home cradling my swollen right hand. I was hurt, but I was still pretty happy. When I got home from school my dad saw my broken hand. "What happened?" he asked.

"I got in a fight," I said, and I told him about it.

My father wasn't bothered at all that I had started the fight. In fact, after I was finished telling my story, he simply said, "Next time, keep your fist closed."

That was it. No doctor, no ice because there was no ice in our house, no more conversation. Just a flattened-out knuckle on my right hand, missing ever since that day. I got in a lot of fights after that, and I always kept my fist closed.

By this time, there were fewer than two hundred people in town, so there weren't many people my age. But the other children were no less memorable for that.

We were one short for a baseball team, so our ninth was a girl, Mary Ann Myers, who was the tomboy at Searchlight School. She could ride bareback better than most people could ride with a saddle, and she played baseball better than some of us boys.

Marvin Marshall was one of the Marshalls, a big family whose father was an old man married to a young woman. Today we'd probably call Marvin dyslexic, because he didn't read very well. They'd call on him to read and he'd struggle. School wasn't his thing. He needed help, but in Searchlight there was none.

There was Darlene Cree, who was one of the smartest kids in Searchlight. She'd been kind of a roustabout but married a devout Mormon and converted. She had a half-brother, Junior Cree, who was much older than Darlene. Junior got shot in the ass in Europe in World War I I. He had been in the Italian campaign and in North Africa, and was in the third or fourth wave going into Normandy. He still runs a trailer park in town. And others in town also went off to the great war. My dad's youngest brother, Doug, was a tank gunner in Europe. I remember when he came home from the war he brought a German helmet, a sword, and binoculars, and we got to play around with them. My Uncle Jeff was on Okinawa. We were so proud of our Searchlight soldiers, and so happy they'd made it back home.

Searchlight School was actually two rooms. Grades one through four in one room, and five through eight in the other. The idea was that you'd graduate from one room to the next. But by the time I was old enough to be an upperclassman, we didn't have enough kids in school, and we only had one teacher. So all grades, all subjects were taught in that one room. Which made it tough if you didn't like somebody, or if you struggled in any way, especially with reading. I was lucky to read well.

My favorite author was Jack London, who wrote *Call of the Wild* and *White Fang*. I never traveled out of Searchlight. We never went any-place. Once in a while to Henderson, rarely to Las Vegas. I was twelve years old before I went to Needles, California, which is only 50 miles away. But even though I never left Searchlight, I traveled everywhere in my mind's eye. My favorite place to go was the Yukon, and Jack London took me there.

Math was another story. I was a whiz at basic addition and sub-traction but nothing more abstract than that. Part of the problem was that it was almost impossible to keep teachers in Searchlight. They'd come and then get out of town pretty quickly. But the one teacher that spent several years there was named Mrs. Pickard. She taught all eight grades and was the picture of a rural schoolteacher: Glasses, black hair tied back in a bun, single. I can't remember one thing she taught me, not one. But she was the first person to teach me that it was good to learn, she was the person who instilled in me the desire to read.

Teachers didn't get paid much, and they had to move to the middle of nowhere, and they had to put up with kids like me, so you probably couldn't blame them for not wanting to stick around. And back in those days, all of these tiny remote towns had their own school districts, so there was no support from Clark County or Las Vegas or the state. We were on our own. But Mrs. Pickard bucked the trend and stayed in Searchlight for several years. Which was lucky for us.

Larry and I are less than two years apart, so we were at Searchlight School at the same time. On Larry's tenth birthday, we were on our Schwinns, about to leave for school, when Mom said, Today, you come home for a special birthday lunch and you don't have to go back to school. And it was a Friday, October 31, Halloween, so we'd be off for the weekend. Because it was a special day, I got cut in on the deal, too.

When lunchtime came, we raced home as fast as we could go down the dirt road to get home for the special lunch. It sure seemed like it was important at the time. And Mom's not home. What's this? "She's not here," I turned and said to Larry. "She's probably up at Daisy's." Daisy had been a family friend for as long as we could remember. "Larry, run up there on your bike and check." And Larry tore out after her and hit some gravel going too fast and he went sliding off that hill and lost control, flipped his bike, and broke his leg. He could get up but kept falling back down. He didn't realize yet what he'd done, but he wasn't going to be able to walk on that leg. So he was crawling back up the hill and kept hollering after me, Pink! Pink! I was in the house, and he finally got my attention and I opened the door and could see him lying on the side of the road. In that special way that only brothers can be brutal to each other, I thought he was fooling around. "What are you *doing?* You're supposed to get Mom at Daisy's for the birthday lunch." Larry said that he had broken his leg. "Stop kidding around!" I said. "Get back on your bike and go get Mom. I'm hungry!" And I let the door slam and went back in the house.

Larry went back to dragging himself up the hill, and was so convincing as an invalid that eventually I figured he wasn't faking and decided to help him into the house. So much for the special lunch. As we made our way inside, he was in so much pain that to this day I remember his screaming anytime he tried to move. There was a part-time nurse in town, one of the Hudgens family. She came and checked out the leg, and pronounced it broken.

When Pop came home from work, he quietly went in to talk to Larry. "Are you in pain, son?" he asked. "Do you need to go to the doctor?"

"No," Larry replied.

This was just as well, because Searchlight had no doctor. The nearest would have been at St. Rose de Lima Hospital in Henderson or maybe in Boulder City, but even if we'd had the best doctor in the country, there was no money for it.

Larry would be laid up lame for weeks. Because he was ten, he mended pretty quickly and was hopping around the house on one leg before too long. But the leg was never set, and healed crooked. Larry always had a sense of humor about it, though, and says that he blames his lack of football prowess on that busted leg.

It wasn't just us. No one saw the doctor. If a medical condition simply couldn't be ignored, most often the afflicted had to take matters into his own hands. My parents both had terrible teeth. My dad's teeth would hurt him so much, and when the pain became unbearable, he'd pull them with vise grips. He said it didn't hurt as bad as the toothache.

My mother had a few teeth, but one by one they fell out. She had to gum her food. She couldn't eat the meat we had. We ate a lot of potatoes. Rice, beans.

That always bothered me and I am confident that it must have bothered her. So later, in high school, when I started working and earning a little money, I wanted to get my mother some teeth. I knew there was a big-shot dentist in Las Vegas named J. D. Smith who had married a woman from Searchlight. I went to his office and told him I would like to get my mother some teeth. And he just looked at me and said, "You know there is no credit." I was so insulted that I just walked right out of there. I wasn't looking for credit. To hell with you, I thought. Next I went to Paul Marshall, who was a dentist in Henderson. I had no connection to him but I wanted to help my mother. I said, "Dr. Marshall, I want to get my mother some teeth. She has no teeth."

He said, "Well, it costs about two hundred and fifty dollars."

I said, "Fine." And I got my mother teeth.

There are a lot of people even today just like my mother. People who can't get their teeth taken care of or have health problems that they ignore because there's nothing else to be done. No money, no transportation. So they do like my mother. Can't worry about it, she'd say. And maybe have a drink or two.

IN SEARCHLIGHT we made do in other ways, too. When I was ten, a huge fire ravaged what was left of downtown Searchlight, burning, among other things, the grocery store. It was never rebuilt, and I honestly can't remember where we got food after that. We obviously got it somewhere, I'm just not sure where. Around that time, my father told me I could go hunting.

My older brothers each had a .22 rifle. Searchlight at the time also had no place to buy a bullet. I had this bolt-action rifle that belonged to my brother. It held seven shells. I had none. So I rummaged around in some drawers and found two bullets: a .22 long and a .22 short. My grandmother told me that if I could get a jackrabbit she would cook it for us. So I left my house in search of rabbits and was walking down a wash at sunset when I saw him there, sitting on his haunches. I shot and I missed. But the rabbit didn't move. I shot again, my last shell, and I hit the rabbit, but I didn't kill him. So I gave chase. I chased and chased that rabbit. Seemed like for hours. I was tired. He was wounded. But I was gaining on him. I got that rabbit. Took it home. Skinned it. Took it to my grandmother. And she fixed this wonderful rabbit stew, enough for everybody. Cooked it on the woodstove in the house where I was born. Best rabbit I ever ate. I think the chase must have made it taste better. We figured we could make do with nothing, and half the time we did.

As a boy, I had to work for a living. Come summer, I would work with Sharky Myers at his corral. Sharky was a rodeo cowboy, and the son of the man who saved my father's life. He was a nice-looking guy, and had a good personality and a real way with women. He dated Miss Helldorado, Joanne Sandquist. The Miss Helldorado contest was a beauty pageant, but instead of the bathing suit competition, they showcased horseback-riding skills. Sharky was quite a bit older than me, by at least five years, and he always took such good care of me. I don't know why, but he did.

We'd go down to Spirit Mountain south of town, where Sharky and his father, Carl, kept their cattle. Sharky had built what we called an arena. He'd cleared a spot and arranged railroad ties in a big circle, put up fencing, and built cattle chutes like at a real rodeo. I'd haul water and clean out stalls. Spirit Mountain was a magical place. You can see it from great distances, glistening blue. The Indians were the first to call it Spirit Mountain, and if you've ever seen it, you know why.

I worked with Sharky for several summers in addition to my other jobs. Cowboy work is hazardous, and Sharky got hurt a few times. Once he got hit in the face with a windlass crank. So he was all scarred up. I used to go with him to Helldorado with his parents and we'd have chute passes, so we'd sit where the cowboys were, with the horses and other animals. I was always afraid of horses and cattle, but I never let on. He would rope the calves and it was my job to untie them, which I just hated because I've never felt comfortable around big animals.

I had many other jobs as a kid. I did a lot of digging. For a cowboy named Queen, I dug trenches for a water line. I dug postholes with another guy for a power line that was coming in. He couldn't speak a word of English and I didn't know a word of Spanish, but we worked side by side for three weeks and communicated just fine.

Once in a while, I'd help my dad dig graves at the Searchlight Cemetery, which is a wonderful place. Started in 1906, at the peak of the boom. Sometimes he'd get paid, sometimes he wouldn't. He'd take a pick and shovel to the rocky ground. If it was too rocky, he'd single-jack it and dynamite the earth open.

And I drove a truck, too. Of course, there was no such thing as a driver's license for a thirteen-year-old, and this job tested my skills pretty severely. Some men were drilling a well, and a well needs water. So I drove the water truck. My first time on the job was at night. I missed my turnoff on a steep, narrow road. It was a hot summer night and I was pouring sweat. The steering wheel was wet. My shirt was soaked. I brought the big truck, heavy with water, to a slow stop. There was no room to turn around. I knew I'd have to back it up. I had never done anything remotely like this before. I can't say how long it took, but it seemed like forever before I got back to the road. When I got back to the job, the men didn't want my excuses. They were angry that I'd taken so long.

It was just after this that I rolled our '42 Mercury and totaled it. That's what they get for letting a kid drive. It was a nice car, too. We didn't always have cars. My dad once had a brand new Studebaker, but it was repossessed after six months. In the Mercury, I was driving my cousin Jeff and my brother Larry down to the river and was going too fast. Nobody cared about the car, though. As poor as we were, my parents didn't care. They never said a cross word about it. They were just relieved that nobody was hurt too badly.

But life wasn't all work. There were times of actual joy. And even the rough-and-tumble characters of Searchlight could be kind.

I remember a man named Willet Barton. He killed a man in a claim-jumping deal. Somebody had tried to take his mine away from him, and Willet shot him. People were kind of afraid of him, I guess, because all the kids had heard that he was a killer. Willet liked me for some reason. And in this little yard of his, he cultivated figs—he had two trees—and this man who had such a fearsome reputation would share his figs with me. I don't really know why. Maybe it was because I wasn't afraid of him. But I didn't care why. I just loved the figs, and I couldn't believe that something so sweet could be born of the hard rocks beneath our feet.

Pop Payne, who made the star on the ceiling in the front room of our house, would cut my hair and fill me with stories of his life as a major-league umpire. This meant that he'd been to all those places I had heard about on the radio, and it made Pop Payne a very important person in my world, as I lived and breathed baseball. A man named Elwin Kent would also come by the house with his hand clippers and cut our hair. He'd had polio and was hunchbacked. Every now and then, my father and his friends would pick up Elwin by his hands and feet and try to stretch him out to get rid of his hump. Elwin was always of good cheer about this, and my dad and his friends meant well, but it didn't work, of course.

For music, my Uncle Doug could play the steel guitar. And my mother would sing every chance she got. Even at funerals. My dad would make fun of her. He'd say, "Somebody died, so now you can sing." I'm sure he was just jealous, because she had the most pleasant voice.

I, on the other hand, could not sing. Even my mother said so. She'd say, "Okay, at the Christmas program, just move your lips or you'll get a beating when you get home." So I would move my lips, but I wouldn't sing a word. I only got one spanking from my mother, but she threatened me a lot. My dad never gave me a spanking.

On weekends, a western band would come through town. One of the whorehouses, the Searchlight Casino, would be converted into a dance hall for the night, and the grown-ups would go swing-dancing or square-dancing.

Searchlight had no town hall, and so no place for people to gather. When I was a little boy, somebody found an old secondhand building somewhere and hauled it into town. It was pretty rickety, just one big room, and it became our town hall. It was pretty nice. And it's where I saw my first movie. Once in a blue moon, some kind person with the school district would get a two-reeler, always a western, often Roy Rogers, and we were convinced that life didn't get any better.

And Christmas would come.

My mother would have done anything to make sure that we kids had Christmas. She would beg and borrow and I can remember that more than once she got the postmistress to open the post office in the middle of the night on Christmas Eve so we could get our packages—she would delay buying them because she would have to scrape money together to pay the COD, or cash on delivery. In those days, when you'd order from a catalogue, to pick up your merchandise you'd need to pay the postmistress.

And the annual Sears catalogue was always a major cultural event at our house. Everything that existed in the wide world was in that book. Everything. Fancy clothes, baseball stuff. We'd pore over it, studying it to see how those other people out there lived. It's hard to describe the pleasure this gave us—it was almost as good as Jack London. But mostly we just looked at it and dreamed, because we never ordered much out of it.

But when you did get a gift, from the catalogue or elsewhere, you hung on to it. No matter how short it was or how badly it fit or how it wasn't your favorite color. To this day, I hate to return a gift. Because when I was a kid we didn't return gifts. When you get a gift, you say thank you. And if it doesn't fit, you make do. On top of all else, Searchlight taught me this: When you get your hands on something, you keep it.

And when Christmas was over, the catalogue doubled as toilet paper.

ONE DAY, when I was about fourteen, my dad obviously had had something to drink. It was summer, because I was home from my first year away at high school in Henderson. It was daytime. He was being mean to my mother. He started hitting her. That was it. I just looked over at my brother and said, "Larry, let's take him." So we did. We jumped him. I took him high, Larry took him low, and we pinned him to the floor. He was like a rock. My father was a big man, and I'd always been afraid of him. "Get *offa* me!" he yelled as he kicked and writhed. Down in the mines my father was more than a match for solid rock. I'd never conceived of a physical task he couldn't do. Except on that afternoon in Searchlight, he couldn't get my brother and me off of him. "Stay *down!*" I said. My father lived a hard life. He wasn't a bad man. But I'd be damned if he was going to do that to my mother again. It was the first time that we had ever done anything like that. We'd never been big enough. We didn't want to hurt him, we didn't hit him, but we took him down and weren't about to let him up. Oh, he was mad—being challenged under his own roof like that. He struggled there on the floor, cursing the ceiling. For fifteen minutes it went on like this.

All of a sudden, he stopped struggling and started laughing, which we thought was kind of odd. Larry said, "What are you laughing about, Pop?" He said, "You have to let me up sooner or later." We may have been big enough to take him down by then, but we were still afraid of him and he knew it. But then, in silence, we all got to our feet. I figured there was a good chance that Larry and I were going to get it. But to my surprise and relief, nothing happened. My father understood physical strength. That's the world I was raised in. He judged people by what they could do physically, and he taught me to do the same. Larry and I were becoming men, and he wouldn't be able to carry on like that in front of us anymore. Those days were over. We had taken him down, and he would never look at us the same again.

As my father left the room, I caught my mother in the corner of my eye. She had what I remember to be a look of pride on her face.

Looking back, I realize that this was when my father began to seem kind of old to me, even though on the calendar he wasn't that old at all. Things just began to catch up with him.

A few years later, all my brothers and I were home in Searchlight for a family gathering of some kind. We were grown, so the kitchen was smaller than ever, and we're standing around talking when we look up and there's my dad stark naked. I guess he had been drinking or something and got up and there he was. Now, to everybody there I don't think it meant anything. And it shouldn't have to me either, but damn, I was humiliated for him. It was just family. I shouldn't have cared that much. But I did. There was my father, and in such a state. That's why—and I'm sure it's not fair—but that's why I've never had much sympathy for people saying, "The reason I'm so screwed up is because my parents are screwed up. I would have been stone sober if my parents hadn't done this or had only taken me to church more often." That's probably a shortcoming on my part, but I'm just not very sympathetic to those kinds of stories.

I GUESS SOME PEOPLE might consider it to be kind of an unusual background, but this is where I developed my values. Much atten-

tion is paid in public life to the importance of the collection of at-
tributes that we call character. Somewhat less attention is devoted
to consideration of where character is born. But I suppose you
could say that Searchlight gives the lie to some of the prevailing
theories. I am here as a witness to say that character, and values,
come from places you wouldn't necessarily think to look. Because
some of the men and women of greatest character that I will ever
meet in my life came from this place of hard rocks and inhos-
pitable soil.

Trace the footsteps back far enough in anyone's story and you'll
find a pioneer. These are the pioneers in my story. Why they came
here to Searchlight is rather easy to understand; why they stayed and
persevered is maybe a little harder. Mining the earth is just about the
hardest job under the sun, and when the returns begin to dwindle,
the gold is less plentiful, the checks start to bounce—I guess it might
seem to a hard-rock miner like my father that the earth itself is fighting back, exacting its revenge.

Like a lot of young people, I was, quite frankly, embarrassed about
my home, my family, where I came from. And it wasn't until much
later in my life that I came to the realization that who I was, who I
am, is best understood by looking at the tiny high-desert town
of Searchlight.

It took me years to come to this, because that part of my life I had
always put away somewhere. I didn't want anyone to know that I
came from that little place that only had one teacher and no indoor
toilets. That wasn't something that I would ever talk about. But as
time went on, I was drawn back to my hometown, and I started talking about it. This awareness, of course, is not unique. We all have our
homecomings, and this was mine. I suppose when you leave a place,
reject it, you begin to see it clearly, maybe for the first time. You

begin to hear its voices, and maybe even appreciate what it was you were so determined to leave.

My temporary estrangement from my hometown when I was a younger man has its roots in many of the things that I now love most about Searchlight. In modern-day America, it was remote, very quiet, an outpost from the complicated world. Its physical desolation was, and is, stunningly beautiful. And the people there are special characters.

When I was a boy, we had a burly lawman in town, a deputy sheriff named John Silveria. He was known and feared for his toughness. He didn't worry about being nice. If you got out of line, Big John served as judge, jury, parole and probation officer all in one. But he was the object of more hero worship than fear. Every kid in Searchlight seemed to want to be like him.

But it wasn't Big John who made sure that my life of crime was brief. It was Willie Martello, the whoremonger.

It went like this: When I was in high school, sophomore or junior year, a friend of mine named Ron McAllister and I came over from Henderson, and we were kicking around in Searchlight, with not much to do, when we noticed cases of redeemable bottles stacked up behind a casino. Well, we looked at them and we saw dollar signs. We just stole them, as many as we could carry, a case of them, two cases. The perfect crime committed in broad daylight. The next time I saw Willie, he had a serious expression on his face that I wasn't used to seeing. He looked at me and said, "You know, I saw you steal those bottles, so I could have gotten you in big trouble. Pinky, you should never steal anything from anybody. I didn't get you in trouble because I think you could amount to something. Don't you do stuff like that."

And I remembered that always. It was a good, lasting lesson for me. It may sound unusual, but I didn't learn many of those kinds of lessons from my parents. They never taught me things about basic honesty—maybe that's why I had to learn about it from the whore-monger.

But this lesson my mother did teach me, and it's the most impor-tant thing I've ever learned: She taught me to have confidence when sometimes I had no business having confidence. She taught me that no one was better than me, even if it wasn't true. She taught me that I could handle anything that the world could throw at me, what-ever it might be.

# THREE

# THE MINORITY

I CAME TO BE LEADER of the Senate Democrats the hard way. On election night, 2004, my family and my top staff and I gathered in a third-floor suite at the Rio Hotel in Las Vegas to receive election returns from across Nevada and from around the country. It was one of those suites that they normally give to the high rollers, and while I'm not a gambler, we were cautiously optimistic about our chances and were ready to celebrate. The projections coming in throughout the afternoon were excellent. If the exit polls were to be believed, undecided voters all over the country were breaking that day by significant margins for the Democrats. Not only did we stand to gain seats in the Senate, but most important, John Kerry would be our new President. At last, crucial equilibrium would be restored to a nation badly shaken by the attacks of September 11 and increasingly disillusioned by President Bush's conduct of the war against Islamic terrorism.

I was up for reelection that day, and had not often won by comfortable margins—my last election in 1998 had been decided by a mere 400 votes after an excruciating recount. "Landslide Harry" they called me. But this time my campaign had been vigorous and well run, and if the recent polls were any indication, I was going to be fine, and my fellow Nevadans were going to honor me with another six-year term representing them in the U.S. Senate.

One race we were all paying close attention to was in South Dakota, where Tom Daschle, the Democratic leader of the Senate, was in a tight race for reelection. Senator Daschle had typically been reelected comfortably, but these were not typical times, and with President Bush running strong in his state, there was some cause for concern. Running against Daschle was former Congressman John Thune, who had run for the Senate two years earlier and narrowly lost to Democrat Tim Johnson. So here he was trying again. Through the fall, Senator Daschle had kept a small lead. But the White House and the Republican Party had pulled out all the stops to beat him. Earlier in the year, when Thune had been home in South Dakota exploring a race for governor, President Bush himself made a trip to Sioux Falls to appeal to him to instead take on Daschle. And, in an unprecedented breach of Senate protocol, Senate Majority Leader Bill Frist went to South Dakota in the spring to personally campaign against his Democratic counterpart.

Most astonishing, the national parties had turned South Dakota, a state with fewer than a million people, into far and away the most expensive race in the country, pouring $35 million into the two campaigns. And that figure doesn't include the money spent on advertising by independent groups on both sides. Pity the poor people of South Dakota, for their state became host that year to a titanic struggle, and a bloodbath ensued. And it was Tom Daschle who took the brunt of it. He was attacked for having a nice house in Washington, as if that somehow meant that he'd gone native and wasn't the boy from Aberdeen anymore. He was attacked as the "obstructionist-in-chief" of the Bush agenda. And Daschle, a devout Catholic who attended Catholic schools as a child, was attacked in a door-to-door smear campaign that informed Catholic voters that because of Daschle's position on abortion, they risked committing a mortal sin if they voted for him. And as has happened to a disgusting degree in the years since 9/11, Daschle was attacked as being insufficiently steadfast in his resolve to defend America in a time of peril. Hardball politics is one thing, but I find the our-opponents-are-traitors tactic perfected by Karl Rove and the Republicans in this election to be repulsive and un-American.

Tom Daschle by this time had been the Democratic leader for a decade, and he had become a great friend to me, so these attacks were hard to watch. He had worked his way up through the leadership. In the first year of the Clinton administration, Tom and I had had the idea to go to the White House and recommend that President Clinton appoint George Mitchell of Maine, who was then Senate Majority Leader, to the Supreme Court. "Why would I do that?" the President responded. "There's a Republican governor in Maine. He'd appoint a Republican to replace him." Well, we hadn't thought of that, but on the walk back to the Capitol, I had said to Daschle, "Tom, when a leadership position comes open, you should run for it. I think you'd do well." And sure enough, after George Mitchell unexpectedly retired from the Senate in 1994, Daschle had become the Minority Leader, and in 1998 I had become the Minority Whip. All of us who have stood for election and spent any time at all in Washington, D.C., know what a brutal sport full-contact democracy can be, and one just has to accept that as part of the job.

But so far in the twenty-first century we have seen the national security of the United States—and war itself—politicized to a terrible degree by the White House and by the President's party. Along the way, they have engaged in a level of mendacity and secrecy that is unprecedented in American history, and they've done much of this just to gain political advantage. On November 2, 2004, Senator Daschle, who as a young man had worn the uniform of his country during his years of service in the Air Force, was in their sights. Through it all, he had maintained a small lead in the polls—too close for comfort, really, for a sitting Democratic leader—but we nonetheless remained confident of his reelection.

We were so confident of the outcome that a couple of days earlier, at a strategy meeting convened at my old high school friend J. J. Balk's house in Henderson, we hadn't even considered how to respond if the worst-case scenario—a Kerry loss coupled with a Daschle loss—came to pass. We had cycled through our agenda for the meeting when Susan McCue, my Senate chief of staff, suggested that we plan a response in case that very thing happened. But I shook my head no. "Let's not even talk about that," I said. I suppose that it was a function as much of superstition as of confidence. But the rest of the room felt the same way. Daschle's lead was up to 6 points or so, comfortable enough to see him through Tuesday. Why invite bad luck?

But fairly early on Tuesday evening, we realized just how wrong the network exit-poll numbers had been. Earlier in the afternoon it had seemed as if Kerry was on his way to easy wins in Ohio and Florida, and was even competitive in the Republican strongholds of the Deep South, but those numbers—and all the other numbers— were disastrously wrong. Senator Kerry had made a bad mistake by not answering the ridiculous charges leveled by the so-called Swift Boat Veterans for Truth sooner and more effectively, charges that by election day had left a significant number of Americans confused as to whether Kerry had ever even served in Vietnam. And so now, instead of telling the story of a sweeping Democratic victory, the actual returns painted on the electoral map a sea of red in the middle of the country. We just hadn't given those states a compelling reason to vote for Democrats, and if we didn't engage those Americans, immediately, we would have to get used to being in the minority in the Congress and in the country for a long, long time.

The early euphoria drained from the Rio in Las Vegas, just as it did from Democratic election-night gatherings all over the country, replaced by a funereal atmosphere. Kerry hadn't yet conceded the election, as there were still hundreds of thousands of provisional ballots to be counted in Ohio, but given the margin in the state, those ballots seemed unlikely to change the outcome. So his concession was just a matter of time. My focus then shifted to the Congress. And the question then became: How bad is this going to get? The answer: Worse.

I had been monitoring South Dakota all evening, and had been on the phone regularly with Daschle's chief of staff, Pete Rouse, who after the election would go to work as chief of staff for the dynamic young freshman senator from Illinois, Barack Obama. Rouse was a realist, and he knew that in a U.S. Senate contest in which fewer than 400,000 total ballots had been cast, a margin of just a couple thousand could be insurmountable. After all, Thune had lost to Tim Johnson by only 524 votes two years earlier. This time around, Thune's margin had inched up throughout the night, and with the vast majority of the ballots counted, hovered around 4,000 votes.

It wasn't until about 2 A.M. in South Dakota that we knew that Daschle wasn't going to make it. I hung up the phone from my last conversation with Pete Rouse. "Well, Tom Daschle is going to lose," I said to the room. The news was greeted by a stunned silence. Then the phone in our suite at the Rio rang. It was Tom, calling from the Sheraton in Sioux Falls, where he and his family had gathered. "Harry, it's not our night," he said simply. "But I want to congratulate you on your reelection." Because it was so late, he would not concede the race to Thune until the morning, but it was over. And at such a difficult time for him personally, he thought to congratulate me. I am not easily given to emotion, but now my voice was full. "This is devastating news, for the country and for me as your friend," I told him. "Tom, you are like a brother to me."

I hung up the phone, and couldn't help but feel a sense of deep sadness and foreboding. Daschle wasn't to be our only loss that night. We lost open Democratic Senate seats across the South—the Republicans elected David Vitter to assume John Breaux's seat in Louisiana, Johnny Isakson to fill Zell Miller's seat in Georgia, Mel Martinez to Bob Graham's seat in Florida, Jim DeMint to Ernest Hollings's seat in South Carolina, and Richard Burr to John Edwards's seat in North Carolina. The only Republican seats picked up by Democrats were in Illinois, with Obama's victory in the seat being vacated by Peter Fitzgerald, and in Colorado, which elected Ken Salazar over the heir to the Coors beer fortune, Pete Coors, when Ben Nighthorse Campbell retired.

This meant a net loss of four Senate seats for the Democrats. In January, the Republicans would have the White House, a larger margin in the House, and an advantage in the Senate of 55 to 45.

An election day that had appeared to start very promisingly had ended up a Republican blowout. This had become a national security election, and the White House had swept to victory on a wave of fear. We even had a color code by which the government would instruct the public on how afraid they should be. Two weeks before the election, Dick Cheney had warned of nukes in our cities if John Kerry was elected. Somehow, Democrats had not been able to tell a better story.

It was getting late in Las Vegas, and the dispirited crowd in the ballroom was thinning by the minute. The irony of such a devastating day is that I actually had won reelection in Nevada with 61 percent, the most comfortable margin of my career in the Senate. Although I wasn't much in the mood to celebrate, I needed to go say a few words to the die-hard Democrats who had stayed. These were friends of many years. We'd been through tough races together and lots of great victories, too, and they deserved my thanks. Serving in the United States Senate is the honor of a lifetime, and Nevadans had entrusted me with six more years. They deserved my thanks, too. So joined by Landra, my wife of forty-five years, our daughter Lana, and all four of our sons, Rory, Leif, Josh, and Key, I made my way to the ballroom, said a few words, and went back to the suite to make a decision.

For six years I had worked closely with Tom Daschle as Democratic whip, and in that time I had practically lived on the Senate floor. I would often schedule meetings with my staff in the cloakroom just off the floor so that I could remain aware of what was happening on the floor. I had thrown myself into the job, gained a refined understanding of Senate rules, and worked hard to be fair both to members of my own caucus and to Republican senators. The Senate is a body dramatically different from the House: its manners are more courtly, its pace is more deliberate, and it operates to a significant degree by the unanimous consent of its members. In the House, the majority rules absolutely. Not so in the Senate, where a single member in the minority can hold up business if something is not to his or her liking. And so it is a very personality-driven institution. My interest, of course, was primarily the Democrats. In counting votes for Senator Daschle, I had become intimately familiar with the diverse members of the Democratic caucus—with their main areas of policy concern and expertise, with the local political forces that shaped their decision-making, and with their distinctive personalities. I would reserve the breast pocket of my suit jacket for their notes, requests, and complaints, and by the end of most days that pocket would be full. They are an extremely talented, impressive, and diverse group. We have a caucus that reflects the broad ideological spectrum of the country, from liberal to conservative and everything in between. While the Republicans claim a big tent, the Democrats actually have one. In fact, the Republican Party in the age of George W. Bush has come to be so narrow and so dominated by the far-right wing of the party that other voices are seldom heard and no longer welcome. But the Republican Party is not my concern.

My concern early on the morning of November 3, 2004, was who would lead the Democrats in the Senate during the next Congress. Was I going to run to replace Tom Daschle as Senate Minority Leader? Who would be the one to try to turn back this Republican tide, to rein in their horrible excesses? The next day, Karl Rove would be hailed as a genius who had forever redrawn the electoral map and ushered in the era of the permanent Republican majority. George W. Bush would again go around talking like the consultant-in-chief, blustering, "I earned capital in the campaign, political capital, and now I intend to spend it."

I would not sleep that night. It was late, and few remained in the suite at the Rio. Landra was still up. We've been together since high school, so of course no important decision would happen without her. In times of triumph and trouble, Landra is without fail the first person I turn to. Our children were there with spouses, and a couple of our granddaughters were snoozing in their pretty dresses in an adjoining bedroom, dishes of ice cream melted beside them. And a few members of my staff, bleary from lack of sleep, were still there as well.

At about 4 A.M., Susan McCue, a young woman from a big working-class family in New Jersey, stood before me and said, "You've got to make a decision. Do you want to be leader?" It was late, and in moments the sun would rise on the East Coast. Soon I would need to start calling Democratic senators to tell them I was running to replace Daschle and ask for their support. If not me, then who? "Senator, I know that when I have momentous decisions to make," Susan said, "sometimes I'm flooded with doubt. I can't help but feel somebody else is more worthy."

I looked up at Susan, smiled, and said, "I don't have moments like that."

It had been a long, difficult night, and we'd had nothing to laugh about, but now the room broke into laughter, a welcome break in the tension. The decision had been made.

It felt unseemly, given that Daschle hadn't even conceded his race yet, but in two hours I would sit and call the members of a stunned and demoralized Democratic caucus. I wasn't entirely sure what I was going to say.

We would turn this around the best we could.

IN FACT, we had been trying to turn this situation around since just after the 2000 election.

Ever since the election had ended in the infamy of the United States Supreme Court declaring that the ballot counting in Florida was to cease and that George W. Bush was President, the U.S. Senate was evenly divided, 50–50. This was extraordinary. It had been more than a century since such a thing had happened, and it required an unusual reorganization of the Senate, with equal numbers of Democrats and Republicans on committees and equal budgets.

Given that Dick Cheney was the incoming Vice President, though, and as President of the Senate would tilt the balance to the Republicans, Trent Lott of Mississippi would still be Majority Leader.

But almost as soon as the ink was dry on the power-sharing agreement between Lott and Daschle, I started picking up grumbling from some of the few true moderates left among the Republicans in the Senate that strict ideological obedience was being demanded of them, and that the new occupants of the White House were taking a hard line against dissent from the party line of any kind. For instance, anyone questioning the wisdom of the administration's single domestic initiative, the President's massive proposed $1.6 trillion tax cut that disproportionately favored the richest Americans, giving little or no tax relief to middle-class Americans, would be regarded as an enemy by the President's men, and revenge would be exacted. And these tax cuts would be graduated over ten years so that the biggest hits to the federal budget would come just as the baby boomers were starting to retire. We had just spent a decade making hard choices and getting our fiscal house in order, and this new crowd was sweeping into Washington determined to wreck it all over again.

During this period, we were just beginning to get a true sense of the zeal with which the new leadership in Washington would seek to attack and starve the institutions of our government. And this point bears repeating: As important as it has been to President Bush and his ideological brethren to favor the rich in their tax policy, with working people shouldering the burden, it is more important to the ideologues that they starve the American government, because, quite simply, they view government as the enemy, the source of all that is bad.

Ever since the ascendancy of Ronald Reagan in 1980, it has been popular and easy for candidates to run against Washington and the very institutions they are seeking to lead. For these titans of public service, these profiles in courage, the more viciously you can tear our government down, the better. An entire generation of politicians had learned that cynical lesson so well that in 2000 we elected a President for whom this government-is-the-enemy notion was an article of faith. Well, during his presidency this simple-minded political credo has become a self-fulfilling prophecy. Their logic has been circular: A) Government can't do anything right, so, B) elect us, and we'll prove it to you.

This political strategy has been a disastrous success.

The problem with this approach, of course, is that it attempts to obscure the fact that the American government is the greatest force for good in the history of mankind. No amount of cheap political demagoguery will change that fact. But when you so degrade the institutions of our government, you play a very dangerous game, because when you have the power of the presidency, you can make it thus. When you say, over and over, that government is the problem, it becomes the problem. So much so that when you are in charge of it, you don't know how to run it. And you have such contempt for its functions that you appoint partisan hacks to run lifesaving agencies, which is what President Bush did when he appointed Michael Brown to run FEMA, and Brown was then revealed as incompetent in the critical days after Hurricane Katrina wiped out much of the central Gulf Coast in late August 2005.

I am as much a believer in the genius of the American free-enterprise system as anyone, but it was not the market that built the Interstate Highway System, sent man to the moon, or conceived of Social Security, the greatest social program since the fishes and the loaves. It was not the market that saved the planet in two world wars or dammed mighty rivers to electrify Appalachia and the West. Those things, and so many others, were brought to you by the genius of the American government. And what is the American government but an expression of the will of the American people? The Republicans sometimes talk about our government as if it's some kind of alien landing craft, come to impose an alien order. This, of course, is paranoid nonsense. It is this kind of thinking that ought to be considered alien. Because when we've got elected officials in Washington so blinded by ideology that they cannot abide the thought of government helping someone—like, for instance, insuring an uninsured child— then something is terribly wrong. And when at the same time you've got right-wing activists given carte blanche in the halls of power, such as Grover Norquist of Americans for Tax Reform, whose favorite saying is that he wants to shrink the government to a sufficient size so that it might be drowned in a bathtub, then you've got a recipe for disaster. A recipe for a diminished America. You begin to do serious harm to the very idea of American greatness.

That is the situation we faced early in the Bush presidency, and a few seasoned senators in the President's own party were chafing. And that's when we began to seriously consider that one of our moderate Republican colleagues might have just had enough and could be persuaded to switch parties.

There were two possible candidates for such a switch, for very different reasons. Lincoln Chafee of Rhode Island was by this time simply so out of step with his party that he was no longer very welcome in it. It was a reflection of the rightward march of the Republicans that the traditionally moderate Northeast Republicans were becoming a very rare species indeed. So Senator Chafee seemed a likely prospect. The only thing preventing him would be family tradition. Chafee's father, John, had represented Rhode Island in the Senate as a Republican for twenty-three years.

The other possible candidate was John McCain of Arizona, whose family had been slandered so maliciously by George W. Bush and company during the campaign for the Republican nomination the year before that he was known to still be furious. And McCain had over the years established himself as a maverick in Washington, a senator who sometimes seemed to delight in defying the orthodoxies of his own party, especially on high-profile issues such as campaign-finance reform, tobacco litigation, and immigration. In the Presidential campaign of the year before, McCain had given a fiery speech in Virginia attacking the "agents of intolerance" among the religious right. In South Carolina, one of his campaign slogans had been "Burn It Down," echoing Stokely Carmichael from the sixties. The Republican establishment in South Carolina had recoiled in horror at McCain's perceived radicalism and had instead burned down McCain's campaign. So we counted this unpredictable conservative as a possible candidate to disentangle himself from the Republican Party. But as damaging as the experience of the 2000 campaign had been for him and his family, McCain was known to still harbor Presidential ambitions. And a man without a party does not get elected President. In turn, McCain would later climb right into bed with those same "agents of intolerance."

Of course, the Republicans were looking for prospects of their own, and were openly wooing Zell Miller of Georgia, whose friendship in the Senate with the party-switcher from Texas, Phil Gramm, was becoming well known. So time was of the essence. Whoever struck first would win, because a senator in the majority would be very unlikely to switch parties, no matter how estranged he or she might feel ideologically. There were recent precedents for such a switch, all bad for Democrats. During Bill Clinton's first term, Richard Shelby from Alabama and Ben Nighthorse Campbell of

Colorado had both switched to the Republicans after run-ins with the White House.

In the spring of 2001, I began to have discreet conversations on and off the Senate floor with a few of the GOP moderates, who had by then become known as the "Mod Squad." In addition to Chafee, who said that he was interested, Arlen Specter of Pennsylvania and Olympia Snowe of Maine seemed to me to be genuinely flattered by the overtures, but I felt they were unlikely to make such a move. And then there was the junior senator from Vermont, Jim Jeffords.

I had talked with Jeffords on several occasions, because I knew that he was unhappy with the size and scope of the Bush tax cuts, and was worried that consequently Bush wasn't serious about funding public education. The Congress was in the process of passing Ted Kennedy's education bill, which had become known as the "No Child Left Behind" law, but the President included very little funding in his budget for the increased standards the bill called for. So No Child Left Behind left a lot of kids behind. And even worse for Jim, there was nothing at all in the budget for disabled students or special education, which had become Jim's premier cause. Jeffords had established a reputation as a Republican who did not hesitate to cross over and vote with the Democrats if that was where his conscience led him. Whether it was taxes or his deep passion for education or his progressive views on environmental policy, Jeffords did not feel much constrained by fealty to party, and his party had taken note. He had voted against the 1981 tax cuts, and against the confirmation of Clarence Thomas to serve on the Supreme Court. And when Jeffords had been supportive of much of President Clinton's domestic agenda, including then–First Lady Hillary Clinton's health care overhaul, Senator Gramm suggested trading Shelby for Jeffords, so that the "Republicans might be rid of him."

Most of my conversations with Senator Jeffords were casual, on the Senate floor where everybody could see. Hidden in plain sight. This happened five or six times, over three or four weeks. At the end of one such talk, I had told him, "The issues you stand for are the ones we believe in in the Democratic Party. Jim, this is beyond you and me. This is for your country."

And then, late one Monday afternoon in the middle of May, he and I were talking on the Senate floor when Jeffords said, "I think I might be interested in switching." He had said that he would never become a Democrat, but that he was inclined to go home to Vermont and register as an Independent and return to Washington and caucus with the Democrats. This was an earthquake. I immediately went to Tom Daschle's office, walked in, closed the door, and said, "I think Jeffords is really willing to switch parties."

Tom was stunned. He looked at me and said, *"Naw. Are you sure?"*

"I think he is," I said. "I'm going to meet him in the morning to talk about the details."

"I've got a tough schedule in the morning," Daschle told me.

"Well, I think he could do it," I said. "He's right on the verge. I think you'd better come with me."

So Senator Daschle rearranged his schedule. I had set up a meeting with Jeffords for the next morning at 7 o'clock. There exist in the bowels of the Capitol dozens of small private offices used by senators, called hideaways. And that is exactly what they are, hideaways from meetings and ringing phones and buzzing BlackBerrys where work can be done. The three of us would meet in Jeffords's hideaway office early the next morning to hear him out.

We sat down and he immediately said, "I want to do this, but I'm concerned about several things." He was worried about making sure his Vermont dairy farmers received fair price supports for their milk, and that they were protected from any payback from angry Republicans. This wasn't an idle concern. Because he'd shown insufficient zeal for the President's tax cut, the White House had already threatened the program that Jim's farmers relied on. Jeffords's next concern was that he wanted to make sure that his staff was taken care of. And last, he wanted to make sure that his seniority wouldn't be affected. Jeffords had by this time been in the Senate for thirteen years and was chairman of the Health, Education, Labor, and Pensions Committee. The instant he defected he would be stripped of all committee assignments by the Republican leadership and he would lose his seniority. He would be foolish to throw away that kind of influence heedlessly. We'd have to make some kind of accommodation.

At that time, I was the ranking Democrat on the Environment and Public Works Committee. If power shifted to the Democrats, I would be in line to become chairman. In his time in the Senate, Jeffords had become a leader on environmental issues, and his keen interest in the environment was one of the things I found most admirable about him, because it had only served to further isolate him in his own party. It takes a brave man to walk his own path like that. When he raised his concern about seniority, I said, "Jim, I've been thinking about that. I'll have my hands full as assistant majority leader. You can have my committee. You can have my chairmanship. We'll give it to you."

I don't think Jim could quite believe his ears, but with that, the deal was done. Jim Jeffords was going to leave the party he had belonged to his entire life, and shift control of the United States Senate to the Democrats in the process. Never before in the history of the country had power in the Senate shifted for any reason other than death or an election.

But first, Jeffords would have to tell the Republican leadership and his family in Vermont.

On that score, it was unanimous. His wife was opposed. His children were opposed, and threatened to say so publicly. And his staff was opposed. But that was nothing compared with the opposition of his Republican colleagues. Late the following Monday, Jeffords confided his plans to Olympia Snowe, who immediately called White House Chief of Staff Andy Card to raise the alarm. Snowe left a message, and wouldn't hear back from Card until noon the next day. By then, Jeffords had been approached in the men's room off the Senate floor by Pat Roberts of Kansas, who was chairman of the Intelligence Committee. "Jim, how are you?" Roberts asked him. "I hope some of the stories I've been hearing are not accurate."

"I've got to do what's in my heart and mind," Jeffords answered. After that, it was open season on Jim Jeffords, and his resolve would be tested severely.

Senators work hard and bide their time, sometimes for decades, to gain a full committee chairmanship, and the Republicans were not going to take this lying down. Several of his colleagues encircled Jim on and off the Senate floor and took turns cajoling and browbeating. A few of them seemed on the verge of tears. Chuck Grassley of Iowa was overcome with emotion. The rest of them got mad as hell. This would effectively kill off the Singing Senators, the barbershop quartet Jeffords sang in with Trent Lott, Larry Craig, and John Ashcroft. Did he really want to do that? Don Nickles, the Republican whip from Oklahoma, asked him what kind of funny water he'd been drinking, which I'm sure was an effective tack to take. "Just don't screw up the tax bill," Phil Gramm told him. The Vice President met with Jeffords, but made no headway. "You'd better talk to him," Cheney told the President. Jeffords went to the Oval Office and reminded the President of his pledge to be a "compassionate conservative," and admonished him to not just be responsive to the interests of his conservative base, for the good of the country, lest he be a one-term President. "I hear you," Bush told him. The President would later tell Trent Lott that he didn't think that he had been very persuasive.

The stress and the vitriol of his colleagues was taking a toll on Jim, and of course Daschle and I were worried that his decision would not hold.

In the middle of all this, I went to him to see how he was holding up. "How are you, Jim?" I asked.

"Well, I think I'm still going to be with you, Harry," he said. "But I have to hear these guys out. They're friends of mine, and have been for a long time."

Jeffords was scheduled to go home to Vermont on Wednesday evening, May 23. That afternoon, a few Republican senators had a meeting with him just off the Senate floor, a wrenching last-ditch effort to keep him in the party. "We can fix this," Chuck Hagel of Nebraska told him. "Give us a chance." Word came down that Lott would create the new position of "moderates' representative" for Jeffords in the Republican leadership. But that only served to underscore Jeffords's problem with his party, not solve it.

In any case, it was too late. Jim had made up his mind. It was an agony for him that I will probably never fully appreciate, but the next morning at a hotel in Burlington, he made history. "I became a Republican not because I was born into the party but because of the kind of fundamental principles Republicans stood for—moderation, tolerance, fiscal responsibility," he said. I watched him give his speech with Daschle in the Capitol suite that has been the Democratic leader's suite of offices since Robert Byrd was Majority Leader. And as I stood there, transfixed, I couldn't help but notice that he spoke of his party in the past tense, as if paying tribute to someone or something that had died. Jeffords did not do this easily. The easier course by far would have been to do nothing. "Their party—our party—was the party of Lincoln," he said, mournfully. His meaning was raw and clear and bracing. George W. Bush had an ideological ancestry, but Abraham Lincoln certainly wasn't in his lineage. This President belonged to a party that Jim Jeffords no longer recognized. It was a moment that carried great power, and took unbelievable courage.

But Jeffords was just getting to the heart of the matter. "Looking ahead, I can see more instances where I'll disagree with the President on very fundamental issues—issues of choice, the direction of the judiciary, tax and spending decisions, missile defense, energy and the environment, and a host of other issues, large and small.

"And the largest for me is education. I come from the state of Justin Smith Morrill, a U.S. senator from Vermont who gave America its land-grant college system. His Republican Party stood for opportunity for all, for opening the doors of public school education to every American child. Now for some, success seems to be measured by the number of students moved out of public schools."

And then he said it.

"In order to best represent my state of Vermont, my own conscience, and principles I have stood for my whole life, I will leave the Republican Party and become an Independent. Control of the Senate will be changed by my decision."

Senator Daschle's office erupted in a great cheer. "Congratulations, Mr. Majority Leader," I said to Daschle. But as happy as we were at the political victory that we had just achieved, we stood in awe of what we had just witnessed.

Afterward, well, many people hated Jeffords passionately, and he accepted their scorn—and even their death threats—with great equanimity, just as he was levelheaded about the hero worship that came his way as well. In Washington, he would walk down the street and people would spontaneously applaud and cheer as he passed. Since then, he has told me that the switch was something he had been mulling for twenty years.

When it would come time for reelection, in 2006, Jeffords announced that he would retire. He had some encroaching health matters to deal with, and his wife, Elizabeth, was also ill. Upon a senator's retirement, it is tradition in the Senate to honor them and their service to the country with floor speeches. When Jim Jeffords retired in 2006, only one Republican senator could be stirred to say something nice about him. Senator Chuck Grassley of Iowa, who had lost his chairmanship of the all-powerful Finance Committee when Jeffords left the Republican Party, called Jeffords "my friend." It was a moment of true grace, at a time when grace seemed hard to come by.

After that, Jim got sick quickly, and although he is not old, something has taken his memory.

When he decided he couldn't run again, we talked together alone. I said to him, "Jim, when did you first get elected to the House?" His eyes searched the air for the answer, and then he looked at me and said, "I can't remember."

Memory is a kind editor, and a wondrous thing. It tells us our stories differently over time, smoothing out the roughness, removing bitterness, taking away hurt, keeping the people we love young. But sometimes capricious memory abandons us altogether, as it has done with Jim Jeffords.

But let it be remembered that the good senator from Vermont had the eyes to see what was coming with this President, and he wanted no part of it.

I will never forget his act of bravery. I will never forget what Jim Jeffords did for his country.

· · ·

THE REPUBLICANS were furious.

But while Trent Lott circulated a document that became known as their "Declaration of War," in which he railed at this "coup of one," and vowed to deliver on their "mandate" as if they were still in the majority, we got to work.

We would work with dispatch to increase funding for education and make No Child Left Behind something more than a Potemkin bill. And we would pass a Patients Bill of Rights in the Senate, immediately. The bill, cosponsored by John McCain, John Edwards, and Ted Kennedy, was an ambitious and overdue piece of legislation that did several things that federal law did not: It guaranteed access to specialists, required the continuity of medical care so that patients would not be forced to change doctors in the middle of treatment, ensured a fair and timely appeals process for health-plan grievances, and assured that doctors and patients could openly discuss all treatment options without interference from health plans—and the bill made all of these provisions enforceable.

The bill had strong bipartisan support in both houses of Congress, but with the Jeffords defection still fresh and Lott's war just declared, the Patients Bill of Rights had to be passed in the Senate with considerable Republican opposition.

Meanwhile, the President had been systematically withdrawing the United States from the world. Since the Second World War, the United States has been at the fore in conceiving of the covenants that have governed the conduct of the civilized nations of the world, helping the human race avoid a third world war in the process. Our commitment to peace and our fervent belief in the rule of law had made us the vigilant stewards of a peaceful world. And the world has relied on our filling this role. John F. Kennedy, who had been President at the peak of the great existential struggle of the Cold War, struck the balance perfectly when he said, five months before his assassination, "So, let us not be blind to our differences—but let us also direct attention to our common interests. . . . For, in the final analysis, our most basic common link is that we all inhabit this small planet. We all breathe the same air. We all cherish our children's future. And we are all mortal."

But during the first half-year of his presidency, Bush had cheerfully trashed several of our standing agreements that had for decades contributed to the stability of the planet. He canceled the Comprehensive Test-Ban Treaty, withdrew from the Anti-Ballistic Missile Treaty, ignored the Biological Weapons Protocol. He rejected any effort to create an international criminal court, and he rejected the Kyoto Protocol, which had been negotiated by Vice President Gore. He had disengaged completely from the Middle East peace process. The full significance of this impulse to shun the world and abrogate international conventions would not become clear until much later.

In the summer of 2001, President Bush was establishing himself as an American leader who didn't much care what the world thought. It was, to say the least, a strange way to come to power. Typically, American Presidents of both parties have turned to the world with an extended hand and soaring rhetoric. But George W. Bush was pulling up the ladder behind him. Either he didn't understand what America meant to the world, or he was determinedly forging some new and as yet undefined role for us. It was hard to say, because he wasn't talking much. And he was not much more forthcoming to the American people. His presidency had begun with no exhortations to greatness, no generational rallying cries. No "Ask not what your country can do for you, ask what you can do for your country." No "bridges to the twenty-first century." Instead, his refrain was nothing more than a blunt-instrument appeal to narrow self-interest: "It's your money!" As if he were not President of the United States at all but one of those men you see on television hawking for an everything-must-go warehouse sale. But this warehouse sale was divesting the American people of the future.

At the same time he would signal his disregard for science when he announced a tortured position on embryonic stem-cell research that served mostly to limit the horizons and curtail the ambition of some of our most brilliant scientific minds. A significant cohort of our best scientists believed that unlocking the secrets of stem cells was putting us at the threshold of an age of miracles. When our government should have been challenging the best young American minds to go into the sciences and lead the world in this revolution in medicine, the President was instead drawing the shades, content for the rest of the world to take up the slack.

In the summer of 2001, George W. Bush's America was a place of contracting imagination and diminishing returns. A place where you'd better get yours while you can, because who knows about the future. The President had campaigned as "a uniter, not a divider," and had arrived in the capital vowing to "change the tone" in Washington. I suppose you could say that he was keeping that promise, just in a much different way from what anyone had hoped.

On more than one occasion that summer, Tom Daschle came away from a White House meeting and told me, "I think the President really hates it here. I think he really hates his job. I don't think he's going to last long."

And so this is the way it would be. Polls showed that, as ever, the

American public favored Democratic ideas over those of the President and his party by significant margins. Now, in 2001, with the Senate back under Democratic control, we would work toward consensus on health care and education, and we would be in good position to counter the excesses of the Bush agenda. As the August recess rolled around, as Congress and the President headed home, things were looking up.


THE AIR-TRAFFIC CONTROLLERS describe that kind of day as "severe clear."

Not a cloud in the sky, no hint of fall, September 11, 2001, dawned like a summer day in Washington.

Every Tuesday, the Democratic leadership meets to plan the week's business. This week's meeting was going to be on an area of growing concern—protecting Social Security from the Republicans, who had been floating trial balloons on various ways to spend the fund on other things. That wasn't going to happen, not as long as we were in the majority, anyway.

The meeting is always held at 9 A.M. sharp in Room 219 of the Capitol, across from the Democratic leader's office. That morning I was a few minutes early, and I was the first one there when John Breaux of Louisiana came in in a hurry. "Turn on the TV," he said. "There's something going on in New York." Like the whole world, Breaux and I, by this time joined by the rest of the Democratic leadership, stood there watching the television, mystified at how a pilot could have misjudged so badly on a severe clear day. Senator Daschle came into the room and said that retired Senator John Glenn had just been in to visit him, and Daschle had told him of the accident in New York. Glenn, of course, was one of the greatest of all test pilots before going into space. His immediate response had been, "Pilots don't fly into buildings. That's no pilot."

Then came the massive explosion in the other tower.

Almost immediately, the Senate sergeant at arms ran in and grabbed Daschle and took him outside. Then the TV was reporting a fire at the Pentagon. At that moment, Senator Robert Byrd looked out the window of his office facing the Washington Monument and he saw what the television was reporting. The Pentagon was burning. In 219, Senator Patty Murray of Washington State looked out the window and yelled, "Smoke!" Things were now happening quickly. Daschle came back in and said, "We've got to evacuate the building. There's a plane heading toward the Capitol." It was a disoriented Congress that streamed out of the venerable old building. Senator Byrd was very reluctant to abandon the Capitol to fate and almost had to be carried out.

I went from there to my home, to make sure Landra was okay. My longtime aide Janice Shelton lives a great distance away in Virginia, so I took her with me. I was home just a short time when Daschle called and said, "You've got to come back down to the Capitol. They want us here. The Congressional leadership is being evacuated from the city." As I left I told Landra that I didn't know when I would talk to her next. Such was the chaos that throughout the rest of the day, senators from our caucus would call my home and ask Landra where I was, who was in charge, what was the plan, was there a plan? I was the Majority Whip. In any given situation, I was the point man, and under normal circumstances would have had an answer for them. But normal life had ceased. And I was impossible to reach. Members of Congress had dispersed and were congregating in ad hoc offices throughout Washington. There was no plan for such a day, and it was humbling that the government of the United States could be rocked so thoroughly by an act like this. The traffic had been no trouble on the way home, but by the time I was returning the capital city was in a full-bore panic. Brian McGinty was with me. Brian's the member of my security detail that has been with me longer than anyone else. With sirens screaming, we drove back to the Capitol on the sidewalks. The Capitol Police directed us to the west front of the Capitol, which was swarming with police all in black wearing flak jackets, assault weapons at the ready, fingers on triggers. They loaded the leadership of the United States Senate on a military helicopter—the Senate Majority Leader, Tom Daschle; the Minority Leader, Trent Lott; the Minority Whip, Don Nickles; and me—and delivered us to a secret location in Virginia where we would join the House leadership and spend the day communicating with Vice President Cheney, who was in the bunker under the White House. The President was in the air.

As we boarded the helicopter, it was 10:30 or so. Two minutes before, the north tower of the World Trade Center in New York had shuddered to the ground, killing untold innocents, debilitating the center of the world economy, and producing a horrible noxious cloud that would cover lower Manhattan and not dissipate for days.

By early evening on the 11th, we decided that it was important for us to return to the Capitol and demonstrate to the country and the world that the government of the United States was still standing, that our bewilderment at the stunning devastation of the day was matched by our unity and resolve. We met on the steps at sunset. Dennis Hastert spoke, and vowed that when we figured out who was responsible, they would "pay the price." Tom Daschle spoke, offered prayers for the dead and for the living, and said, "Congress will convene tomorrow." And then Barbara Mikulski of Maryland said, "Let's sing 'God Bless America.' " So the Congress of the United States stood on the Capitol steps, and in our uneven voices, we sang.

At that moment, there was nothing else to do.

Someone had declared war on the United States.

And so we were at war.

THE BOMBING of Afghanistan commenced less than a month later, on October 7, with near unanimous support. I had never seen political Washington so united in common cause. The culprits had been identified, and al Qaeda's barbaric hosts in Kabul had been warned: Give up Osama bin Laden or else the Taliban will also be regarded as an enemy of the United States. And so be it.

After the fall of the Taliban, and with the hunt for Osama bin Laden still on, the White House turned its attention to Iraq, and to the threat Saddam Hussein posed to the world because of his nuclear ambitions and his alliance with terrorists. For much of 2002, Vice President Cheney made the case that Hussein had harbored al Qaeda operatives and was eager to turn over his weapons of mass destruction to Islamic terrorists to use against America. Cheney signaled that another war was coming, although the President assured the Congress and the country that he had not made up his mind what he intended to do about the problem, and that his intention was to exhaust peaceful means before doing anything else—continuing the economic sanctions leveled against Baghdad years before and making sure the UN weapons inspectors were allowed to complete their work. I knew that President Clinton had been gravely concerned about the Baghdad regime for interfering with the weapons inspectors, and for flouting the will of the world, so I took these claims by the White House very seriously.

Committing our nation to war is the most serious responsibility a President has, and no President wants war. At least, no President ought to. President Eisenhower, who knew something of war, said, "Every gun that is made, every warship launched, every rocket fired signifies, in the final sense, a theft from those who hunger and are not fed, those who are cold and are not clothed." And as President Kennedy said, "The United States, as the world knows, will never start a war."

But September 11, we were being told, had changed that calculus, had changed everything, and today the greatest threat to our existence was something that yesterday we had never recognized as much of a threat. As the march of globalization connected the world as never before, fanatical nonstate actors lurking in the shadows of failed states could start wars with us and slink back into their caves. That's certainly what had happened with bin Laden and his primitive sponsors in Afghanistan. Great-powers war was suddenly a thing of the past. The twentieth century was assuredly over. And, moreover, the end of the Cold War had awakened Russia from its Stalinist slumber and unleashed black-market criminals on its loosely guarded nuclear arsenal, and now weapons-grade material was to be had by any terrorist for the right price. Confidence was high that Saddam Hussein was trying to get his hands on this material. The Vice President said so, repeatedly. The President would say it as well.

No, the United States could never again sit back and wait for an attack. We must act preemptively or suffer the consequences.

In the early summer of 2002, at West Point, the President announced this doctrine in a speech:

"If we wait for threats to fully materialize, we will have waited too long.

"Homeland defense and missile defense are part of stronger security, and they're essential priorities for America. Yet the war on terror will not be won on the defensive. We must take the battle to the enemy, disrupt his plans, and confront the worst threats before they emerge. In the world we have entered, the only path to safety is the path of action. And this nation will act.

"Our security will require the best intelligence, to reveal threats hidden in caves and growing in laboratories. Our security will require modernizing domestic agencies such as the FBI, so they're prepared to act, and act quickly, against danger. Our security will require transforming the military you will lead—a military that must be ready to strike at a moment's notice in any dark corner of the world. And our security will require all Americans to be forward-looking and resolute, to be ready for preemptive action when necessary to defend our liberty and to defend our lives."

In August, Cheney made his case for war before the VFW convention in Nashville, applying the President's doctrine of preemption specifically to Saddam Hussein:

"What he wants is time and more time to husband his resources, to invest in his ongoing chemical and biological weapons programs, and to gain possession of nuclear arms.

"Should all his ambitions be realized, the implications would be enormous for the Middle East, for the United States, and for the peace of the world. The whole range of weapons of mass destruction then would rest in the hands of a dictator who has already shown his willingness to use such weapons, and has done so, both in his war with Iran and against his own people. Armed with an arsenal of these weapons of terror, and seated atop ten percent of the world's oil reserves, Saddam Hussein could then be expected to seek domination of the entire Middle East, take control of a great portion of the world's energy supplies, directly threaten America's friends throughout the region, and subject the United States or any other nation to nuclear blackmail.

"Simply stated, there is no doubt that Saddam Hussein now has weapons of mass destruction. There is no doubt he is amassing them to use against our friends, against our allies, and against us."

In addition, Cheney repeated several times in the fall of 2002 that a linkage had been established between Hussein and al Qaeda, that the lead 9/11 hijacker, Mohamed Atta, had met with Iraqi intelligence officials in Prague. His implication was clear: Saddam Hussein knew about 9/11 before the fact, and may have had a part in it.

And in September, the President's national security adviser, Condoleezza Rice, famously said of the danger posed by Hussein, "We don't want the smoking gun to be a mushroom cloud."

In October, the President spoke to the nation in prime time, and the wolf was at the door. The drumbeat for war from the White House was now deafening.

It was in this atmosphere that Congress set about the business that fall of considering whether or not to give the President the authority to take military action on Iraq. Classified briefings only reinforced the case coming from the White House. Iraq, they said, posed an imminent threat to us and to the world. We must learn the lesson of September 11, 2001, and not be surprised like that again. We must as a nation employ the President's new doctrine and make war preemptively to deliver the world from this gathering threat.

I had come to know that President Bush was an arrogant man, and acted as if he had something to prove. What on earth does a man who has achieved the presidency have to prove? But I had no reason—yet—to believe that he would lie to our nation. Our country had a long and sordid history with the Iraqi dictator, most of it awful. He was a hideous tyrant, a proven mass murderer, a figure the world would be well rid of. And I was very concerned about the stability of Israel if he got the weapons our intelligence services and the White House claimed he was seeking. It was inconceivable to me that our national leadership, whatever our differences, would trivialize matters of war and peace, life and death.

So the Congress asked for and received assurances from the White House that military action would only come as a last resort, and that the United States would first seek the legitimacy of the United Nations before taking action. And on October 11, 2002, I voted for a resolution, H.J. Res. 114, which stated, "... The President is authorized to use the Armed Forces of the United States as he determines necessary and appropriate, in order to ... defend the national security of the United States against the continuing threat posed by Iraq."

I was joined in my vote by seventy-six other members of the Senate. I was comfortable in this decision because I had become convinced of the threat. I sincerely believed that such a strong statement from the Congress would make it crystal clear that the United States was serious in this cause, and that this vote could actually have the effect of averting war by convincing Hussein to open up again to a full regime of UN weapons inspections. Certainly he was crazy, but perhaps he wasn't a fool.

And I also believed that, as his father had done in advance of the first Gulf War, this President would gather the nations of the world around him before going to war, should it come to that. Between Hussein's invasion of Kuwait in August 1990 and the beginning of the first Gulf War in January 1991, the first President Bush had sent his Secretary of State, James Baker, around the world numerous times to construct a mighty coalition to oppose Hussein, including the majority of Arab states.

President George W. Bush, as it turns out, would only send his Secretary of State to perform at the United Nations.

And on February 5, 2003, when Colin Powell testified to the gravity of the threat before the UN Security Council and the entire world, the case was resoundingly made. Certainly a man such as Powell would not lend his good name and reputation to such a cause unless his list of particulars was completely sound.

Many of us in Congress knew well that Secretary Powell was not in lockstep with the White House on this emerging Iraq policy or on anything else for that matter. And that fact only buttressed his credibility as he strode onto the world stage to indict and convict the Baghdad regime. At that instant, the war clock began to tick. I cannot overstate the influence his presentation had on me and others in the Congress; serious men and women, with sober judgment, had their doubts swept away by Colin Powell.

What we, of course, didn't know at the time is that the President had already made up his mind about what he was going to do— before Powell's briefing, before the Congressional vote, before 9/11 even.

Two years later, Paul O'Neill, Bush's first treasury secretary, would tell writer Ron Suskind that at President Bush's very first National Security Council meeting, on January 30, 2001, replacing Saddam Hussein had been at the top of the agenda. "Getting Hussein was now the administration's focus," O'Neill told Suskind.

And what we didn't know at the time was that according to the famous British intelligence document known as the Downing Street Memo, as early as July 2002, "Military action was now seen as inevitable. Bush wanted to remove Saddam, through military action, justified by the conjunction of terrorism and WMD. But the intelligence and facts were being fixed around the policy. The NSC had no patience with the UN route."

And what we didn't know was that half of Powell's presentation was based on intelligence that was already known to be unreliable or false.

The legislative branch of the United States government and the American people had been misled by the executive branch. We would not realize this fact for some years to come, a slow dawning, a sickening feeling, and by then the war had begun to go very badly.

But in all of this, I will never forget the voice of Robert Byrd, who, as debate was coming to an end on the war resolution that October, urged more time. "It would be unpatriotic not to ask questions," he implored. Byrd would be ignored.

He was right.

I was wrong.

And that is a difficult lesson to learn.

People ask me, Are you sorry?

Yes. I am sorry I didn't ask more questions.

But I am also sorry I was lied to. I am sorry that the awesome power that the President has at his disposal was abused so. I am sorry that Senator Byrd wasn't allowed to ask his questions. And I am sorry that when Colin Powell realized that his honor had been compromised and his reputation damaged by a White House bent on war, he did not resign his office.

ON MAY 1, 2003, President Bush landed on the deck of the USS *Abraham Lincoln* just off the coast of Southern California and famously declared that "major combat operations in Iraq have ended." MISSION ACCOMPLISHED read the banner behind him. I found every element of this highly politicized event to be enraging. "Some hotshot, huh?" I said to Richard Verma, then my chief foreign policy adviser, as we watched the carrier landing and the President strutting across the deck wearing his flight suit. "This is *incredible*. One of our aircraft carriers is being used as a political prop." But worse than that, of course, is that the President's pronouncement that day turned out to be about as correct as everything the White House has had to say about the Iraq campaign since. The tragic irony was that at this point the real war was just about to begin. The flowers-and-sweets fantasy of the neocon authors of this war policy was about to get a horrible dose of reality. And American soldiers would pay the price.

The drive to Baghdad had been something to behold, a testament to the stunning prowess and professionalism of our fighting men and women. But once they had toppled the regime and set about the task of finding Saddam's WMD, there existed a vacuum where a government had just stood, and Washington had no plan to fill that vacuum, nothing to put in its place. The planners had all been ignored in favor of the fantasists.

Well, chaos loves a vacuum. And so chaos it was.

ROOM 407 of the Capitol is the room where classified briefings are offered to members of the Senate. It is here, in this room, where we gather to learn the best intelligence that our various intelligence agencies have to offer on myriad situations around the world. And it is here, in the late winter of 2004, where members of the Senate filed in to look at stacks of photographs that had been taken at one of Saddam Hussein's most notorious prisons, Abu Ghraib. They were horrible pictures, pictures of sexual humiliation and explicit sex acts. Pictures of degrading and violent treatment of prisoners. And pictures that can only be described as documenting torture.

The pictures on the table in Room 407 were not pieces of evidence against a brutal dictator. They were a lurid and incredible record of the treatment of prisoners at the hands of Americans. And of graphic sex between soldiers and guards while supposedly on duty. They were sickening. How did this happen? What could possibly be the explanation? Was it aberrational? And who was being held accountable?

The President had been talking regularly about the crucial hearts-and-minds element of the war that he now had taken to calling the "central front in the war on terror." I thumbed through these pictures and I thought, So much for hearts and minds.

I couldn't believe the level of mismanagement and carelessness and malice and failure of leadership.

And although the President and the Secretary of Defense would try to blame these grotesque acts on "rogues on the night shift," these images did not represent an aberration. In late 2001, when then–White House Counsel Alberto Gonzales was establishing the extrajudicial military tribunal system for dealing with prisoners, he had issued the first opinion of many such opinions stating that "enemy combatants" in this new kind of war would not be regarded as prisoners of war and so would not be afforded protections specified under Common Article 3 of the Geneva Conventions, to which the United States had been a proud signatory in 1949. In the face of general outrage, the White House had backed off this "Presidential finding," but I held in my hand clear evidence that this pernicious idea had survived and was governing, or at least influencing, our treatment of prisoners under our control. We would later come to know about the "torture memos" issued by the Office of Legal Counsel at the Justice Department that had defined torture so narrowly as to allow almost any treatment of prisoners, U.S. law and Geneva Conventions be damned. This was a national disgrace, and was certainly not the American way of war.

In the American Revolution, at the Battle of Princeton, British soldiers mercilessly bayoneted wounded Continental Army soldiers that they found helpless on the battlefield. But when Washington's irregulars prevailed and took hundreds of the redcoats prisoner, Washington would not hear of vengeance.

The American soldiers asked for permission to reciprocate and show the prisoners no quarter, but Washington told them, "Treat them with humanity, and let them have no reason to complain of our copying the brutal example of the British army in their treatment of our unfortunate brethren." In his book *Washington's Crossing*, David Hackett Fischer writes that General Washington "often reminded his men that they were an army of liberty and freedom, and that the rights of humanity for which they were fighting should extend even to their enemies."

And it was not just the father of our country who said this. Every great commander in every existential struggle in our history has understood that we Americans are different from our enemies. A civilization that values the dignity of man does not torture, does not sanction torture, and does not engage in Orwellian doublespeak to obscure its activities when it "takes the gloves off," as Donald Rumsfeld said, or walks on the "dark side," as Dick Cheney said. Torture doesn't make a leader tough or patriotic, it makes him despotic. We don't have despots in America. And most important, this is no way to protect America. Torture compromises our soldiers and puts them at terrible risk, which is unpardonable.

These are the hinges of history. It is when we are threatened that we are defined. History will not spare us in Congress, any of us, for our complicity in this period. And we ought not be spared. At times Democrats have been too afraid of being seen as weak to do the right thing, from the war-authorization vote forward. At times we have just been outnumbered by a Republican caucus determined to give the White House whatever it wants, with no questions asked. So when this chapter of our history is written, it will tell the story of a Congress that at crucial moments—the shameful elimination of habeas corpus rights for prisoners comes to mind—has been compliant in the face of an out-of-control White House.

Within a couple weeks of "Abu Ghraib" becoming an unfortunate addition to the American vocabulary, the Senate leadership was briefed by Tom Kean, the former Republican governor of New Jersey, and former Democratic Congressman Lee Hamilton, who had cochaired the 9-11 Commission and were days away from issuing their much-awaited report.

I asked these two men, "Just who are these terrorists?"

"Here's what we're most worried about," Governor Kean said. "There are a finite number of people in this world—a few thousand—who want to kill or harm Americans and Western interests in some way. These people cannot be rehabilitated, they can't be counseled out of the wrongness of their beliefs or actions. They either have to be killed or captured."

"But there are millions of people in the world who sympathize with what the bad guys are doing," said Congressman Hamilton. "And this is the group of people that you must spend your time and energy on. Because they could either be with us or they could turn their energies into aggressive actions against the United States and our interests for decades and generations to come. We could lose them."

"We have to offer them a better deal than jihad offers them. This is largely a nonmilitary struggle, it's an ideological struggle," said Kean. "We have to win these people over. You *have* to *win* these people over."

The White House had opposed the bipartisan 9-11 Commission investigation, just as it has opposed all inquiries on behalf of the people into activities of the Bush administration. Cooperation from the executive branch finally came only grudgingly, not in the spirit of openness, but as if the President and Vice President were somehow reluctant to discover and learn everything possible from the event that has defined American priorities and the American relationship to the rest of the world ever since.

But this briefing from these two men, one from each party, has stayed with me since that day, and to a great degree I view American power through the prism that Kean and Hamilton gave me. It is foolish not to consider how the millions in the Muslim world that Kean and Hamilton describe experience American power. What does Guantánamo do to those people on the fence? Abu Ghraib? Water torture? Illegal wiretapping? News that we've rendered suspects to secret CIA prisons, at least thirty of whom have died and been ruled homicides? News that we've used "enhanced interrogation techniques" pioneered by Torquemada?

WE WOULD TURN this around the best we could.

November 3, 2004. It was not yet dawn in Las Vegas as I sat in the high-roller suite at the Rio in my pajamas and began to dial Democratic senators back East, tell them that I was running to replace Tom Daschle as Minority Leader, and ask for their support. I was tired, and not entirely sure how these calls would go. I had been a member of the Democratic leadership in two successive elections in which we had lost senators. In 2002, we had lost the majority that Jim Jeffords had given us in an election that had been much the same as that of the day before. Another 9/11 election, another election in which Democratic patriotism and courage had been slandered by hacks. As the Democratic whip, I probably knew and understood the caucus better than anybody else, but would they trust that I was the one to lead us out of this mess?

I knew that Chris Dodd of Connecticut was also running to lead the Democrats and would have some support, including his longtime friend Ted Kennedy.

But as I began making those calls, I took strength from my colleagues. Tom Daschle was like a brother to me, I told them, but time was too short to hold a wake. We had to get organized, and fast. George W. Bush was at the peak of his power, and was determined to complete his radical agenda. First in the line of fire: Social Security. I told my Senate colleagues that as Democrats, our diversity should be our strength. Our caucus covers the spectrum from Ben Nelson of Nebraska to Barbara Boxer of California. We can't expect Nelson to vote as if he were from California or Boxer to vote as if she were from Nebraska. And we would no longer cede any part of our country to the Republicans. We had to engage the middle of the country, define ourselves rather than be caricatured by the Republicans, and make a claim for the country's votes. Give them a reason to vote for us again. We would go after Senate seats in "red" states. And we would aggressively go after Republicans who held Senate seats in "blue" states.

Robert Byrd said yes. Jim Jeffords said yes. Chuck Schumer of New York said yes, and offered to call others on my behalf.

Some senators had committee requirements. Ron Wyden of Oregon wanted Finance. Jack Reed of Rhode Island wanted to stay on Appropriations.

Some had suggestions for engaging the majority and the White House. Hillary Clinton, who is as tough and smart as any senator I've seen, told me that we needed to establish a "War Room" to combat the Republican noise machine and take our message to the country. No more Swift Boats. This was excellent advice born of hard experience. We would act on Hillary's suggestion quickly.

Patty Murray of Washington said yes. Russ Feingold of Wisconsin said yes. Herb Kohl of Wisconsin said yes.

Now was not the time for Democrats to get in a circle and start firing. That would be a surefire way to ensure that we'd be in the minority permanently.

Bill Nelson of Florida said yes. Barbara Boxer of California said yes. Daniel Inouye of Hawaii said yes.

We would not let the President and his allies in Congress privatize Social Security.

Ben Nelson of Nebraska said yes. Dianne Feinstein of California said yes. Barack Obama of Illinois said yes.

And what we lacked in numbers, we'd make up for with a comprehensive understanding of the rules of the United State Senate. And we would strengthen the committee system. I would empower senior senators, who ran the committees. The Republicans had a 10-vote majority, so we'd have to be nimble.

Dick Durbin of Illinois, Ken Salazar of Colorado, Evan Bayh of Indiana, Debbie Stabenow of Michigan, Jay Rockefeller of West Virginia, Daniel Akaka of Hawaii—all yes.

There were now forty-four Democratic senators. With Jim Jeffords in the caucus, forty-five. By late morning I had more than the twenty-three commitments I'd need to be elected Democratic leader of the Senate.

I showered, got dressed, said a prayer, and was ready to face the day. It was then that Senator Dodd called and very graciously told me that he was not running and that I would have his support. Then the

President called. "Be straight with me," he said, "and I'll be straight with you."

"Thank you, Mr. President," I said. "I always had a wonderful relationship with your father, and I will do my best for the sake of the country to work with you. But Mr. President, cooperation is a two-way street."

With that, I went downstairs to the front of the Lloyd George federal building, where my Las Vegas office is located, to talk to the press, which by then had become a throng, with media organizations from around the world represented. This was a new one on me.

I had not prepared anything to say, but I've learned that a lot of things you do that turn out well are things you do instinctively. You've had a little bit of experience, and you just think certain things are right and certain things are wrong.

"I'm going to do my best to be cooperative with the President," I said. "He just called me, and I appreciate that. He didn't have to do that. We will work together to defend America against all enemies. We will work to reach compromise when we can. And we will oppose him when we must."

His first four years, he had acted with utter disregard for the Congress. "Be straight with me," the President had said, "and I'll be straight with you." A promising start, I thought. Perhaps with a large electoral victory comes magnanimity.

"I won't today dwell on our differences," I said. "But I will say this: I will do everything in my power to make sure that the President does not privatize Social Security."

Well, that's where the instinct comes. In truth, I had no idea if we could stop him. He was on a real roll. And now some people were saying that we had been reduced to a one-party government. Could we hang on? I had talked to Nancy Pelosi, who was the incoming House Minority Leader. We were scared, really scared, but we decided to take him on. And we would fight like hell. It was the right thing to do.

We would turn this around the best we could.

Not long after, the *New Yorker* magazine published this headline: "How a Pro-Gun, Anti-abortion Nevadan Leads the Senate's Democrats."

# FOUR

# THE OUTSIDE WORLD

SHE WAS WEARING SHORT-SHORTS, I remember that. And she was washing the family car.

Her family lived on a nice street in Henderson, and I was just driving around. And that's when I saw her. And I thought, Wow, that's a pretty nice car washer. I was starting to like life in the big city.

She doesn't remember it that way. She remembers seeing me around at school, at the Saturday night dances, here and there. But I remember the pretty girl in the short-shorts washing the family car in her father's driveway. And that's a memory that stays with you.

I was a junior at Basic High School, and she was a sophomore, and she looked like she belonged in the movies. Short dark hair, dark brown eyes, porcelain skin, unbelievable smile. She was smart. And she'd been places. Out of my league, that's for sure. But when you come from Searchlight, you know you're going to have to work twice as hard for things.

When you finished Searchlight School, either you went to high school someplace distant, or you didn't go anywhere and that was the end of your education. Finding someplace to go to high school took money some people just didn't have. Some young men kicked around or went into the mines or other such jobs. Others went to school in Needles, California, some to Boulder City or Las Vegas. Following the good example of my brothers Don and Dale, who had both gone to Basic High School, I stuck out my thumb at age thirteen and hitchhiked the 45 miles north to Henderson, which was then an industrial town of two or three thousand, but after Searchlight it may as well have been Times Square.

And lucky for me that I did, or I never would have met Landra Gould, the chiropractor's daughter.

If one's life is a series of fateful meetings, then I had the two most fateful meetings of my life at Basic High School in Henderson, Nevada, home of the Basic High Wolves. First and foremost, Landra, who, as you'll see, has been my partner in this whole adventure. Born the daughter and only child of Earl and Ruth Gould, who lived at 77 BMI Road. BMI stood for Basic Magnesium Incorporated, and the Goulds lived in a new three-bedroom stucco house, with an indoor bathroom and everything, across from the plant by the Titanium Metals baseball field. To me, Landra's home was like the Taj Mahal. By contrast, the original Henderson town site was put together in a matter of months during wartime and was built to last only twenty years. Those houses were simple, wood, 500 square feet.

Earl Gould—or Doc Gould, as he was called in town—was a large figure in Henderson. He had been born in Russia or the Ukraine (no one knows for sure which) under the name of Israel Goldfarb, and had been brought to America as a child, first to Minnesota. Then he made his way to Los Angeles, and then, following his brother-in-law, he arrived in southern Nevada. His brother-in-law, Fred Kersch, was a pharmacist. He was friends with another pharmacist, Hubert

Humphrey, and when Humphrey was a senator and then Vice President, he would always visit Fred when he passed through Nevada. Kersch told Doc Gould that there were opportunities in Henderson. And so there were. The opportunity I saw was Doc Gould's beautiful daughter. As soon as we became acquainted, I asked Landra to homecoming, but she was already committed. This did not make me happy. Maybe she was just trying to make me feel better, but she said it didn't make her feel very good either. And that wasn't the end of my problems. I knew there were other guys out there vying for her attention.

This Landra Gould would require some effort, as all good things do.

So I tried again and we just went on a regular date, to a movie at the Victory Theater. I borrowed Larry Perryman's car, because I didn't have a car of my own. Larry's car didn't have a starter that worked, so you had to park it on a hill and coast to get it started. So there we were after the movie, on our first date, pushing the car. This is not the way you want things to go. But then, well, I looked over at Landra, and that smile just redeemed the night. She was of such good cheer about it. Who cares about the car! Something that could have been embarrassing became funny. There are moments that turn a life, and that stay with you until the last breath. This was one of those moments for me.

And that was it. Somehow, she would choose me. Landra Gould and I just belonged together.

And then there was Mike O'Callaghan, who arrived at Basic High my senior year there and would become my teacher and my best friend.

He had a wooden leg, I remember that. At least we called it a wooden leg. And the first time I ever saw this remarkable man in action, he was challenging a bully to fight, which really made him my kind of guy. The guy was as big as O'Callaghan, but he could have been five times Mike's size, and it still wouldn't have been a fair fight. Just a few years before, when he was just back from Korea minus a leg and was recovering in a veterans' hospital in San Francisco, Mike and another decorated soldier, a double-amputee Japanese-American, decided to go out on the town. Along the way they got in a fight with a bunch of sailors. The other soldier forgot for a moment he had no legs, and dove out of the car after them. Mike came hobbling around to help the guy. Just a couple of brawling amputees. The picture of them lying in the street was on the cover of most newspapers in America the next day. And in that picture, he looked just like he did when I met him: toughest man I ever met. A real world-beater. The kind of guy who joins the Marines at sixteen. Acts of courage were routine for Mike. And this day early in my senior year was no different.

I was student body president. It was football season, and the football players were standing around, sizing everybody up. And here comes this big man. He walked with a strange gait. He had a comb-over and a barrel chest and he'd left a leg in Korea. Well, as seniors we thought we ruled the roost, but all of a sudden there was a new sheriff in town, come to set us straight.

And there was a football player, Ken Smith, big guy, who had beaten up on some smaller guy, and was talking big about it. Well, O'Callaghan had heard about this, so he went up to Smith, who was well over 200 pounds, with a big shock of red hair, and in front of all of us he said, "I hear you think you are pretty tough, huh?"

And Smith said, "Yeah, I guess I am pretty tough."

"Well, I think you're a chickenshit," O'Callaghan told him. This is a teacher talking to a kid. Mike said, "I bet you wouldn't come down to the Boys Club after school and put gloves on in the ring, because you're a chickenshit." Well, what was Smith going to say? Nobody knew O'Callaghan, he had just gotten to Basic. So we all went down to the Boys Club after school and O'Callaghan and Smith put on gloves and got into the ring, and the brand-new teacher with one leg just coldcocked him. Smith was out like a light. The fight lasted less than ten seconds. O'Callaghan hit him so hard, he crashed down and hit the back of his head and we thought he'd killed him. Well, he wasn't dead, and after that, O'Callaghan was our hero. Nobody messed with him. And when he was around, nobody messed with the little guy either. One of the many things he taught me was that the little guy was worth fighting for.

Mike had been in a trench when the mortar shell hit. February 13, 1953. His squad leader was blown up. Others were killed. Mike was lucky to survive. The citation from his Silver Star reads, "While his company was being subjected to a barrage of heavy artillery from Chinese Communist forces during a night attack, Sgt. O'Callaghan was informed that men on an out-guard post had been cut off by this enemy action. Immediately, he voluntarily exposed himself to enemy fire, located the men and brought them, together with a wounded member, safely back to the trenches."

That's when the 82 mm mortar round hit, blowing off his left foot and mangling his leg. With some telephone wire he made a tourniquet, using a bayonet to twist it tight around his bloody stump.

"He crawled back to the command post," continues the citation, "and from that position, controlled platoon action for the next three and one-half hours, giving orders over the phone. Not until the enemy had withdrawn did he permit himself to be evacuated." They amputated Mike's left leg below the knee. But he wasn't going to let anything stop him. And by the mystery of life he made his way to

Henderson, Nevada, and to Basic High School. And now here he was, not much more than a kid himself, knocking out the bullies. In years to come, I would have the privilege of seeing Mike O'Callaghan take on more bullies than I could count.

THEY CALLED MAGNESIUM the "wonder metal," because it was so light and could be used for so many things. The Germans had used it for making aircraft and munitions during the First World War. And in 1937, Nevada Democratic senator Patrick McCarran, the very powerful, right-wing, anti-Semitic, and anti-black chairman of the Senate Judiciary Committee, convinced his nemesis Franklin Roosevelt that the federal government should support a magnesium refinery in southern Nevada. There was nothing there at the time, and they essentially built Henderson for the war effort. They situated the plant there because there was cheap electricity to be had from nearby Boulder Dam, which would soon become Hoover Dam. And good thing they did, too, because war was just over the horizon. At its wartime peak, Basic Magnesium was processing 5 million pounds of magnesium ore a day. Most of this was put into bomb manufacturing, and Basic became crucial to the American war effort. If gold put Searchlight on the map, it was magnesium that did it for Henderson.

And before long, more than 10,000 workers were drawn to the area for jobs in the defense plants in Henderson, or at the Nevada Test Site, or at Boulder Dam. My friend Donnie Wilson's father had been a miner in Idaho and Arizona and had been passing through town when a man at the plant told him that if he could weld, he could have a job on the spot. Well, miners think they can do anything, so a welder he became, on the spot. Richey Vincent's dad brought his family to Nevada from California. Tom McGinty's dad came over from Oklahoma to make bomb casings and nose cones for rockets in the plants. Jimmy Joe Balk's dad was an excellent carpenter and had uprooted his family in Wisconsin for a job at the Nevada Test Site. J.J. remembers that his father would come home, open the shades, and wake everybody up so that they could all watch the flashes from the nuclear tests together.

One winter, my friend Gary Bates's dad moved his family from Estes Park, Colorado, after their house burned down. They'd headed south and west, looking for someplace warmer, and ran out of money in Henderson. Housing was in short supply. The Bateses put themselves on waiting lists at Victory Village, a development that Gary's dad would call a "white ghetto," and at Carver Park, which was largely a black ghetto. In Victory Village, the buildings were painted white. In Carver Park, which was originally built to house blacks working on the construction of Boulder Dam, they were painted brown. Neither place had any houses available, and the Bateses had no money in any case, and so the family lived out at Lake Mead for six months, camping out of the family car while they scraped together a little money and waited for a house to open up. Gary's father disabled the dome light so it wouldn't drain the battery, and thus, they had a house on the beach. Every morning, Gary's mother would drive his dad to Hoover Dam, where he'd found work, and then drive their homestead back to the lake, where she'd do the wash. A call finally came that there was a place open in Victory Village, and the manager made a deal with Gary's parents that if they would pump kerosene for the other residents, he'd give them a five- or ten-dollar break on the rent, which was a big deal.

Different versions of this same story played out in every family as the fathers of my friends followed opportunity to Nevada. The work was good and purposeful, the pay was reliable, but it was not without its dangers. When you heard the sirens at Basic Magnesium, you knew there'd been some kind of spill, an injury, maybe a death. You knew somebody might have lost a dad.

When I was a junior at Basic High, my own father would return to Henderson to work in the plants. He came back out of desperation, for there was no longer any work in Searchlight. And for two years I would live with my parents in one of the old town-site homes on Magnesium Street. You could get to Magnesium Street by turning off of either Copper Street or Manganese Street. A few blocks away were Gold, Lead, and Zinc Streets, too.

But for my first two years in Henderson I lived during the week with aunts and uncles, and would hitchhike home for weekends. Freshman year, I lived with my father's brother, Uncle Joe, and his wife, Aunt Ray, and then during my sophomore year with my Aunt Jane, who was a wonderful cook. She would make venison that was just delectable; pancakes with Roman Meal, topped with her homemade syrup. And the best hamburgers. Back in the early 1940s, she had put together enough money in Searchlight to buy some meat and some buns and invited people in off the street to try them, and Aunt Jane's restaurant was born. It grew into a nice little place.

Uncle Joe was a wonderful man, but withdrawn, like my father, not somebody you shot the bull with. As for my Aunt Ray, a lot of people in the family thought she was a little strange because she was religious and went to church. And she was a Mormon to boot. This shouldn't have been strange, as there are a great many Mormons in Nevada. But maybe my family was a little strange. And I liked Aunt Ray. She took her role as surrogate mother seriously, and she was strict, which was a new experience for me. I had not had someone express that kind of interest in me before. Her kindness made my transition from Searchlight to Henderson a lot easier than it might have been otherwise. But I never could completely shake the feeling that I was imposing on my aunts and uncles. They were just trying to be nice to my parents, who didn't pay them to support my stay most of the time or were always late in paying them.

A lot of people I met at school showed me exceptional kindness as well. And what great characters. Bernard Cannon would strut around Basic like he owned the world. Lantern-jawed and a star athlete, Bernard was a full-grown man when he was only fourteen. He owned his own car as a freshman. For whatever reason, he made sure I was always taken care of and nobody messed with me.

On the first day of football practice my freshman year, the coaches assigned us a locker and passed out the equipment to us in a bag. More than anything else in life, my goal was to be an athlete. In the locker next to mine was this new guy named Eddie Johnson who had just moved to Henderson from California. He would turn out to be the star quarterback of the team and an all-state third baseman. I began to sort through the gear and pulled out a contraption I'd never seen before. I looked at this strange device, and for the life of me I could not figure out what I was supposed to do with it.

Out of my depth, I turned to Eddie. "What is *this*?" I asked him. Eddie was a junior and I was a freshman. Rather than ridiculing me to the other guys at this moment, as the law of the locker room almost required—"Look at this doofus, he doesn't know what a jockstrap is"—he was instead very kind to me. At that age, cruelty can ruin your whole year, sometimes your whole life. "You wear it like this," he said. "It covers your balls." It took me decades to fully appreciate how Eddie Johnson spared me in that moment, and I'll always remember how kind he was as he explained to me what to do with that thing.

Ron McAllister was a real ladies' man and a world-class character. He was the guy who would go to a party and always end up with the best-looking girl. I was a hick from Searchlight and had never met anyone so slick. Well, he wasn't always so slick. There was the Christmas when one of his neighbors got a new bow and arrow. The kid told McAllister that he could shoot an arrow so high that he couldn't even see it anymore. So McAllister said let's go try it. And sure enough, the arrow went higher and higher and you couldn't see it anymore. But they could hear it coming down, so Ron took off running as fast as he could. The faster Ron went, the louder the arrow got. An inch or two either way and it would've killed him, the doctor said, but Ron caught that arrow in the side of his head as it came slicing toward earth. A near-impossible feat. And a superficial but ghastly-looking wound. His goofy friend, a real cool customer, was frightened at this image, and ran off and left Ron alone. So McAllister drove himself to St. Rose de Lima with his head and the arrow sticking out the window of his low-rider with the leather seats. He would live to fight another day.

It was McAllister who invited me to go to something called "seminary" that happened every morning before school over at the Mormon church. It was religious instruction and some history, but Ron didn't mention any of that to me. His pitch was that all the best-looking girls went to seminary. Well, he didn't have to ask me twice. I was new in town and looking to fit in. And McAllister didn't lie: There were lots of pretty girls at seminary.

But there was something else at seminary. I was so unchurched as to have never set foot in a house of worship of any kind. There was no church in my town. My father hadn't once darkened the door of a church in his life, and it had never occurred to me to do any different. I had never much thought about God, and had only the vaguest notion of what believers believed. But at seminary they talked about this man Jesus, about whom I knew absolutely nothing. I had scarcely heard the name. And I was interested enough in Jesus that I went to seminary at 7 A.M. almost every morning my freshman year. Well, Jesus and girls, I suppose. I would not at all describe myself as religious by the end of that year, but for the first time in my life, I was aware of religion. For the first time, I was receptive. Seminary awakened my curiosity. And very slowly, almost imperceptibly, something that can only be described as a spiritual hunger planted its seed in me. It helped that seminary was taught by Marlan Walker, the Spanish teacher at Basic High, who was one of those teachers that made you excited to go to school. Where Mike O'Callaghan ruled by brute force, Marlan Walker ruled by moral suasion. He was inspiring as a teacher, he arranged student trips to Mexico, he played the guitar, he was handsome, and he and his wife opened their home to a stranger as if he were family.

The Walkers just seemed so . . . happy. This was not lost on me. Who doesn't want to be happy? Were there choices you could make that could bring order to your life and make you happy? This was an as yet alien concept to me, and would require further investigation.

In the meantime, I became indoctrinated in the ways of being a teenager in the 1950s. You had to comb your hair just so—flat on top, longer on the sides, ducktail in back—or you'd look funny. A lot of effort and not a little Vaseline hair tonic or Brylcreem went into the swooping and swirling hair architecture of the day. There was a period when white jeans reigned supreme, sending everybody scrambling for just the right white denim. My mother would starch them stiff. We'd buy Levis for $2.75 a pair and take all the stitching out of the pockets and wear them, of course, with no belt and no cuff. Every Saturday night, there was a dance at Victory Village called "Teenage." And if you didn't care for dancing, it was the place to go and fight, too. Lots of fights on Saturday nights. Well, Landra loved to dance and I hated it. My freshman year Aunt Ray knew I needed some social graces, so she took pity on me and had me take dance lessons. Secretly, I did take the lessons, but I wanted no one to know that I was being taught to dance. I didn't think so at the time, but it was one of the nicest things she could have done for me. I remember desperately trying to keep the beat—one, two, three, one, two, three—and failing. The lessons weren't much, but it was better than nothing. By the time they were done with me, I could do the dip and glide and almost hold my own on the dance floor.

And to truly belong, you went out for sports or ran for some class office or other. My brother Don had been student body president his senior year at Basic, and Dale had been vice president when his turn came.

When I was growing up in Searchlight we didn't have a Bible in the house, but we sure had my brothers' Basic High yearbooks. As a kid, I would sit for hours and study those annuals, and now I was here at the high school of my dreams, the gateway to the outside world. It felt as though life could now begin.

There were so many rich and funny characters I felt lucky to meet, if only for the stories we'd get to tell and retell. Rupert Sendlein had had polio, but he was a big strapping guy, a great football player, a starter at center. His son Robin would go on to be an outstanding NFL linebacker, and his grandson Lyle is now the starting center for the Arizona Cardinals. Oh, but did the stories accumulate about Rupert. One of those we heard involved a beautiful girlfriend of his. One day, they were at her house. Her family had gone to Europe for an extended vacation, and Rupert just took advantage of the situation and basically moved in with her. But her parents came home more than a week ahead of time. So they're in bed, and her parents come home unexpectedly. Rupert had been messing around, and he was wearing his girlfriend's shorty nightgown and nothing else. *"Honey, we're home!"* And Rupert's so startled that he jumps up out of bed in the nightgown, and it's hard for him to move in that thing, and he falls and breaks his leg badly. So as her parents are coming up the stairs, Rupert is writhing in pain on the bedroom floor in the shorty nightgown. I was never quite sure how Rupert got out of that one. But I can report that he survived it.

He did have a pretty hard time explaining his lingerie accident to his friends.

In football I was a left guard and defensive tackle. It wasn't until college that I'd realize that I wasn't fast enough, big enough, or good enough to be the athlete of my dreams, but in high school I went out for football and baseball and threw myself bodily into them. Football practice was grueling, and the coach, Charles Razmic, allowed no water during practice. It's a wonder he didn't kill anyone. It wasn't unusual for me to be bloodied in practice or a game, and I'd wear the blood like a battle wound when we gathered at the Tastee Tavern afterward. I remember one game in particular, sophomore year, against Las Vegas High. Got the hell beat out of me. Blood all over my face. I didn't really mind, though. As strict as Coach Razmic could be, in my senior annual, he wrote: "Best of luck to one who never quit."

In baseball, I was catcher. Sophomore year, we were Nevada state champs. We were also California state champs, beating San Luis Obispo for the CIF title. Rey Martinez, who would later be my chief of staff in the Senate, was the star pitcher on that team. Donnie Wilson, who also would work with me in Washington, swung a heavy bat and was the Nevada state batting champion sophomore and junior years, and they'd both go on to play for perennial collegiate powerhouse Arizona State.

And although I was no Marlon Brando, in the senior play, a mystery called *Double Doors,* I dazzled as Dr. John Sully.

And then there was politics. I really believe that the most important election of my life was junior class treasurer at Basic High. It was the first time I was ever elected to anything, and the feeling of confidence it gave me at a crucial time in my life is hard to place a value on. I had been accepted by my peers.

Senior year, I had no plan whatsoever to run for student body president, but Patsy Lopeman and Cookie Schreck came to me and they said, "We think you can beat Russell Williams." Russell Williams was a genius, one of the smartest guys in school, a great athlete, and tough. Very cocky and self-assured. He won at everything he tried. He had been elected class president every year of high school, and everyone was sure he would be elected student body president senior year. Cookie and Patsy were dreaming.

And I'd been sick. Between football and baseball came basketball season, and I wasn't good enough to make the team. So I got a job at the Cakebox bakery. I wanted to buy a car, so I went to work every morning at 4 A.M. to glaze the doughnuts. Three A.M. on Saturdays. There were big vats where they fried the doughnuts, there was a baker, and then there was a guy who fried the doughnuts. Then you'd get to the lowest rung of the bakery caste system and that was me. My main job would be to take these doughnuts and dip them in glaze while they were hot. To this day, I hate the smell of glaze. A glazed doughnut? No, thanks. It's distasteful.

The guy who fried the doughnuts had very bad teeth and he would always go to the houses of prostitution. And then he would come to work and rhapsodize about his conquests. "Oh, she loves me," he'd say. "I was the best she's ever had."

From November until March of my junior year, I would get to the bakery at 4 A.M. and work until school started. I was a young man with no sleep. I could go to sleep standing up. Then I got sick and had to miss school. I was really sick. I had a high fever and I developed a big sore on my shin that the doctor said was a symptom of rheumatic fever. Landra's parents were very kind to me; they took me in and nursed me back to health. And I was still convalescing when Cookie and Patsy came to me and said, "We think you can win."

Rey Martinez was my campaign manager. This was the first of many campaigns that Rey would manage for me.

And Landra helped me write my speech.

I surprised everybody—no one more than myself—and won.

Rey had been student body president the year before, and he was worried that I might not know what I was doing, so in a letter dated September 29, 1956, he passed the torch. "Hi Harry, what the hell is happening?" he began, before offering the best advice from his own presidency, explaining how to manage the Basic Hall of Fame, and telling me, "Take command when you first start your council meetings and make them respect you and you will get along real fine." Rey would repeat variations of this advice to me countless times over the next forty years. He signed the letter "Ray," but in later years he would take to signing his name "Rey," as his given name is Reynoldo. The joke at Basic among his friends was that Rey Martinez didn't realize he was Mexican until he left Henderson.

In my spare time during senior year, I became a boxer. After Mike O'Callaghan's boxing exhibition earlier that year, a bunch of guys from Basic High started boxing at the Henderson Boys Club with O'Callaghan as coach.

By then I weighed 190 pounds. We all trained together—Richey Vincent, Steve Sendlein, Bernard Cannon, the Hardison brothers— and a number of my friends had fights for the Boys Club, but I didn't. O'Callaghan arranged no fights for me, and would only let me spar. It took me a while to figure out that he was doing me a big favor, because at 190, I was a heavyweight. I would have had to fight real heavyweights, big men, and they would have hurt me. Even at 175, I would have had to fight the light heavyweights. But I liked to fight, so I trained hard and learned to box. O'Callaghan would work us hard. To get us in shape he would take us to the road between Henderson and Railroad Pass and drive behind us as we ran. He couldn't run because of his wooden leg, so he'd pace us in his car. I was a lot bigger than I am now, and wasn't used to running, so even though it probably wasn't more than three or four miles to Railroad Pass, it seemed like a marathon. O'Callaghan said, "Slow down too much and I'll run you over." And we believed him.

There are sluggers, and then there are boxers. I became a pretty good boxer. I could assess situations well, and I learned to recognize and exploit an opposing fighter's weaknesses. I could hit hard, and I could take a punch. But I never had a bloody nose. I got hit in the nose plenty. Darn thing just didn't bleed. Mike saw that the left jab was my best punch, and I got good with the left hand, working hard on the bag.

Later, in college, I would be ready to fight, but my weight would still be a problem. I was still too small to fight as a heavyweight or a light heavyweight, and far too big to be a middleweight. But I was desperate for some real bouts, so I started running and watching what I ate, and before long I had lost 30 pounds. At 160, I could fight anybody. In Cedar City, Utah, where I'd go once I left Henderson, I'd become a fighter.

One day in my senior year at Basic, I got called out of class and into the school counselor's office. Dorothy Robinson taught government, and she also dispensed career advice. She looked at me and said, "We looked over all of your aptitude scores, and you should be a lawyer." That was it for me. I have no idea if Mrs. Robinson was of such influence with everyone whose path she crossed, but from that day forward, I was going to be a lawyer. I had never seen a court-house. I had never met a lawyer. I didn't even really know what lawyers did. But my course was set. Dorothy Robinson set it. I would not look back.

IN THE FALL OF 1957, at the moment I started college, *On the Road,* a classic of American literature written by Jack Kerouac, was published. I did not rush immediately to read Kerouac's new book, because I was too busy hitchhiking across the American West.

When I'd first hit the road out of Searchlight headed for Henderson, I had been a little anxious, because I was only thirteen years old, and you never really knew who was going to stop to pick you up. Are they going to try to molest you? Before getting in, I al-ways looked at whoever it was and figured if they tried anything, I'd be ready for them. I was a kid, and thought I was a lot tougher than I was. My mother had taught me that if you acted like you could handle yourself, then you could.

But when I stuck out my thumb and went off to the College of Southern Utah at Cedar City, hitchhiking became an avocation. Ron McAllister and another friend from Basic, Tom McGinty, also went to Cedar City, so we often thumbed it together. Not knowing exactly how you're getting where you're going or when you're getting there could be a lot of fun. But more exhilarating is hoofing it between rides under the cathedral skies of Nevada and Utah and California. The West. This was surely God's way of letting us know we weren't in Europe anymore.

One time, McAllister and I took a road trip to Los Angeles with Bernard Cannon. Barney had a beautiful brand-new blue Ford pickup truck. What Ron and I didn't know was that he also had a beautiful brand-new girlfriend in L.A. named Betty "Tex" Conklin. Well, the second we got there, Barney dumped us to spend time with Tex (whom he would later marry). So McAllister and I were stranded and broke on our first trip to great big L.A. We had only enough money for a bus ride to Victorville, California, and would have to thumb it from there. It was Labor Day weekend and on the side of a two-lane highway in Victorville we stood for five hours waiting for deliverance to Las Vegas. My thumb was exhausted. We finally got a ride with a drunk guy. He was drunk as a skunk, too. But we didn't care, we were happy to get a ride with anybody. And he got us out of Victorville and took us all the way to Las Vegas. Each mile closer we got, the more talkative he got. By Vegas he was sober. Oh, what a ride.

Freshman year in college, Tom McGinty and I needed to get to Vegas from Cedar City, Utah. After we'd waited awhile, a woman stopped for us. She was about thirty-five and told us her name was Barbara Smith. She looked weary, a little worn, had dandruff. She asked one of us to drive, so I got behind the wheel, and she sat between Tom and me—it was the fifties, and the cars still had those bench seats. Finally, this curious woman said, "I'm so tired." Well, there wasn't much room to spread out.

"Oh, just lay your head on Tom's shoulder and go to sleep," I told her. Tom and I would always remember her dandruff on his shoulder. She was kind of a sad woman, not bad-looking but a little scroungy. And a little mysterious. She took us to downtown Vegas, dropped us at Fifth and Fremont, and then turned around and went back the same direction she had come from. Maybe she was just look-

My mother, Inez.

Inez and my father, Harry, a year before his suicide.

The house in Searchlight where I was born.

Me as a baby with my older brothers Don, twelve, and Dale, ten, in 1940.

About age eleven, up on a gallows frame at the Western, one of the mines I worked with my father.

With my brother Larry (*right*), summer of 1956. They called me Pinky, a nickname bestowed by my cousin Cal Blackmore when I was a baby.

As a student at the College of
Southern Utah.

At George Washington University Law
School, with daughter Lana, about 1962.

In my Capitol policeman uniform, with Nevada's sole congressman, Walter Baring,
and the Nevada Cherry Blossom Princess. On November 22, 1963, I sat with
Baring as he told me Kennedy had been leading us down the path to Communism,
and it was probably a good thing he was murdered. That's what he said.

My first day as a
Nevada lawyer, 1964.

Announcing my candidacy for Nevada lieutenant governor, 1970.
When I won, I was the youngest lieutenant governor in the country, and the youngest ever in Nevada.

RENO
PRESS CLUB

Campaigning for lieutenant governor.

U.S. House candidate Reid, 1982.

*(Lee Zaichick)*

Riding in the Boulder City Fourth of
July parade, with Landra and Key.

Campaigning for Congress. With Landra (*left to right*) are Leif, Josh, and Key, who look less than entranced. (*David Lee Waite*)

Being sworn in to Congress by Speaker Tip O'Neill, surrounded by (*left to right*) Landra, Leif, Key, Josh, and Rory.

Breaking ground with Governor Mike O'Callaghan,
my lifelong friend and mentor.

With Majority Leader
Senator Bill Frist, just
after the "nuclear option"
was taken off the table,
May 23, 2005.
(*Joe Raedle/Getty Images*)

Flanked by Senator Charles Schumer (*left*) and Senator Dick Durbin (*right*) moments after getting the news on November 9, 2006, that George Allen had conceded to Jim Webb in Virginia—giving control of the Senate to the Democrats.

(*Karen Bleier/AFP/Getty Images*)

Working the phones, making calls to other senators late into the evening as the all-night debate on the Iraq War raged on the Senate floor, July 17, 2007.

(*Doug Mills/The New York Times*)

ing for boys who were more adventurous than McGinty and me, but Barbara didn't seem to be headed anywhere.

LEAVING HENDERSON meant leaving Landra, which wasn't easy. We had become serious, and every chance I had, I went home to see her. Doc and Mrs. Gould had taken me in when I was sick, and had always been exceptionally kind to me, but this was about to change abruptly. Landra was their daughter and their only child. They were observant Jews. I was a goy with no religion. This was an irreconcilable combination. Making things worse, when I was supposed to be away at school I was still occasionally showing up at their door. Landra and I were not exactly being subtle about it, and when it became clear to Earl Gould that his daughter was in danger of marrying a non-Jew, he cast a wary eye on me, and I was no longer so welcome around his house. This problem was not going to go away easily.

Meanwhile, I fell in love with Cedar City, Utah, a beautiful town about the size of Henderson with a stately old campus more than a hundred years old surrounded by tall mountains and covered in trees—*trees!* I had never seen so many trees in my life. All manner of pine and fir and spruce and, of course, cedar. I had never been anywhere, especially on my own, and the first place that you make your own is in a way your first home. Cedar City was a good home. Not being Mormon, I was a minority in the heavily Mormon town, but I didn't much care, as nobody bothered me about it, and in any case I was really starting to like Mormons. I got good grades and was freshman class president.

Soon after arriving, I learned that an athletic career wasn't in the cards for me. I'd made it to Cedar City on a football scholarship, but early in the season I was laid up with a busted foot. I was sitting on my bunk looking at the brace at the end of my leg and listening to the football game out the window when I came to the realization that I could get good grades, and that I felt good about learning. I actually wanted to try to do well in college. This feeling was new to me.

It got cold in Cedar City, which is something else that was new to me. In fact, no sooner had I gotten there than I experienced a weather-related disaster. With my hard-won Cakebox bakery savings and my work at the Standard gas station, I had bought a car. Nothing fancy, but a car with four wheels. A Pontiac. I had never lived in a place as cold before. I knew that in cold places you're supposed to drain the radiator before a freeze so that your engine block won't break. But it was September. It doesn't freeze in September, right? Well, it was September when the first freeze of autumn 1957 came to the mountains of southern Utah, and I woke up the next morning the proud owner of a car with a broken block. A car that would never move another inch, other than to be towed to the junkyard. So after one week in Utah, no car. Not so fast, Pinky Reid, fate seemed to be saying.

When I graduated from high school, Mike O'Callaghan had gotten together with a few businessmen in Henderson and come up with a scholarship for me. It was the first and last time anything like that had happened in Henderson, and it sure made things a little easier for me once I went away to Cedar City. But I would still need to work throughout college and law school to make my own way. I tried night work in a service station. Man, you've never been cold until you've worked through a winter on the night shift at a service station in Cedar City, Utah. It felt like an arctic outpost. Then I was a night janitor at the school. In the summertime, I pumped gas, was a warehouseman, changed oil, and drove an oil truck.

McAllister, McGinty, and I roomed together in the dorms. Dorm living was four people per unit, two on each side with a little kitchen in the middle. It was a tiny little apartment. The three of us flipped a coin to see who would get stuck in the room with the odd guy who would be our fourth, and sure enough, it was me. We called him "The Spook." He was tall and serious and considerably older than us. He'd already been in the Army, served in Korea. His name was Larry Adams, and in actual fact, he was a wonderful guy, but we drove him crazy because we were so obnoxious. You'd think we hadn't been raised right. Or maybe we were just exuberant.

McAllister and McGinty were such good friends to me. Whereas Tom and I came to college to play football, Ron came to play. Tom made the team and played a lot. Ron was into girls, literally. And as ever, you could always count on something strange happening with McAllister. From the time he was thirteen, he was very hairy. Hair covered his chest and back. Often, we would hold him down and set his chest afire. I can report that there was no pain involved, just a terrible smell.

And poor Larry Adams had to put up with us. He was mature and very quiet. He'd seen a lot of the world, and had had experiences we couldn't understand and didn't care to understand. We were so rude to him. We didn't care if he was our roommate or not—it didn't matter to us. And he indulged our bad behavior. I'm not sure that I would have.

In the Reid family tradition, I was never much at letter writing, but around this time, I wrote home:

Dear Folks,

    We were in Price, Utah, I received a letter from you before we left this morning. What do you mean you only have gotten one letter from me? I have answered every one of your letters. Too bad about Mrs. Yeager. [I guess she had died; an old family friend.] It's really cold up here. It snowed most of the way up. It's only about 10 days until I will return to Nevada. I got a letter from Larry. I'm going to start boxing Monday.

The nerve damage in my foot may have ended my football career, but it wouldn't stop me from boxing. So I started to train again, and this time would get some real fights. I trained at the university gym in Cedar City. And that's why I was never real good on the small bag, because the small bag would make too much noise and interrupt basketball practice, so I didn't get a chance to use it as often as I would have liked.

There was an old fighter at Southern Utah named Kent Hoyt, and he finished the job on me that O'Callaghan had started. He would be my sparring partner and teach me so much. He'd been a professional fighter, and had the busted nose to prove it.

A manager named Spike Bybe found me, and over the next two years, I had fifteen or twenty fights, mostly in Utah—Hurricane, Kanab, Beaver, Price, Cedar City, maybe St. George—but I also fought in Las Vegas. I'd go anywhere and fight anybody. I had boxing shoes. I was a full-fledged fighter.

And I sparred many, many rounds with professional fighters, which is kind of dumb, because you can get hurt, especially sparring out of your weight class. I remember one very good middleweight named Armand Caudal, who was a pro. He was fighting Don Fullmer. Spike got me to spar with him. I can still remember my forehead being sore afterward. But I didn't care. Like the blood from football, the black eyes and soreness to me were badges of honor to wear the next day, and I'd fight every chance I got.

It got to where my roommates were calling me Puppet, because anytime Spike Bybe called me, I'd go.

In Kanab, I fought a guy named Al Swiderski, who would turn pro afterward. He was much bigger than I was. It was a set-up. They said my fight couldn't go, as my opponent hadn't shown up. They also said that if I took it easy on this inexperienced fighter, I could have a fight. We hurt each other pretty bad, and he took the decision. This was the first time I ever had broken ribs.

And I fought another professional named Andrew Richard, who was an Indian. I fought him at least twice. They called these fights exhibitions, and they threw me a little expense money. Those were my only purses.

Spike was always in my corner. And he'd get me mentally prepared to fight. When the other guy was big, he'd look over and say, "Oh, man, look at those muscles. Don't worry, you got him. He's *muscle-bound. He can hardly move.*"

And it helped. Even though it was not true. But I believed him. The bell would ring, and I would spring to my feet thinking, I can take this guy. I won much more than I lost because of Spike's advice.

THE ONLY PERSON I could be moved to write to regularly was Landra. All that year, we wrote back and forth. She was still in high school, and so was living at home, and my letters were cascading out of Earl Gould's mailbox, a reminder courtesy of the U.S. Postal Service that I was deeply in love with his daughter. I had tried half-heartedly to date other people, just as she had, but that just wasn't working. And in any case, Landra had her best friend and spy, Deanna Williams, who was the future first wife of Ron McAllister, to monitor my activities and report back regularly. When it came time for

Landra to decide on a place to go to college, she began to express serious interest in the College of Southern Utah. I thought this was an excellent choice. But there was no chance that Doc Gould was going to stand for that.

Miraculously, Landra was awarded a full scholarship to the University of Nevada, Las Vegas, which was nowhere near Cedar City, Utah. We will never know if Earl Gould had worked the levers to make this possible, but UNLV's generosity obviously solved his problem. At least temporarily. This would not be the end of it.

Things would come to a head before Landra would start a single class at UNLV. That summer, I returned to Henderson, where I lived with Barney and Betty (formerly known as "Tex") Cannon. I intended to see Landra as much as I possibly could. College hadn't cooled the relationship, it had intensified it. We were going to be together, and there was nothing her father could do about it. Of course, he did not see it this way. She lived under his roof. Seeing her meant pulling up in front of 77 BMI Road and knocking on Earl Gould's front door. I didn't have a thing in the world against him. As far as I knew the only thing he had against me was that I wasn't a Jew. It was his obligation to put an end to this relationship. To be faithful to my heart, I had an obligation to make sure he failed. And as has happened in every small-town replay of the Montagues and Capulets throughout time, a little violence broke out.

We were double-dating with friends the night I fought Earl Gould. I didn't go over there intending to lay a hand on him, but that's what happened. It started just inside the front door. "You can't come here anymore," he said. "I don't want you to see my daughter." He was red in the face and pretty worked up. I was there to pick her up and he was blocking my way, talking too much. He started pushing, and I threw a punch, and then the whole mess spilled out into the front yard. It wasn't a very fair fight—he was smaller than I was. It's hard to say what goes through your mind as you start a fistfight with your future father-in-law. Do you have a flash of how important this man will become to you? Do you know how much you will come to love and respect him? Will you be given a glimpse of what fine grandparents he and his wife will be to your children? Do you know that somewhere, in the future, you will wear the ring from his finger in his memory? Not exactly. Life must be lived.

First comes the pandemonium of the yelling and pushing, and crying, and the sting of a punch just landed. Love comes later.

Who could guess that this would turn out anything but bad?

But then, as has been the case since that night, I turned around and found Landra by my side. We got in that car and we took off. I have no recollection where we went or what we did that night.

LIKE MY FAMILY, Landra's family, and the families of most of my friends, Wing Fong's family had come to southern Nevada the long way—in Fong's case, the incredibly long way. He had been just a boy in 1939 when he was drawn from China to Las Vegas to work with his uncles at the Silver Café downtown, which the family had started a few years before, at the peak of the Depression. Fong had worked like a slave, learned English, gone to college in California, and returned to Las Vegas in the mid-fifties to open his own place, Fong's Garden, on East Charleston just off Fremont. It quickly became known as the best Chinese food in town, some say the best food in town, a terrific place for festive gatherings.

On the evening of Saturday, September 12, 1959, Landra and I had our wedding dinner at Fong's Garden. We chose Fong's because we really knew of no other place. It was an intimate, happy affair. We left our friends after our wedding and dined alone, because when you're eloping against her parents' wishes, you generally don't alert the media. Although by now Doc Gould knew well that something was wrong. When they'd come home the day before to find their daughter gone, along with all her belongings, they had commenced to calling everyone they thought might know of their daughter's whereabouts. Landra was not a rebellious girl; she'd never done anything remotely like this before. With her parents, she was quiet, even shy. Something bad was happening, they thought.

Months in the planning, the wedding had gone off without a hitch. The secret had remained a secret to all but those gathered at the church for the unusual ceremony. Most important, behind the secret there was Marlan Walker, who had counseled us on married life and performed the ceremony at the Mormon church in Henderson. When he'd heard rumors of our elopement, he'd said to my friend Ron McAllister, "I'll save them the twenty-five dollars for the justice of the peace. We'll do it at the church." And even though Landra was a Jew and I was a nothing, this wonderful man had taken it on himself to break all the rules and offer us the sanctuary of his church. If man might frown on such arrangements, God apparently did not. And lucky for us, in addition to all else that he did, Marlan Walker was the bishop of the LDS ward in Henderson, and could legally perform such ceremonies.

Ron Mich'l, our good friend from Basic High, had stood guard just inside the door to the room as we exchanged vows. Six and a half feet tall, Ron had been an all-state basketball player at Basic and would go on to be the star of the Utah State team. But on this night, our large friend kept his eyes peeled for Earl Gould. We were too close to being married for anything to go wrong now. Since the beginning of summer, Landra and I had been planning this. We'd worked hard and hoarded every penny. I worked three jobs that summer—I pumped gas, drove a truck, and worked as a warehouseman. In Cedar City, I had planned ahead and bought insurance so that we'd be covered if we had a baby. We'd checked every detail and kept it secret. And Landra had even prayed over this, and she had never really prayed about anything before in her life. But after that, she felt such certainty and peace about our decision. We both did. And after dinner, we would be on our way to Utah State in Logan, where I'd been offered an academic scholarship to finish my degree. My brilliant wife would postpone her education for mine. I'd study, she'd work.

We bid Las Vegas farewell there at Fong's and headed north in a '54 Chevrolet. What I remember most about that car is that it leaked air around the accelerator, and in the wintertime it seemed my foot would literally freeze. But our wedding night was balmy. We'd spend it at a motel in Mesquite, Nevada, but not before pulling off the road at a pay phone so that Landra could call her parents to tell them what we had done, to confirm their darkest fears.

It is tradition among Orthodox Jews that if a member of the family marries outside the faith, you sit shiva for that person to mourn their passing. There was a very real possibility that Landra was now dead to her parents.

We'd done it. It was real. This was a hard call to make. The conversation was short.

"We're married," Landra told them. "I wanted to give you the address of where we're going."

"This is not what we wanted. I did everything I could to stop it, and that was my right," Earl Gould told his daughter. "But now it's done. You are our only daughter. We're going to try and make this thing work."

Henderson was a small town at the time. Almost everyone knew everyone else. When Doc Gould found out that Marlan Walker had married us, he went to him.

"How could you do this?" he asked him. "I thought you were my friend."

"ARE YOU MEMBERS of the church?" the man on the other end of the line asked me. We needed a place to live, and he had one. On arriving in Logan, we found our student housing to be deplorable, so Landra and I went to the local newspaper and they showed us some classified ads that were to run in the next day's paper. This man, Matthew Bird, was advertising a basement apartment in his family's home, and I called him to tell him that my wife and I had just married and to express interest in seeing the place. "Are you LDS?" Mr. Bird asked. He would have preferred it if we were Mormon. I told him no. "Well, come on by," he said. We passed the interview.

Logan, Utah, was founded by Mormons in 1859, and probably 90 percent of the students at Utah State were Mormon, so Landra and I were somewhat of a rarity. In any case, the Birds were so charmed and intrigued by Landra—they had never met a Jew before—that they gave us the place. We didn't smoke or drink, and I guess we seemed a decent bet. Not long ago, I received a letter from Matthew and Louise Bird's daughter-in-law, Twila Bird. In it she quoted some passages from Louise Bird's journal. Her entry from October 7, 1959, reads:

> We rented our apt. on the evening of Sept. 16 to Harry and
> Landra Reid, from Las Vegas. He is here to study at the U.S.U.

preparing for a law course. . . . They were practically on their honeymoon when they arrived, had been married five days. She is a beautiful little dark-eyed Jewish maiden who had to elope to marry out of her race. Her maiden name was Landra Gould. She thinks her folks have forgiven her now.

The Birds lived upstairs. They were a good-sized family, but by this time only one child was still at home. One evening I needed to use their phone, as we didn't have one, and I knocked on the back door and looked and there they were, all kneeling on the floor. And I thought, What is going on here? Mr. Bird told me that they were saying their evening prayers. They were really devoutly religious people. And they were generous to us, which was very welcome, as Landra and I struggled quite a bit financially.

I would major in history and political science, and got started with classes immediately while Landra went in search of a job to support us. Many of the jobs in town had already been taken by students, so she had to cast a wider net, and found work 50 miles away near Brigham City at Thiokol Chemical, where they tested rockets for the space program that was just then being born. The world was just a couple of years away from President Kennedy's declaration that by the end of the 1960s Americans would land on the moon, and Thiokol was hiring.

For the next year or so, Landra would rise when it was still dark and do a lot of commuting, about ninety minutes each way. Thiokol had a shuttle bus that would drive around Logan and pick up people to take them out to work.

Her bus driver was a part-time Mormon missionary. His name was McPherson. One day he said to her, Would your husband allow me and my companion to come by your apartment and teach you about Mormonism? We'd like to tell you about the Church. So when she came home and said, Do you care if these guys come by? I said, I guess not. So they came over. Their first visit became many visits.

And that's when we opened the door to our heavenly father. Yes, we were married, but now we would reconcile our disparate backgrounds in a union of spirit and understanding, and in a recognition that there was more to life—more to existence—than what we could see. More than just us. It was as much choice as revelation. A simple act. And our choice was made so much easier by the people we'd met, who set an example for us—Marlan Walker, Aunt Ray, the Birds, and even the crazy man who lived next door to the Birds. He was expert in scripture, and referred to Satan as "Old Horns." A nice man, with a wonderful spirit, who, we later learned, had struggled with mental illness and had been in and out of institutions. There were many others, who didn't so much speak their religion as live it. We would start a family soon. For my children, I would do anything to avoid the path that my parents had taken. This was to be a very different path.

Brother McPherson was an impressive man. His fellow missionary was even more so. He was a paraplegic. This man labored on his walking sticks with such effort that sometimes it was hard to believe that he could keep it up. But every week for months they came, and we would ask a mountain of questions. And more and more, the questions just fell away. And more and more, their faith became our faith. It felt good. And one day after a lesson, Landra said, "Do you think this would be good for us?" We joined the Church in February 1960.

All the professors I had at Utah State seemed as if they had been put there just for me. But two teachers helped change me from who I was into who I would become. Leonard Arrington was an economist and author who was the first great Mormon scholar, and would become the first official historian of the Church. Dr. Arrington saw something in me and took me under his wing, and before long had me helping him grade papers.

And during my first quarter, Harmon Judd, who was my political science professor, called me into his office and said, "You obviously have a good mind, but your grammar is atrocious. You really should do something about it."

My parents were uneducated, and Searchlight had had one teacher, whose attention was fractured over eight grades at once. So other than learning to read well, I had not learned much of anything in Searchlight. I hadn't been overly taxed in high school, and had gotten by with my stunted education in proper English until I met Dr. Judd, who would stand for it no more. And just as with Mrs. Robinson in Henderson, I didn't question him. I figured he was trying to help me. So I started taking every basic English and grammar course I could, even diagramming sentences, and Harmon Judd's advice utterly changed my relationship to the English language, which happens to be the sole means I have to communicate my thoughts and feeling to the world. Because he bothered to tell me something I desperately needed to hear, my life, and my prospects, improved immeasurably. A lawyer has to be able to string words together in a way that tells a story and is persuasive. He has to be able to write. I had not learned these things, and would not have if not for Dr. Judd.

As ever, we struggled with money, especially when Landra got pregnant and could no longer work. But on March 12, 1961, we hit paydirt with the birth of our baby girl Lana, all 4½ pounds of her.

When it came time to pay the hospital bills, I found out that the insurance policy I had bought didn't cover pregnancy after all. The bills amounted to hundreds of dollars, a lot of money I didn't have.

So I called the agent, Dixie Leavitt, in Cedar City. "Mr. Leavitt,"

I said, "you sold me an insurance policy and it doesn't cover the birth of our baby. The only reason I bought it and have continued making payments is that you told me it covered pregnancy."

And with no hesitation, Leavitt said, "If I told you that, then send me the bills." So I sent him the bills and he paid them. When a lot of people might have said, "Sorry, you should have read the fine print," Dixie Leavitt answered with such profound decency that I will never forget it. His son Michael would become governor of Utah and now serves in the Bush cabinet as secretary of the Department of Health and Human Services.

When my studies in Logan were done, and it was time to go, Louise Bird wrote this in her journal:

> June 8, 1961
>
> Harry & Landra are about packed to leave after commence-
> ment Sat. We are expecting a lot of these two young people. Hope
> some day they will be prepared to serve our country, and the Lord,
> helping to stop Communism & spread the gospel in some
> foreign land.

IN THE MEANTIME, the indomitable Mike O'Callaghan, who while still at Basic High School had gotten himself involved in Democratic Party politics, had risen to become chairman of the Nevada Democratic Party.

There was no law school in Nevada. I had applied to many schools and had been accepted at several. I even had been offered a scholar-ship to attend the University of Santa Clara Law School, but O'Callaghan was of the mind that Washington, D.C., was the place I ought to go. In fact, many aspiring lawyers from Nevada had made their way to George Washington University or American University or Georgetown. As often happened, I would follow Mike's advice, and I decided on GWU. With my young family, I was going to need a job while I went to school, so Mike wrote a letter to Nevada's lone member of the House of Representatives, Congressman Walter Baring, about a patronage job for me. I was at O'Callaghan's house when the reply came from Baring, saying that regrettably there was no job to be had. To make matters worse, Baring had spelled my name R-E-E-D. Mike was a man of great passions, and at that moment, steam was coming out his ears. So he picked up the phone, pretty quickly got Congressman Baring on the phone, and said, "You son of a bitch. This is one of my best students. And you don't even have the decency to spell his name right? What's wrong with you? I'll tell you what. I'm sending him back to Washington. He doesn't have a job, but you're going to give him one, right?"

And that's how I became a United States Capitol policeman.

I would go to law school at GWU full-time, and work full-time in uniform at the Capitol on the 3-to-11 shift. At the time, Capitol Hill cops were being transitioned from a group of essentially untrained security guards to a better-trained and more professional force. But still, a good part of my time on the job was spent giving directions to tourists and assisting members of Congress home when they'd had one nip too many. My most dangerous duty was directing traffic on Constitution and Independence Avenues, where the old trolley tracks could give the cars a pretty unsteady ride as they flew past—which was exciting, to say the least.

I joined an interesting group of guys on the force, several from Nevada. Like me, they held patronage positions. Most of them were also in school. B. Mahlon Brown III would become U.S. attorney. Tom Steffen would go on to be on the Nevada Supreme Court. I would serve in Congress with Jim Bilbray, who was also from Nevada. Jim must have been 50 pounds lighter then, and in his uniform looked a little like Barney Fife. He was very intense and took the job very seriously.

Sometimes it seemed that members of Congress were too important to notice the janitors and cops who served them. Part of my time I was stationed to the front desk in what is now called the Longworth House Office Building. At the time it was known simply as the New House Office Building. All coming in and out of the building had to pass by me, and most often I felt pretty invisible. But two members of Congress were exceptional by being civil. Henry Gonzalez from Texas, who served for many decades and whose son Charlie now serves in his seat, was always so nice to me. "Can I get you something?" he would ask as he walked by. "Drink or a sandwich?" John Lindsay, a member from New York who would go on to be mayor of New York City, was the same way. Very decent men. They would notice you and take interest in your life.

Which was a welcome change of pace, because Washington was a hard enough place to live in. Landra and I couldn't believe how expensive everything was. When I had heard that my police salary would be $5,500, I thought we'd have it made in the shade. With that kind of money in Nevada, we'd have been on easy street. But in Washington, in 1961, that salary allowed you the luxury of barely scraping by.

I had made almost straight A's in college without unduly exerting myself. So the analysis, reasoning, and abstract thinking of law school came as a shock to me.

And the schedule was killing me. I'd leave our apartment in Arlington, Virginia, at 6 or 7 A.M. and get to Stockton Hall at GWU to study. And then classes until about 2. Get to the Capitol, get the uniform on, and report for roll call. Off at 11:15. Home by midnight. Start over at dawn. Saturdays, I was in a study group in the morning with three other students, and worked the evening shift at the Capitol. Sundays I didn't study. I spent that time each week getting reacquainted with my little family.

After the first year, I had doubts that I could carry on this way for three years. Our Buick transmission died. We found out that Landra was pregnant again.

It was then that I decided to go to have a talk with the dean of students, a man by the name of Potts. I would tell him about managing the demands of law school, fatherhood, and a full-time job, and that I wasn't sure that I could keep it up. I guess I was looking for advice—certainly I wasn't the first such student he would have encountered—but moreover, I was probably hoping for some assistance from the wealthy university. I'm not entirely sure what I thought this Potts fellow would say. But it sure wasn't this: "Mr. Reid, maybe the law is not for you. Why don't you just quit law school?"

To be fair to Potts, I suppose he may have been employing some sophisticated reverse psychology to make me angry and to motivate me. But I rather suspect that he was just being a jerk.

From that point forward, I would take as many courses as I could. I piled on the courses. I would take full course loads in the summertime. I wanted to get done with George Washington University Law School and get my family out of that miserable town as fast as possible and back home to Nevada. And I didn't care if I ever saw Washington, D.C., again.

Luckily for us, the local Mormon bishop agreed to have the Church pay for a new transmission for the old Buick. And luckily for me, I had Landra, who would not let me give up.

And then—as if to confirm the ill will I was beginning to harbor against Washington—came a terrible day. On one of the most fateful days in American history, I was at school when I heard about the shooting in Dallas. I quickly raced to the Capitol. What on earth was going on? Was President Kennedy going to die? It seemed the world was falling apart. Later that afternoon I sought out my Congressman, Walter Baring, who kept the habit in the evening of taking a cocktail in his office. And it was there, on the evening of November 22, 1963, that I got one of the greatest shocks of my life.

Like everyone I knew, I had been awakened to the idea of national purpose and public service by John F. Kennedy's campaign for the presidency. I had started a Young Democrats Club at Utah State, and had organized students for Kennedy. My efforts were modest, but a week before his inauguration, President-elect Kennedy had sent me a personal letter to thank me. It was an extraordinary gesture. The letter hangs in my Capitol office today.

But on the evening of Kennedy's death, I sat with Congressman Baring of Nevada as he nursed his drink. And I was shattered. Then Baring said something that I will never forget. He was a conservative Democrat, reactionary actually, one of those guys for whom there was a Communist behind every bush. Fluoride was a Communist plot. And Kennedy, too, had been leading us down the path to Communism, Baring told me. It was probably a good thing that he was murdered. That's what he told me.

It was time for me and my family to go home.

# FIVE

# SOCIAL INSECURITY

FORGIVE AND REMEMBER, I suppose you could say.

Forty-two years later, I finally set foot on the campus of the George Washington University Law School again. The occasion was to deliver the commencement address for the class of 2005, and to tell the story of my disaffection with the place that had disappointed me so. And also I wanted to apologize for having held a grudge for so long.

It is true that I had been upset for four decades, and in that time could not be stirred to answer an invitation or a piece of fundraising mail from anyone at the university. The source of my scorn was simple: Success in my life, given my background, was unlikely enough without being kicked by Dean Potts while I was down. Now, if he was trying to clear me out like a weed among the orchids, then he picked the wrong guy. But how many others had folded in the face of his disregard? And what if I had?

So as I ascended the dais on that May afternoon in 2005 to receive my honorary doctorate in the law, I didn't exactly have a song in my heart. But I wasn't angry anymore either. And I devoted the first half of my speech to telling the audience the story of my unpleasant law school experience.

"I last set foot on George Washington's campus in January of 1964," I began. "That is the time I graduated from law school. In the forty years since, I haven't been back to campus or returned a letter. I've been holding a grudge."

Here, the audience laughed. I hadn't meant for it to be funny. Maybe they thought I was joking. I continued. "Law school was hard for me—I worked six full days a week as a policeman at the U.S. Capitol, and I was a full-time law student.

"At the time, my wife and I were very young and didn't have a lot of money. We had a young daughter, and my wife was pregnant, and wasn't able to work. With my job at the Capitol, we managed to get by, but just barely.

"Then one fateful day my Buick Roadmaster's transmission collapsed.

"So here we were: No way to get to work. Too many bills. And now a car needing its own help.

"Seeking assistance and counsel, I sought one of the law school deans. After I explained my situation, he looked me in the eye and gave me this advice: 'Why don't you just quit law school?'

"Since that day, I've harbored ill will toward this school."

An uproarious laugh from the crowd startled me. I stopped and looked out at them. I guess I can see how they might think this was in jest, but as before, the line had not been intended to elicit laughter. Oh well, at least they seemed to be enjoying the story. "He was only one man," I continued. "But his words stung and they stuck with me for years.

"In retrospect, I should have gotten over it sooner. I'm sorry I didn't. So I apologize to the entire faculty, administration, and all of the law students for my pettiness."

Another huge laugh line, not meant to be funny.

"It's not how I've tried to live my life," I said.

And that last line is true. It's not how I've tried to live my life. And it actually felt good to bury the hatchet at GWU. They were very gracious in receiving me. And so it was over. In any case, I had neither the time nor energy to hold on to past resentments. I guess that forty years was enough. In 2005, there were far too many battles to fight, on far too many fronts. I had quickly put together my leadership team. For the top three positions, I had lent my support to the eloquent Dick Durbin of Illinois to be the assistant minority leader, and the irascible and intelligent Chuck Schumer of New York to lead the Democratic Senatorial Campaign Committee. Hardworking Debbie Stabenow of Michigan was chosen by the caucus to be the secretary. Equally brilliant, they were all brimming with ideas and, like talented siblings, were slightly competitive.

I had called Chuck a few days after the election and asked him to take over the DSCC because I wanted to immediately begin focusing on 2006. He had agreed, but he had conditions. "I don't want to let any red-state Democrats retire in 2006," he told me, and he said we should use relentless pressure if necessary. All our losses in 2004 had been red-state retirements. I agreed completely. Next. "No contributions to incumbents in safe seats, because it just doesn't make sense." We were two for two. "We have to recruit candidates and get involved in the primaries." This was the biggest change of all. It had never been done before, but Chuck was absolutely right. If we ever hoped to win back the Senate, we simply couldn't leave things to chance. Last, Chuck said that if the DSCC was funding a campaign, then the DSCC ought to exercise some control over how the campaign was run. Bingo. Senator Schumer and I were in complete agreement. The rebuilding would begin. And not a moment too soon. The Republicans now had a 55-vote majority. Their new mantra was "60."

My leadership style would be somewhat different from Tom Daschle's. Whereas Tom had centralized control of the party's priorities in the leader's office, I wanted to empower the ranking members on the various committees, give them more autonomy, and place trust in them. I also wanted to establish a bigger and broader leadership group to better harvest the talent and take advantage of the diversity of the Democratic caucus. This would also be something of a change from Daschle, who tended, more often than not, to keep his own counsel. As his whip, I had been very close to him. But he rarely branched out very far beyond me. I resolved to cast a wider leadership net.

It is hard to overstate just how devastated the Democrats were after the election debacle of 2004. There was a great and growing fear that with the President at the peak of his power, and the Democrats at an absolute low ebb, untold further damage could be done to the country. The war in Iraq, which in early 2003 Donald Rumsfeld had said would last "six days, six weeks. I doubt six months," was entering its third year, and things were not going well. I had supported the war initially, had voted for its authorization believing that military action would be taken only as a last resort, and once it started I had been willing to give the President time to manage an extremely difficult situation. But things on the ground had deteriorated to such an extent, so many of our soldiers were being killed and maimed from all sides, and our mission was becoming so ill-defined that a dramatic reassessment of the U.S. mission in Iraq was due. One aspect of leadership is adapting to changing realities and new facts. But no one in Congress was doing the people's oversight or asking any questions about the war at all. With the Republicans in total control, and with Congress abdicating its Constitutional obligations to balance the White House, it would be hard to do anything about this while in the minority. But we had to try.

Just after the 2004 election, two days before Thanksgiving, I made a trip to Bethesda naval hospital to visit the wounded. I had been out there many times before, but this was the first time in a while. There had been a fierce battle in Anbar Province days before, and a dozen or so members of a Marine battalion had just arrived at Bethesda, forty-eight hours or less from the field of battle. Rear Admiral John Eisold, who was the attending physician at the Capitol, had come with me, and he led me back into the intensive care unit where the Marines were receiving care. The room was hushed. Some family members of the wounded were arriving as we walked in, looking stricken and confused and afraid. With the exception of one Marine, the whole unit was hooked up to machines and unresponsive. I walked up to a few of the Marines and took a hand and held it. Sometimes there was a slight squeeze back. More families quietly walked in, parents, brothers, sisters. Many fell to tears. Most of the Marines were missing limbs. Most of them had traumatic brain injuries. I made my way around the room, and as I came within reach of one young man, he reached out and grabbed my hand. He was conscious, but he was pretty mangled. He looked up at me. "We're counting on you, sir, to do the right thing," he said. I leaned over, reached down, and touched his face. "Young man, I will do everything I can for you," I said.

A soldier I had visited an hour earlier had two badly injured legs. One leg was held in the air by a pulley contraption. The other was badly disfigured. "We need to get you better-armored vehicles," I told him.

"Fuck the new vehicles," he said. "I was blown through the top of my Stryker. And look at me. We don't need new vehicles. We need to get out of Iraq. *Now.*"

I know that in war, people get maimed and killed. I know that. And when the cause is clear, that is simply the heavy cost we pay for our liberty. But the searching looks on these young men's faces have stayed with me, and I have never felt the same about the war since.

I began to feel that we no longer knew what we were doing in Iraq. And if we had no defined mission, or a mission whose definition was constantly changing, then the default mission is just to survive. And in greater and greater numbers at the time, our soldiers were not surviving. The insurgency was exploding, but even if we had been taking no casualties at all, what were we there for anymore? Did we know? Or was our military presence in Iraq becoming the mission unto itself? The President would take to saying, "As the Iraqis stand up, we will stand down," but President Bush had already said a number of things that had ended up not being true. His credibility on the subject was somewhat suspect.

With this in mind, I went to the Pentagon in early February 2005, to meet with Secretary of Defense Donald Rumsfeld. I wanted to tell him of my concern that the American military mission was creeping in several bad directions, and I wanted some clear answers about the situation in Iraq. My third purpose was to offer him help. This, after all, was an American problem, and it ought to have an American solution, without regard to party.

But as with many things in life, the crucial first step is the admission that a problem exists in the first place.

As I entered into Rumsfeld's inner sanctum, I felt as if I were passing from objective reality into a place where only sunny thoughts were allowed. He greeted me in a bomber jacket, full of the vim and the vigor for which he is known, as well as the broad smile.

"Mr. Secretary," I said, "I am not in the habit of visiting cabinet secretaries, and in fact I can't think of a time that I've done so. But I am so concerned about the state of play in Iraq that I wanted to see you in person."

I wanted him to know that this was not a casual courtesy call. I was the incoming Senate Minority Leader and I knew that this war was going to consume a lot of the Senate's time. I would need to work with Rumsfeld and I wanted that work to commence that very day. But instead there unfolded one of the most perfectly reality-free meetings of all my time in Washington. "Great, appreciate your help. Everything's fine, going well," he said. "We've really routed the terrorists." The situation is where we want it to be, he said.

Of course, this is the same man who, in one of the great rationalizations of all time, pronounced just after the invasion, as chaos was enveloping Baghdad and everything that wasn't set in cement was pillaged, "Stuff happens. . . . Freedom's untidy, and free people are free to make mistakes and commit crimes and do bad things."

It is true, stuff does happen. But we must try to mitigate the bad stuff with a good plan. And in early 2005, there simply was not much of a plan of any kind. That's what I was in the secretary's office to talk to him about, but he was having none of it.

"Mr. Secretary, this war is paralyzing our country," I said. "The only way to solve this is in a bipartisan way. That's why I've come here today."

The expression on Rumsfeld's face turned, as if a cloud were passing behind his eyes, but then the sun came out again. He was practiced at the art of avoidance, and his conversation style was to bob and weave, polite all the while, and throw out the odd non sequitur.

"Isn't Bill Frist a nice man?" he asked at one point, connected to nothing. "He seems like a nice man."

Yes, Senator Frist is a very nice man. But I hadn't come to discuss that.

"I need you on BRAC," he said at another point. BRAC stands for the Base Realignment and Closure process, which was an important part of Rumsfeld's plan to transform the Pentagon. "I really need your help to make sure this BRAC process does not get derailed by the Congress."

I supported the BRAC plan, and told him so. But it was clear that the Secretary of Defense thought that a war that was spinning out of control, tying down so many of our assets, making us less secure, and risking or taking so many lives should be of no concern whatsoever to the Senate Minority Leader. And so the smoke screen.

But I wasn't the only one who was being smoked out—the entire country was.

On leaving, I told Rumsfeld that I would soon be going on a trip to Iraq to assess the situation firsthand.

"Great, great, important that you go," he said.

He seemed, though, as if he couldn't have cared less.

This was a bad situation, and getting worse. Did he care about the facts? Was anyone in charge?

IT WAS 6 A.M. and already blistering hot in Kuwait as we waited to board the plane to Baghdad. We wouldn't be allowed to stay for more than a day in Iraq on this trip, as it was just too dangerous, and after the first briefing we'd have to chopper everywhere, as the roads were too treacherous to drive on. We—a delegation of senators from both parties—were here to meet the prime minister and get an overview briefing by the commanding general, George Casey, as well as by General David Petraeus on his progress in the training of Iraqi security forces.

General Petraeus delivered his briefing to the Senate delegation in an armored vehicle on a short secured road from the airport to the training facility. They called this vehicle the ice cream truck, because it looked like an ice cream truck, albeit an ice cream truck hardened against roadside bombs. The staff that accompanied us on the trip followed in a somewhat less armored van, which could not have been comfortable. On arrival, we watched some Iraqis training, followed by a live-arms demonstration.

General Petraeus's report to us was glowing. The training is going spectacularly well, he said. And he walked us through what goes into diplomatic security, and they demonstrated someone getting kidnapped, and the Iraqis took target practice. Here, come and watch these Iraqi recruits, watch them fire a weapon, watch them run and jump. We're going to field a big army and a big police force, Petraeus told us. This thing is in good shape. The Iraqi army is standing up.

Remember, this was 2005.

General Petraeus is an outstanding soldier, a scholar of war and strategy, and he is very smart and persuasive. But it did not take long for us to learn that what he told us was not actually the case at all.

This tends to give one a jaundiced view of such reports going forward.

One thing I won't forget about this trip to Iraq is the look in the eyes of some of the soldiers. It was the same hollow look one saw in every face on September 11. I think about that every day, because there are soldiers that have been there for years on multiple tours, and you can't live under those circumstances forever.

And you cannot come away from spending time with American soldiers without being awed and impressed by what our military does on a daily basis. The professionalism of our soldiers and Marines is stunning. We had lunch with a bunch of Marines who couldn't have been more than a few months out of high school, and I believe them to be the most thoughtful and poised eighteen-year-olds to be found anywhere. Their sacrifice and integrity are deeply moving, and their service to their country is unstinting.

We must serve them back. We must do right by them.

We must only ever risk their lives for a good and honest reason.

BACK IN WASHINGTON, there was an issue of even greater urgency than the war, as hard as that may seem to fathom.

The White House was manufacturing a "crisis" in Social Security because the President was bound and determined to privatize the program. It was Bush's number-one domestic priority. When President Bush ran for Congress in the 1970s, he wanted to privatize Social Security. Social Security is a government program, and Bush doesn't like government programs. Well, there was no crisis in Social Security. The program was going to be solvent well into the middle of the twenty-first century. No, this had more to do with Bush and his ideologues wanting to drive the last nail into Franklin Roosevelt's coffin. And Congressional Democrats had to make sure that this goal was never realized. If we didn't, and allowed President Bush to deliver on his promise of diverting money from the Social Security trust fund to private investment accounts, it would, in addition to adding trillions of dollars to the national debt, be the beginning of the end of the greatest social program in history.

My view on this is simple: Private accounts for Social Security are a Trojan horse for ending Social Security. As long as I have breath, I will fight that.

Nancy Pelosi had succeeded Dick Gephardt as Minority Leader. She and I meet every Tuesday evening, and early on we had decided that this was our line in the sand. We would oppose this with every-thing we had, and we wouldn't negotiate an alternative proposal.

Nancy and I first met when I was a member of the California Congressional delegation. Allow me to explain. I was the lone Democrat from the state of Nevada when I arrived in Washington after the election of 1982. Seeing me alone over there, my friends from California said, Why don't you join us? And so I did. Every Wednesday morning, I attended the meeting of the California delegation. And during my second term in Congress, I was elected secretary-treasurer of the California delegation. Even after I was elected to the Senate in 1986, my name remained on the their stationery for a few years. And being accepted as a member of that delegation gave me clout that I wouldn't have had otherwise, as California has by far the largest delegation in the Congress. Nancy wasn't a member of Congress then, but she was a real mover and shaker in northern California.

I was already in the Senate by the time she came to Washington, and we would have occasional dealings. But it wasn't until I became Democratic leader in the Senate and she ascended to replace Dick Gephardt that we got to know each other very well. We've worked hand-in-glove on many issues since then. We talk sometimes three or four times a day. She is an outstanding legislator. I have served with some tremendous Speakers—Tip O'Neill, Jim Wright, and Tom

Foley, as well as the Republican speakers Gingrich and Hastert. And with no hesitation, I say that Nancy Pelosi is the best among them.

Well, she and I would be put to a severe test, because the President was putting the full power of the White House message machine behind the effort to privatize Social Security. He had a budget for the effort that was reported to be in the $60 million range. And when after the election he said, "I earned political capital, and I intend to spend it," it sent a shudder through the Democratic rank and file. Though Bush was prone to bluster, this was not bluster. We were in for the fight of our lives. And if we didn't prevail, I was convinced the consequences would be devastating, and that history would write that this was a wrong turn down a bad road, taken by zealots who didn't understand what makes America great, who didn't understand that when we invest in "human capital" in this country, the return on that investment is and has always been enormous. Just ask the GIs who returned from the theaters of battle in World War II to receive benefits from the GI Bill, got themselves educated in record numbers, and went on to be present at the creation of the greatest economic engine in the history of the world—the American middle class.

My memories of growing up in Searchlight are of my grandmother. Her name was Harriet. She was born in England. I didn't know either of my grandfathers or my other grandmother, but I did know Harriet Reid, the mother of nine children. Grandma was short and quite fat. She loved to sit and talk and tell me stories, which I still remember. But the thing I most remember about Grandma is that she was an independent woman. Why? She was independent because every month she got what we used to call her old age pension check. Well, of course, that was her Social Security check. When I was a boy growing up during World War II, that program was in its infancy, not yet ten years old. And that check gave my grandmother the ability to stand on her own two feet, and not be destitute or dependent on the fortunes of her children.

And so from my boyhood on, I have seen the capacity of Social Security to utterly transform lives. I believe Social Security is the most successful social program in history. It not only provides the "old age" pension check, it also provides for widows, orphans, and the disabled. Those who were arguing for privatization were dead wrong, in my view. But at that moment, they held the upper hand.

So the risks were huge, and the outcome was far from certain. But this was the right fight. This was for all the marbles. There wasn't an issue that better or more clearly demonstrated the elemental difference between the parties. In their hearts, the true ideologues among the Republicans genuinely believe that the government should get out of the Social Security business altogether, that this program that has raised the standard of living for hundreds of millions of people since its inception should be eliminated. In my witness, Democrats usually aren't so afraid that the government might actually help someone. Thus, the battle lines were drawn. To say that it was going to be nearly impossible to stop the President was something of an understatement.

This would have been a titanic struggle even if we'd been on an even footing with the Republicans, but we were at an historic disadvantage. In the Senate, they held a 10-vote majority—55 to 45—which meant that they would only need to peel away five Democrats to support their bill to make it filibuster-proof. Social Security was in grave danger.

I decided that the key to this effort would be Max Baucus, the senior senator from Montana. Senator Baucus was the ranking Democrat on the Finance Committee, which made him the natural point person on this. He and the Finance Committee chairman, Republican Chuck Grassley of Iowa, were extraordinarily close, and had organized the committee in such a way that if the two of them did not reach consensus, legislation wouldn't proceed. They had partnered on the first two rounds of tax cuts early in President Bush's first term, so much so that it infuriated Tom Daschle. He and Baucus had never been particularly close—Baucus was the only Westerner to vote against Daschle in his race for Democratic leader in 1994, which Daschle had only won by a single vote—and they had been driven farther apart on the issue of taxes. By the end, they really couldn't stand each other, and had had several extremely testy exchanges on the floor and in private as a result.

I had to get to Senator Baucus and let him know that we needed for him to take the lead on the issue. This was crucial, and time was of the essence. Max and I are friends, and I thought he'd make a perfect first line of defense on Social Security. And making him the point on this would also vest him in the success of the strategy and prevent him from making a deal with the Republicans. I had to make sure that he knew how crucial it was that he not negotiate with either Senator Grassley or the President on this, and that he tell them that in no uncertain terms as soon as possible. If we were going to stand a chance, the Democratic caucus would have to present a united front. What we did not need was Democratic senators floating alternatives to the President's plan. That would change the terms of the debate from "This is a terrible idea" to "Our version of the idea is better than your version of the idea." And the door would be open.

It's ironic and worth noting that this had been the strategy that the Republicans had used to effectively counter the Clinton health care initiative in 1993. "Health care is not, in fact, just another Democratic initiative," said the conservative Washington fixture

Bill Kristol. "It will revive the reputation of Democrats as the generous protector of middle-class interests." Therefore, he said, the Republican mission should be not to deal, not to compromise, not to amend, but to kill health care reform, lest, heaven forbid, someone's life be improved and a Democrat get credit for it. So the Republicans had simply offered no alternative, and the plan sank of its own weight.

Kristol's cynical point is well taken. I certainly harbored no fear that President Bush would be seen as a conquering hero by the middle class if he managed during his presidency to ruin Social Security, but just as the Republicans did with health care in 1993, we Democrats resolved not to deal, not to compromise, not to amend, but to kill the President's plan to privatize Social Security in 2005.

At a small White House meeting in early December, two Democrats and two Republicans—the chairman and ranking member from the House Ways and Means and Senate Finance Committees—met with the President to go over his priorities. Bush had told them that the time was right for him to move on private accounts, and that he intended to take his fight directly to the American people, who had just reelected him. He intended to keep the campaign going and tour the country in the new year until he'd convinced the people that Social Security wasn't untouchable.

Congressman Charlie Rangel, Democrat of New York, had exploded at the foolishness of the idea. Senator Baucus had been more measured, but no more supportive of Bush's plan. "Mr. President, I can't sell privatization to my caucus," he said. "Why don't you form a commission on entitlement programs, and we can put everything on the table?"

Bush wasn't about to settle for a commission, and dismissed Baucus's proposal out of hand, repeating his line about having and spending his political capital. It was becoming clear to Max that the President's proposal had nothing to do with the well-being or long-term solvency of Social Security. Instead, it was all about the politics of privatization.

"Well, private accounts are a place I can't go, Mr. President," Baucus said again.

Just over a month later, Bush began his privatization tour in Montana. And the White House didn't have the courtesy to tell Max that the President was coming to his home state. Baucus read about it in the paper. If this was a move intended to intimidate Baucus, it had the opposite effect.

The same day that Bush was to appear in Great Falls, Max held a raucous antiprivatization rally to preempt the President, and the battle was joined. Senator Baucus then returned to Washington, and told me, "Whatever we need to do to beat this thing, I'm in."

I had followed Senator Clinton's advice and had my staff establish a "War Room" to try to aggressively make up for the Republicans' superior numbers with smart messaging and quick maneuverability. This strategy's first big test would be Social Security. I told Senator Baucus that I wanted his chief of staff, Jim Messina, to be in charge of the effort.

At the time, no one had taken on and beaten Bush. He was undefeated in legislative fights; he'd gotten everything he wanted. "Look, we have to win this," I told Max and Jim. "And we can show Democrats that it's okay to stand up to him and that we can beat him."

By March, a new organization, Americans United to Protect Social Security, was running its first ads, and by April, the organization had a footing in twenty-nine states. Organized labor was integral to that effort. AARP was there, too. Americans United would track President Bush's movements as he crisscrossed the country making his case. Wherever he was flying on his big fly-around, organized protests greeted him. Wherever he got press, we also talked to reporters and did editorial board meetings. Whatever state he was in, if the home-state senator was a Democrat, he or she would call in to radio shows or do TV interviews, and if there wasn't a Democratic senator, surrogates from neighboring states would be on the spot. Several senators countered the President's fly-around with their own fly-around. Our message: The President is trying to foist a policy disaster on the American people, he is not telling you the truth about it, we are not going to let him do it, and we are not backing down.

In the Democratic caucus, Senator Baucus and I kept a watchful eye out for members who might be wavering. Ours is a diverse caucus, and there were members who were open to the idea of private accounts. We are legislators, problem solvers, and deal makers. Normally, there is no shame in wanting to compromise. I've tried to do it at every opportunity in my time in Washington. But not this time.

Karl Rove had blithely predicted that it would be easy for the President to bring moderate Democrats to his side, but he got not one.

Ben Nelson of Nebraska and Joe Lieberman of Connecticut had early on seemed receptive to the President's idea, but held fast in the end. And when Dianne Feinstein of California, who was also sympathetic to the White House's position, signaled that she might propose an alternative plan, Senator Baucus quickly convinced her to abandon the idea.

Every Tuesday at the weekly meeting of the Democratic caucus, we would air video compilations of the coverage our efforts were getting so the senators could see how well our sustained opposition was being received out there. Remember, we had just lost the White House when we thought we were going to win it. We had been wiped out in the Senate, and the House looked worse. I had never seen the Democrats lower. But as spring progressed and we continued to shadow the President around the country on his "Sixty Cities in Sixty Days" privatization tour, our confidence grew. We went from being braced for defeat in December, to being cautiously optimistic as Americans United began to spread the word, to, by May, realizing that we were actually winning. By the time the President wrapped up his tour, it was all but over. He did not return to Washington triumphantly. In fact, he had hurt his cause.

Social Security was more popular than ever in the land.

We knew we had won when the White House simply stopped talking about it.

It is hard to describe the feeling that came over me at this disaster averted. I suppose you could say it was like a patient, having been given six months to live, who comes to find that it's not true; the doctor was terribly mistaken, and all is well.

As with everything else, President Bush was convinced that his diagnosis for America was right. And that's why it's always essential to get a second opinion.


THERE WOULD BE no time for victory laps.

Because all that spring, at the very same time that we had mobilized to save Social Security, a storm had been gathering at the Capitol that threatened the very institution of the Senate itself. It was over the rights of the minority to influence debate, as had been the design of the founders. This stands in stark contrast to the House of Representatives, where the majority rules absolutely. The Senate was meant to be a counterbalance for the passions embodied in the House. If some Republicans had their way, and overruled the Senate parliamentarian and the rules of the Senate were illegally changed so that the majority ruled tyrannically, then the Senate—billed to all as the world's greatest deliberative body—would cease to exist.

So the Senate itself now hung in the balance. And in apocalyptic fashion, the Republicans had taken to calling this gathering storm the "nuclear option."

# SIX

# THE CASES
# NOBODY WOULD TAKE

I DIDN'T CARE if I ever went back to Washington, D.C.

Mike O'Callaghan met me at the airport in Reno. In his hand was a fifty-dollar bill, a denomination of money I'd never seen before. It helped pay for my trip, and it allowed me to take the bar exam. Mike had by this time become my best friend and father confessor. I could count on him without fail and he could count on me. And so there he was, on the spot with the money I needed and didn't have. It was September 1963. I would finish school in January, and I had petitioned the Nevada Supreme Court to be allowed to take the bar early, even though I had not yet finished school. The exam was given only once a year, and I was so broke that I couldn't wait until the next September. The bar exam is graded on the curve. At the time there weren't that many people taking the bar in Nevada, fewer than fifty on that particular day. I had studied the list of my fellow test takers, and I knew most of them. Given that about 50 percent pass the bar in Nevada, I sized up those people taking the test and figured I had studied harder and was smarter than at least half of them. I knew it was hard, but I thought I could do it.

Henderson had never had a homegrown city attorney before. This point was not lost on my father-in-law, who was a man-about-town in Henderson. Dr. Gould advanced my cause before the city council. Our newfound religion may have caused him a little heartburn, but otherwise he had somewhat reconciled himself to his daughter's being married to the no-account from Searchlight. "Look, you've never had anybody from Henderson that's ever gone to law school," he told the city council. "You should give my son-in-law this job." They gave me the job, which was part-time. I would be the town prosecutor, counselor for the city council, and jack-of-all-trades for the city of Henderson. And when I wasn't doing that, I practiced law at a four-man firm in Las Vegas. Between my law practice and the city attorney's job, I worked about seventy-five hours a week.

Vegas in the mid-1960s was an interesting place, to say the least, a place where the intoxicating glamour of celebrity and the lawlessness of the Wild West perched side-by-side atop a mountain of mob cash. Enter the richest man in the world, Howard Hughes, skulking around and buying up casinos from the mobsters, and you've got quite a place to practice law. I wasn't aware of much of this at the time, and only later, when I was appointed chairman of the Nevada Gaming Commission, would I become much more familiar with organized crime than I ever cared to be. But just home from Washington and a new lawyer, I was still unaware of the sometimes evil world.

Singleton, DeLanoy & Jemison was the best firm in Las Vegas, and I was lucky enough to get a job with them. William Singleton, Drake DeLanoy, and Rex Jemison were three of the best lawyers in town. Because Las Vegas was still a relatively small community I knew a lot of people, so I did well right away. Working for wages, I wasn't getting rich, but I wasn't doing bad for the time. I was able to bring in a lot of business, and that's what law firms like. They trained me well. Rex Jemison was the brains not only of that operation but of the whole Nevada legal fraternity. He was brilliant and somewhat eccentric.

By the time I stopped practicing law—in 1982, when I was elected to Congress—I had tried more than a hundred jury trials. That's almost unheard of today. I had good success, and I took a lot of cases that no one else would take. I took them because it's really just sort of my nature. Somebody would come to me and say I can't find anybody to help me. And I would try to help. The guys I worked with sometimes didn't like the junk that I brought in, but they couldn't do much about it because I brought in a lot of other business that redeemed the long-shot cases. But that's the thing: They weren't always long shots. Sometimes these people were actually being railroaded, or felt such a total alienation from the legal system that I felt an obligation to at least try to help them. Often in life, a court of law is a place of last resort.

Early in my career, there was a case called *Martinez v. Safeway Stores.* Joyce Martinez was a cocktail waitress at the Hacienda Hotel. She wore one of those skimpy costumes that left little to the imagination while she passed out drinks to the gamblers. She was an attractive woman, and young, in her mid-twenties. While she was working one day, the Las Vegas police department came into the casino full-force and arrested her. They took her in her little skimpy outfit to jail for writing bad checks at a Safeway store. She came to me, after having been to numerous lawyers, and said, "No one will take my case. I didn't write those checks." I liked Joyce Martinez. She had nothing.

I knew people like her. She seemed like a real person, a law-abiding citizen who was genuinely bewildered at having been arrested, not to mention angry. She told me the details of her case, and I thought that I should try to help her.

And sure enough, the lawyers for whom I worked said, "What the hell are you doing?" But they couldn't stop me, and I filed the law-suit. In those days it was extremely rare that anyone would even try to get punitive damages in a case. It could happen, but it didn't happen often. And as I proceeded through the case, I became convinced that she hadn't written the checks. They had probably been written by her ex-husband, with whom she was on bad terms. But the facts didn't affect anybody's opinion of my case. Every step of the way, people made fun of me for filing suit against a powerful corporation on behalf of a cocktail waitress.

The court was not happy. What are you doing? the judge said. The attorney on the other side also ridiculed the case. What kind of a piece of junk is this case? And my own firm, too. Please, *please,* spend your time on more worthwhile things, they'd say. But I didn't listen.

I presented my case to a jury. I asked for actual damages, showing that she had suffered emotional distress. The jury agreed. But I also decided that Safeway had gone too far and needed to be punished. If I could get punitive damages for Joyce Martinez, it would be a warning to others not to engage in similar conduct.

When you have a punitive-damage claim, you are allowed to delve into the defendant's financial status in detail. The jury in this case had the obligation to see what the company was worth and what it would take to financially punish the corporation. So I called in the big shots at Safeway and went through their financial statements, and boy, did I strike paydirt. That jury came back quick—twenty minutes. They compensated Joyce Martinez with a verdict unheard of in Las Vegas at that time. I was vindicated, as was my client. We both did well financially. In fact, at the time, we were told that Joyce's award was the largest in history in a case of malicious prosecution.

Safeway had been violating the law, and they'd been bullying and intimidating people like Joyce Martinez. If the company had been following the law, they would have had to notify her by mail that she had written a bad check. If they had been following the law, they would have given her an opportunity to explain the facts. But they hadn't done that. Not in this case, and not in many others, the evidence showed. They had routinely skipped that step, and they knew it. They knew somebody in the city attorney's office and had filed all these cases, breaking the law in the process. But this legal action stopped them from doing that. As a result of Joyce Martinez, Safeway stores changed their business practices nationwide.

In keeping with my enthusiasm for unpopular causes, I took the case of a woman whom I will call Barbara. She was a tall, attractive woman, probably in her late twenties. She was a prostitute, a lady of the evening. At the time, she had been living in a very exclusive apartment complex called Tropicana Estates, and she had gotten behind on her rent. The man of her dreams had worked at the Nevada Test Site, and had been killed driving home from work—on the two-lane highway called the "Widowmaker" because the traffic was intense and the accidents frequent. And one day, long after his death, while Barbara was out, the landlord locked her out of the apartment, put all her earthly possessions in a truck, and hauled them off to a warehouse.

After Barbara had paid the back rent and moving charges (which took her several weeks), she went to the storage facility to pick up her belongings, which, she discovered, had just been dumped on the warehouse floor. All of her clothes, dishes, and personal items were wet, spoiled, and broken. And some were missing.

Well, she came to me, and again, this is one of those cases that nobody wanted me to take because she had lost everything.

And the possession that she treasured most—pictures of her now dead lover—were gone. She was heartbroken. So I filed a lawsuit for wrongful eviction. Just as in the case of Joyce Martinez, the defendant had broken the law. To properly evict someone, you have to go through a legal process, get an order from a judge, warn the tenant, and then evict. You can't just throw somebody out of her home.

So we went to court, and I asked for compensatory and punitive damages, just as in *Martinez v. Safeway Stores.* And as before, everyone was belittling my case. A woman with loose morals and behind in her rent—why should anyone care about her? What right does a prostitute have to seek damages in a court of law? The same judge who criticized me in the *Martinez* case really blasted me this time. The jury disagreed. They felt she had been treated terribly. The landlord should have followed the law. As a result, she had lost something unrecoverable. How can you replace destroyed photographs of someone who is dead? So my presentation to the jury was, How would you feel if the thing you cared about the most, photographs of the person that you loved, was destroyed because someone broke the law? And that's what had happened in this case. In less than an hour, the jury returned a nice verdict for Barbara.

On another occasion, a young black man and his mother came to see me. His name was Whittemore, and he was no more than twenty-one. His mother called him her baby son, I remember that. All four of his brothers were then or had been in prison. There had been a robbery out at the Twin Lakes Shopping Center, and three robbers had walked into a clothing store, demanded money, and then shot the clerk. It was a bad scene. Whittemore wasn't suspected of being the gunman, yet he was the only one charged in the case. A witness had identified him in a lineup. So that's the case. And once again, no lawyer wanted to handle it. I took it because his mother asked me to represent her "baby." She paid me little, but I knew I would do better than a court-appointed lawyer. So I worked on the facts of the case and I thought I could prove that the young man couldn't have been at the scene of the crime. I had some excellent alibi witnesses. So I went to Ray Jeffers, who at the time was the chief deputy in the Clark County District Attorney's Office, and I said, "I'd like to make a deal on this, you know, either plead to some lesser crime, or . . ." Jeffers cut me off.

"I could win this case standing on my head," he said. End of conversation. Well, I regarded this as something of a challenge, so I went to work even harder. I thought Whittemore was wrongly accused. So we took this young man to trial, presented the case, and he was acquitted. Because he was innocent. Mrs. Whittemore was happy, her baby boy wasn't a criminal.

I loved the law. I worked hard and could identify with the jurors. Things were going well. And these cases had the effect of improving the way people treated one another. When it works best, that's what the law is for. I found that juries in the vast majority of cases arrived at the right result, but not always for the right reason.

And then one evening after Landra and I had caught a late movie on Fremont Street, a banner headline caught my eye. A few years before, I had been elected to the Clark County Hospital Board, so I knew nearly every doctor in southern Nevada. Which made the headline all the more intriguing: LAS VEGAS DOCTOR MISSING—MURDER. I didn't know it at the time, but this story would become the most challenging and bizarre case of my lawyer life.

I placed a dime in the paper rack, and in the crowd on Fremont Street, stopped to read. The story said that Martin Payne and his wife Emmalyn were believed to have been murdered in their home near Jackson Hole, Wyoming.

Many thoughts came to my mind. Payne had been a prominent Las Vegas doctor for fifteen years. In fact, he was the first orthopedic surgeon in town, and was at one time chief of staff of a large local hospital called Sunrise. Mrs. Payne was involved in many charitable endeavors, and had her own newspaper column. Las Vegas had gotten a bit too big for the Paynes and they'd left town a few years before and settled around Jackson Hole. It's great business for an orthopedic man up there, with ski accidents in abundance.

In spite of the Paynes' positions of prominence, all those who knew them believed them to be a strange couple. It was one of those almost mysterious things; they were both just a little odd. Martin loved to make little people feel even smaller. Many of his patients recalled that if an injury didn't heal fast enough for the doctor, he would call them malingerers and would on occasion refuse further treatment. Attorneys who represented insurance companies loved to have Dr. Payne testify, because he thought all people who brought lawsuits were phonies. When he did testify, he would come to court in his blue jeans and revel in reciting his never-ending qualifications. At his home, he had a doormat that read "Stay Away."

Dr. Payne was a great practical joker, yet he rarely laughed. Emmalyn and Martin were totally without affection toward friends, neighbors, their only child Russell, and each other.

And Russell, I remembered him.

I had first met him when one of the senior lawyers at my firm told me to handle a case for the son of Dr. Payne, who was one of his clients. The charge was reckless driving. As I did almost all the criminal work for the firm, I saw this sort of case routinely.

At age twenty-three, Russell Payne was prematurely bald and had very thick eyeglasses, a very sharp and cutting sense of humor, and an excessive air of self-confidence. Yet girls considered him very attractive. He was smart and clever and had breezed through his studies at USC. Now back in Las Vegas, he was known to run with the show crowd on the fabulous Strip, where his associates were showgirls and other men who chased showgirls.

Shortly after the reckless-driving case was disposed of, Russell Payne had given me a call. There had been a new case involving him filed in federal court in Las Vegas. The case was called *United States of America vs. Four Machine Guns and One Silencer.*

His parents having recently moved to Wyoming, Payne was living with his eighty-three-year-old grandmother in Las Vegas when three federal agents with guns drawn and badges flashing executed a search warrant at her house.

In one of the bedrooms of her home on Isabella Avenue, the agents found and seized a Thompson submachine gun with ammunition clip; one submachine gun, a .45-caliber (grease gun) with clip and extra barrel; one Browning automatic rifle with ammunition clip; one Browning .50-caliber machine gun; one homemade .45-caliber silencer; caps; black powder; and some dynamite.

Payne obviously liked his guns. The federal agents were curious as to where and why he had acquired all his toys.

After an investigation, the U.S. attorney didn't file criminal charges. Instead, his office initiated a civil forfeiture proceeding to seize and destroy the guns. At the hearing, his father displayed a droll wit testifying for his son:

Q: Would you tell the court where your house
   address is.
A: Wilson, Wyoming.

Q: And how long have you lived there?
A: Since 1964.
Q: And do you know Russell Payne?
A: Yes. He's my son.
Q: And have you raised Russell Payne?
A: I think.

I forgot about the headline about the Paynes' disappearance until the next night, when I was awakened from a sound sleep by Gary Bates, an ex-con and professional heavyweight prizefighter from Henderson, who announced, "You've got to help Russell." Bates, a very big, handsome, and quite articulate palaverer, was a friend of Payne's. He had been Sonny Liston's sparring partner and would go on to have fights himself with world contenders such as Gerry Cooney, Jerry Quarry, Ron Lyle, and Ken Norton. Bates told me he had called Payne in Jackson Hole, where they were holding him in jail for drunk driving, but that he was also under suspicion in the case of his missing parents. Bates had told the jailer that he was Payne's lawyer, and they had let him talk to Russell.

Always excitable, Bates was now in high dudgeon. He said that Jackson Hole was "a toilet run by Nazis and that Payne was their Jewboy." He said he was afraid that Payne was going to the ovens without a reason. When Bates finished, I said, "I can't help unless he calls me."

He called, collect. Payne sounded calm but afraid.

An attorney who does criminal work of any magnitude and volume must first find if the person in trouble can pay for his services. In my experience, many could not. If they cannot pay, the lawyer has a pat, routine statement whereby he recommends the public defender—you know, the lawyer the government provides for those who can't afford their own lawyers. But Jackson Hole didn't have a defender program at the time.

The only time I had been near Jackson Hole was when I had passed through Wyoming in 1965 while on a family vacation to Yellowstone National Park. The most exciting thing to happen on that trip was that Landra, Rory, and Lana all got the measles. I frankly don't remember much about that trip. But what is there to remember when the car is little more than an ambulance? I remember Jackson Hole being very small. Anyway, because of Jackson Hole having no public defender, I had to remember to not give the routine speech on "if you have no money, go to a public defender." If Payne didn't have any money, well, that was his problem.

But he did have money. He told me that he had a yellow 1967 Corvette, and a homemade motorcycle worth more than $3,000. And he also owned 10 percent of the corporation that owned all his parents' assets. He wanted to hire me to come to Wyoming.

I talked to the lawyers I worked with and, as ever, none of them felt I should take the case. It's too far, and there's no money in it. I was able to convince them that one trip to Wyoming wouldn't hurt. Some cases just feel good to a lawyer. This one had the right vibes for me, so I convinced my colleagues that there was some money in the case, even though I didn't believe it myself.

This was a trip that in the months to come I sometimes would wish I had never taken.

Payne had told me on the phone that people had already tried to kill him. He said he couldn't talk more or explain but he was afraid. I should come fast, and bring protection. He was convincing. I believed him.

I couldn't fathom how, in a modern civilization, people would not understand that a person is innocent until proven guilty. I re-member learning this in law school.

Jackson Hole would quickly show that some people are guilty until proven innocent, and maybe even then they aren't innocent.

I had carried a gun as a policeman, and because of the kind of law practice I had—robbers, burglars, dope addicts, and disgruntled divorcées—I had developed the habit of always having a loaded gun in my desk drawer. In northern Nevada, a few years before this, a couple of lawyers had been shot dead by an angry husband in a court-room. Another disgruntled client shot up a hotel with a gun he had hidden in a cast on his arm. So I threw a pistol in my suitcase and headed for Wyoming.


THE CITY OF JACKSON HOLE knew I was coming. The rich oddball who was in their jail had sent to quick-buck Las Vegas for his Mafia-backed lawyer—this was the word on the street in town when I pulled in.

I stepped off the plane with my empty briefcase and gray flannel suit into a town full of cowboys and cowgirls. Blue jeans and boots as far as the eye could see. I asked the first airport employee I saw where I could pick up my luggage. "Out there," came the reply. He pointed to a place outside the small terminal. I asked the next per-son I saw how I could get to town. "Out there," he said, pointing to a small car-rental stand. Okay, I get it, nobody wants to talk to me. I rented a car and headed into town.

"Where's the jail?" I asked the first person I met on the board-walk.

This guy saved his syllables and just pointed me in the right direction.

Jackson Hole was an Old West town, but its jail and courthouse were new. It didn't seem quite right. The sheriff met me at the door. "Son, I'm glad you came to help this poor sick boy. Nobody 'round here wanted to be no lawyer for the s.o.b."

Boy, was he right.


IT WAS THE SUMMER OF 1969, and by this time I had been practicing law for five years. In that time I had met some superb lawyers, but no one like Rex Jemison.

Rex had gotten to Las Vegas at a very early age, with his parents and sister. His father was a compulsive gambler. Because his dad continually gambled away all the family's money, including his stepmother's earnings as a schoolteacher, Rex and his sisters were left alone most of the time, and broke.

What his father wasn't around to notice was that his son was a genius. To fill the time, Rex's sister, who was a couple of years older, started taking the boy to the city library, which was then pretty small. In short order, Rex had made his way through the entire collection, and that just whetted his appetite for more. This is not hyperbole. He read all the books. As it turned out, he was one of those people who could process an enormous amount of information much quicker than most normal people. Word was that Rex Jemison could read faster than humanly possible.

Well, the brilliant boy became a brilliant if eccentric lawyer.

Among associates, Jemison became known as "Mysto," for his extraordinary, even mysterious, ability to do research on any legal problem, and "El Fado," for his disappearing act whenever an office party or any social event took place. If he did ever make it to anything, after a couple of drinks he would just up and leave without announcing his departure.

Over time, Rex developed a unique trait: He could work on only one problem at a time, but when he turned his attention to something, he shut the world out, and his focus was laser-like. He refused to see or have clients during these periods, and would hole up like a hermit and think his way through the problem.

Russell Payne was the lucky beneficiary of Rex's brilliant focus. His life would depend on it.


BY THE TIME I got to Jackson Hole to see Payne, theories of the crime were flying fast and furious. Dr. Payne's Toyota Land Cruiser had been found, its interior smeared thick with blood. Almost all of Jackson believed that Russell had killed his parents, but the papers also explored the possibility that Dr. Payne, the oddball physician, had murdered his wife and killed himself or simply disappeared. Others believed that Russell Payne was being set up by his parents' real killer. And some hippies who lived near the Paynes were being eyed warily as possible suspects. In 1969, hippies made easy targets in Wyoming.

When I got to Payne's cell, he was lying on a cot and was covered with an army blanket. "You can't believe what I've been through," he said. I have got to get out of this place—"

I interrupted him. "What's going on with this DUI charge? If it weren't for that, we could get out of here right now."

He cast his eyes down. "I don't know," he said.

Payne was a mess. Only in his mid-twenties, he had felt compelled to undertake the concealment of his encroaching baldness. He had gotten in the habit of growing the hair he had very long and swirling it up, over, and around his head. To this he would apply copious amounts of hair spray, and then color in the remaining bald spots with black Shinola shoe polish. He hadn't shaved. The jail had confiscated his Coke bottle glasses, and so he had been forced to wear his prescription sunglasses. Add to this the dishevelment of a few days' rough treatment in jail, and Payne looked like a real train wreck.

The local district attorney informed me that, as I was not licensed to practice law in Wyoming, I'd need to partner with a local lawyer if I planned to represent Payne. "Good luck," he added, as he figured I'd never find any takers. Payne was guilty. Capital case. Why bother? I'd have to look outside Jackson Hole.

A wealthy young Wyoming lawyer by the name of Ted Frome had the reputation of not being afraid of taking unpopular cases. Frome lived in a town about 80 miles from Jackson Hole called Afton, and was a rancher and a lawyer. I called him at home. "Mr. Frome, my name is Harry Reid. I am from Las Vegas, and I represent Russell Payne. You've read about him. I must have the association of a Wyoming lawyer. Will you help?"

Frome agreed, even though it adversely affected his social standing in all of Wyoming. He had intestinal fortitude, he had guts. And by saying yes, he made me legit in Wyoming.

Payne may have murdered his parents. But why? And if he had done it, he genuinely seemed to have no memory of it. And other things just didn't add up. Russell, I had learned, had just come back from a long camping and canoe trip with his parents. If he had murder in mind, why wait until he got back to civilization before killing them?

I had learned early in the practice of law that you need all the facts—the law comes later. Harry Claiborne, Nevada's most celebrated criminal defense attorney, later an impeached federal judge, always said, "Work on the facts; the law doesn't matter much." Rex Jemison disagreed. The facts were important, yes, but the law must always complement the facts. But Tommy Benson didn't help matters at all, the facts or the law.

It was summer. The days were long and sunny. The light lasted until 9 P.M. This gave me a lot of time to investigate this case. In the early evening of June 17, I met with Mr. Benson at his funeral parlor. Benson wore a number of hats. He was the county's only undertaker. He was also the county coroner. He also owned and operated a number of businesses, including Benson's Hardware. He was about 5′5″ and stocky. He had a voice that sounded as if he hadn't quite woken up yet, like he needed to clear his throat. His eyes were dark and darted up and down, across and over mine. It was hard to meet his gaze. This darkened funeral parlor was empty of bodies. As Benson did bodies for a living, I quickly realized that he wanted those bodies, and he wanted my help in finding them.

Then he gave it to me real good. He said that shortly after Payne's arrest, he had been called by the district attorney and the sheriff to help with the crime scene at Dr. Payne's house.

"I helped take carpet samples and stayed at Payne's for about five and a half hours. There was blood all over. The kid did it. There was gray matter on the bed frame. Cops had seen blood around the house the first time they came. Blood had soaked through the carpets onto the matting. Payne had missed a lot of spots. Pieces of the mattress were found in the fireplace, where Payne had tried to burn it. All the towels were out of the bathroom and in the dryer." I raised my hand to speak when Benson said, "The kid's also a bastard fag."

As we sat in the small, dark room, Benson said, "Why don't you tell me what he told you? Where are those bodies? They're entitled to a Christian burial."

"Tom," I said, "things just don't add up. Why did the postmistress see Dr. Payne the day after you say Russell killed him?"

"Don't get cute," he said. "That kid's a queer."

He told me everyone in Jackson felt the same way he did. In Wyoming, they don't want the criminals pampered the way they always are in California. He would like me to know that I should keep Payne in jail. If he got out, he may be tried and convicted on the streets.

So I KNEW that I needed to get Russell Payne out of Wyoming. We would never be able to prepare his defense in that hostile climate. Maybe he was insane, or maybe he didn't do it. There was no psychiatrist in the entire state of Wyoming. At the moment, the only charge against Payne was misdemeanor DUI. So we came up with a plan.

Payne had several college friends in Las Vegas who were trying to help him. One of his friends had a father who was pit boss at one of the casinos. This friend had asked his dad what he should do, and his father had said, "Russell's your friend; you'd better help him." And Dad had gotten a loan from the casino where he worked—two $5,000 bricks of American money. As it happens, the authorities in Jackson Hole had set Payne's bail at $10,000, an astronomical amount for a misdemeanor. But of course we all knew that more charges were in the offing. With any luck, we'd have Payne out of there by then. We just needed time to figure out what on earth had happened.

We put up the cash. I had gotten us four tickets on Frontier Airways to Las Vegas, and everyone in Jackson Hole seemed to know it. The prosecutors were in the process of preparing a criminal complaint against Russell Payne for murder, and if they filed the additional charges before we got Russell out of there, it would be over for him. It was a capital crime, and he'd never leave Wyoming. So I bailed him out and headed for the airport. But I went by myself. I figured the Jackson Hole police might be waiting at the airport to arrest him, and so I had several of his friends take Russell and hightail it by car to the nearest border—Idaho. And when I got to the airport, the police were there all right, waiting for Russell. "Where is he?" they demanded. "I don't know," I said. "I don't know where he is." I caught the flight to Las Vegas. Russell's friends had access to a private plane, and when Payne made it to Idaho Falls, he was put on the plane and flown to Las Vegas.

The Wyoming authorities wouldn't get him back without an extradition fight. And with Rex Jemison on the case, I knew that Payne would remain in Las Vegas for a long time.

This would give us the time to have Payne properly tested to get an accurate picture of his state of mind. The mother of one of Payne's friends suggested they get a more seasoned lawyer—Who's this kid Harry Reid?—and contacted Percy Foreman down in Houston. Foreman had never lost a murder case. Murder was his game. He was the Clarence Darrow of his day. Well, we met with the silver-maned Foreman—it was the first time I'd ever seen anyone who wore garters to hold up his socks. I went to pick him up from his room at Caesars Palace, and he sat on his bed in his boxer shorts, and there were the garters. Foreman and I went to the Clark County Jail. We both stood looking through the bars of the interview room at Russell Payne. Foreman spoke like a Baptist preacher. After about forty-five minutes of his sermon, he was interrupted by Payne, who asked, "Mr. Foreman, how much will you charge me?"

And in his sleepy drawl, Foreman said, "Young man, everything you've got." This was Percy Foreman's standard fee for a murder case. It is said that when he died, he had warehouses full of his clients' possessions.

Well, everything was a bit steep for Russell, so he was stuck with me as his attorney.

I immediately contacted the leading psychiatrist in Las Vegas, William O'Gorman. He agreed to work with us, knowing that the police were looking for Payne, as it was all over the news. Murder charges had been filed on the day he left Wyoming, and Payne had become a very recognizable figure in Las Vegas. We sneaked Payne through the back door and into the doctor's office, where O'Gorman spent five and a half hours testing him. Afterward, Dr. O'Gorman called my office. I was awaiting his call. It was after 11 P.M. when he invited me to his office for a debriefing. As I entered the dimly lit room, Payne was told to have a seat in the waiting room, and I was ushered into the doctor's spacious private office. Before I had a chance to sit down, O'Gorman said, "He is as sane as you and me."

And then he got to the heart of the matter. "Do you think he did it?" he asked.

"If they had found the bodies, I think the circumstantial evidence would be great enough that they could and would convict," I said. "He can be placed in his parents' home on the night they disappeared. They found a burned mattress and there is a witness from a store where he bought a new one. They have just about all but the bodies." It is tough to convict someone of murder when no bodies have been found. Dr. O'Gorman and I thought a polygraph would prove helpful.

O'Gorman then asked something interesting: "What medication has he been on?" Mostly alcohol, I told him. And he also on occasion took Quaaludes. Additionally, Russell told me that his father had prescribed him a relatively new drug called deanol, also called by the brand name Deaner. Dr. Payne was vehemently opposed to Russell's drinking and had read in a medical journal that Deaner showed promise in curing alcoholism. He had been drinking at least a fifth of vodka each day. He had a real problem, so why not try this new drug?

"Well, trying to develop an insanity defense is a loser," O'Gorman said. "There's nothing there. Russell Payne can distinguish right from wrong."

A few days after the murder charges were filed in Jackson Hole, they got the criminal complaint down to Vegas. I made arrangements to surrender Payne to local law enforcement.

By this time, my buddy Ron McAllister had become a fine private detective, and in the five years I'd been practicing law, he had done a lot of work for me on cases. He had done so many routine background checks that he had begun keeping track of some of the most interesting names he had run into in his line of work. His favorite was Athol R. Smelly. His second choice was Dern Strange. It seems McAllister had met Dern Strange in the Utah State Mental Institution. Strange had wound up there after returning to his home in Provo, Utah, after a two-day bender, whereupon he attempted to make love to his wife. After she refused him, Dern Strange swore to her that if she would not have him right then and there, he'd castrate himself. She still refused, and he proceeded to perform the surgery. The ambulance was called, and he was taken first to the hospital, and then the mental institution. The interesting—and cruel—thing is that his name really was Dern Strange.

So McAllister had experience that I needed for this case. He was a good sleuth. Over the years, he had developed the strange skill of being able to read documents upside down. He'd stand in front of someone's desk and be able to read and recall the documents before them. He was the best I had ever seen at finding a missing person. He was also very good at serving subpoenas on people trying to avoid being served. He had settled in Utah after his aborted college career, but had made it back to Las Vegas after one of his divorces, and that's when he started working for me. And while I had been trying to get Payne out of jail, McAllister had already been to the Payne house and interviewed about a dozen potential witnesses.

McAllister felt that there was abundant evidence of a brutal crime, but that something just didn't add up. And then there was something else: In a detailed note that he sent me, McAllister wrote that the deputy sheriff of Teton County, where Jackson Hole is located, a fellow by the name of Spence, had told him this: "Says Russell told them he had been taking drugs and drinking vodka and had blacked out and didn't know where he was Wednesday night and that he sometimes blacked out for 2–3 days at a time."

Ron also told me that each night in the Jackson town square they faked a public hanging. This was to impress the tourists that this was still a frontier town, and that in Jackson Hole, Wyoming, they were familiar with executions.

WHEN WYOMING DEMANDED that Russell Payne be returned to face murder charges, I immediately sent a wire to the governor of Nevada, Paul Laxalt, demanding a governor's hearing, which started the extradition process. Laxalt, a lawyer, set a date for the hearing, to be held in Las Vegas. This was the beginning of one of the most calculated stalls in Nevada criminal jurisprudence. I knew that after the governor held the hearing, various legal questions could be raised, mainly because the bodies of Dr. and Mrs. Payne had not yet been found. I also knew that as a matter of law, the extradition papers from Wyoming had to be perfect. If they weren't, the paper war would give me the time to figure out this puzzle.

Now here's where the talented and brilliant Rex Jemison comes in. I had explained the facts of the case to Rex on several occasions. Rex had a rare ability to come up with legal theories when everyone else had failed to come up with a viable idea of how a case should proceed. And Rex had an idea or two about this case.

One of the things I had explained to Rex was the theory that Dr. O'Gorman had introduced me to about the relationship between drugs and alcohol and criminality.

Rex had found a number of cases that involved a doctor in New York City named Alberto Laverne. Laverne was a neuropharmapsychiatrist, meaning that he was board-certified in neurology, psychiatry, and pharmacology. Laverne's testimony was so unique and his scholarship so outstanding that he was featured lavishly in the case law. Rex had zeroed in on one case involving a young man named Tommy Higgins.

Higgins was a twenty-two-year-old oil burner installation and service mechanic. His intelligence was below average. It seems that he began a certain evening in New York with friends and claims he had fifteen to twenty beers, either alone or chased down with rye whiskey, and had eaten nothing all day, and said that this made him feel high but not drunk. After he left his friends and walked to his car, he noticed a young woman he knew crossing the street and offered her a lift. They had never dated. In fact, Higgins was engaged to be married. After she got in the car, Higgins drove her home and parked the car. They talked for a few minutes, and then started kissing, then went into the backseat. Higgins thought they were going to have sex, but she said, "No, not yet, let's go for some drinks."

By his own statement, Higgins said he reached back, picked up a ball-peen hammer, which was there with other tools he used in his work, and started swinging, and struck the young woman in the face and head at least nineteen times. He then returned to the front seat, drove his car a few blocks, and placed her body on the curb, then drove home and went to sleep.

Higgins was easily apprehended. When he was examined in custody, the medical history given to the doctors showed that in the past Higgins had experienced "fits."

What drew Rex's attention to the Higgins case was, of course, the violence of the crime itself. But his attention became fixed on the medical tests that had been conducted on Higgins following his arrest.

Higgins was given the standard physical, neurological, and psychological tests, none of which proved to be particularly illuminating. He was then given what is known as a provocative test. The provocative agent for Higgins was alcohol.

Tommy arrived at the hospital at 2:45 P.M. and was placed in a sitting position. EEG sensors were fixed on his skin. After a blood sugar test was made, he was given a mixture of three ounces of whiskey, three ounces of orange juice, and some sugar. Half a minute later, this dosage was repeated. The examining doctor and those in attendance reported that nine minutes after he had the second drink, Higgins suffered a seizure. His lips started quivering and his whole body then went into motion as he slid off his chair. He then became so violent that four corrections officers couldn't hold him down. Eventually, they handcuffed him to the chair. His pupils were dilated, and his reaction to light was sluggish. When the seizure subsided, he became bewildered and dazed. It was impossible to communicate with him for thirty minutes. Afterward, he was unable to remember anything that had happened during the seizure or during the disoriented period that followed.

The doctors testing Higgins explained to the court the different types of epilepsy. The grand mal, or convulsive type, is characterized by total amnesia, and during one of these attacks the afflicted is so helpless that he is unable to perform any coordinated movements. Petit mal is a mild seizure of brief duration prevalent in children. Psychomotor epilepsy is a type in which the patient is not conscious but displays coordinated and seemingly purposeful movements. Thalamic, or hypothalamic, epilepsy is characterized by strange attacks fitting into none of these patterns. It is also known as rage epilepsy, or furor epilepsy. During the violent state of a hypothalamic attack, the individual is capable of performing skillful, coordinated movements, and can be so adrenalized as to have superhuman strength. These types of seizures, we learned, are often accompanied by partial or complete amnesia. In 1969, rage epilepsy was newly discovered, and little was understood of its effects.

Dr. Laverne, the senior psychiatrist at Bellevue Hospital in New York City, had testified at the trial of Tommy Higgins that a person in the throes of a furor seizure acts like a wild animal. Laverne also testified that he had examined Higgins while Higgins was under the influence of sodium amytal, or truth serum, and that Higgins had described the attack:

"He was in the backseat with Pat Ruland, and she suddenly stated to him, 'Tommy, why are you shaking? What's wrong with you, are you sick?' He then grabbed my arm [Dr. Laverne's] to demonstrate what Pat did to Tommy. She then stated to him, 'You're talking crazy. You're talking nonsense. What's wrong with you?'"

In the Higgins case, Rex Jemison saw possible parallels to the Payne case. Higgins had apparently committed a heinous murder while experiencing an epileptic seizure. Could something have triggered such a seizure in Russell Payne? Rex Jemison thought that we should have Payne immediately subjected to a similar battery of tests to find out.

NO ONE TOOK Rex seriously on this score. You couldn't always follow his leads because he often had far too many. But I thought the tests would be too expensive. And there were no bodies yet. We still weren't sure exactly what crime we were dealing with here. While I went back to Wyoming to get a good look at the assembled evidence, Rex went into one of his trance-like periods of intense concentration. He simply could not understand what had happened that June night in Jackson Hole. And if he encountered something he couldn't understand, he was incapable of letting it go. You or I would simply shrug our shoulders and go on to something else. Not Rex.

He would awake early in the morning with the same problem he had gone to bed with. From a moneymaking standpoint, Jemison was actually not the best. A person who obsessed over a problem as he did, without regard for time, had trouble getting all his time paid for. He spent far too long on most of his cases. Few clients could afford him.

Russell Payne couldn't afford to not have him.

With the Payne case, there were a number of things that bothered Rex. The Higgins case seemed to involve a mental state that could explain Payne's behavior at the time of his parents' deaths. If they were dead. But Payne had no history of "fits" or of epilepsy.

Rex spent hours at the library of the Southern Nevada Memorial Hospital reading all the available literature on epilepsy and Deaner. He found a strange article entitled "Seizure-like Homicidal (Filicidal) Thoughts, as a Symptom of Temporal Lobe Epilepsy." The article had been written in French by a Polish doctor named Dabrowska. Rex had it translated by an ex-Mormon missionary, Carl Christianson, a Las Vegas lawyer who had gone to France on his proselytizing duties. The article told the story of one of Dr. Dabrowska's patients, a farmer. The man was fifty-two and had no history of epilepsy, mental illness, or alcoholism. He was quite sociable and drank only one bottle of wine each month. By temperament, he was cheerful and quite sentimental. He was devoted to his family, especially to his oldest son.

One very warm August day, in a small neighboring town, he drank a couple of shots of vodka and a glass of wine, but was not drunk. He climbed on his bicycle to ride home on a familiar road. He became very disoriented but didn't realize it, thinking all the time that he was traveling in the right direction. Finally, he reached a neighbor's home about a mile and a half from his own home. He couldn't remember how he had gotten there. A couple of months later, while looking for mushrooms near his home, he again became totally lost. His sense of disorientation, Dr. Dabrowska reported, lasted only about five minutes. About two months after that, in December, while working, he suddenly had a feeling he described as "dizziness, rage, unconsciousness, a desire to flee." At that moment, a stunning impulse hit him powerfully: He felt the almost uncontrollable urge to kill his oldest and most beloved son. The urge was so violent and obstinate that he wanted to stop his work immediately and run to the school where his son was and kill him. The man told Dr. Dabrowska that he had had to resist the impulse with everything he had. But that didn't stop him from visualizing his son hacked to death in a pool of blood. The impulse came over him in waves, and each time it lasted for about ten minutes. In the intervals between these fits, the patient felt remorse and despair, and fear that he might actually kill his son. Because of this, he hid all his sharp tools, avoided his son, and even rigged his bed with heavy chains, which he told his wife to use to restrain him if either of them felt he was again becoming delusional.

From this experience, Dr. Dabrowska developed the theory that in one of these seizures the afflicted usually tries to kill the person most beloved to him.

Rex decided he still didn't know enough about Deaner, and so we went to the source. Riker Laboratories in Southern California manufactured the drug, and they had their own library.

Russell had been taking the drug since April, having been prescribed it by his father. While the drug was normally prescribed to raise the IQ of those with substandard intelligence, Dr. Payne had read that Deaner had the effect of reducing the appetite for alcohol. His father had grown worried that Russell was an alcoholic, and he thought that Deaner might be a good treatment. Russell had also read the literature on the drug and was eager to take it, figuring that Deaner might sharpen his intellectual powers, which were already superior.

So as we entered the Riker facility, we were aware of at least two effects of this powerful drug. Could there be more? Could Deaner do things to the brain that nobody had contemplated?

Deaner was a remarkable drug. It was one of the few substances known that could penetrate the blood-brain barrier, which is nature's way of protecting the brain from foreign substances. Deaner also had the capacity to increase the amount of cerebral acetylcholine, which is the chemical that transmits messages from one part of the brain to another. In other words, this was a powerful drug capable of altering the basic chemistry of the brain.

Reading as fast as he could, Rex discovered many things about

Deaner that the manufacturer had concealed from the federal Food and Drug Administration. He found an article published by a medical journal in Australia entitled "Use of Deaner in Behaviour States," written by a prominent Australian doctor named Bostock. It was a frightening story. Dr. Bostock wrote that he had first encountered Deaner when the drug had been prescribed to a subnormal nine-year-old girl. Efforts in therapy for the child had been unsuccessful, so she was given two tablets of Deaner a day. Initially, the family reported an improvement in the girl's attention span. Intrigued by this, Dr. Bostock decided to test the drug on a group of twenty-two children, and found that seven of the twenty-two had suffered temporal lobe epileptic seizures after taking Deaner. The seizures, the doctor reported, were characterized by rage, aggression, destructive behavior. None of the children had a history of epilepsy before taking the drug.

In tests performed by Robert Kugel of the Department of Pediatrics at Iowa State on two boys taking Deaner, one of the boys exhibited a rage that was hard to manage. The other threatened his father with a knife.

Another article, from *The Modern Hospital* magazine, showed that prolonged intake of Deaner in high doses produced spontaneous epileptic seizures in mice.

And then Rex found an article written by a doctor from Emory University that described a stunning syndrome. A Dr. Goldstein from Emory had tested Deaner on rabbits, producing a strange reaction, in that the brain wave patterns on the electroencephalogram indicated a sleeping pattern while in fact the rabbits were moving around and in an agitated state.

How on earth was this possible? And just what hell did this drug unleash in the human brain?

. . .

"DOCTOR, YOU HAVE come very highly recommended," I said into the phone. "I hope you can help." I was speaking to A. A. Marinacci in Los Angeles. Dr. Marinacci had spent years developing a procedure for testing the effects of drugs and alcohol on criminal behavior. He did it empirically, using an electroencephalogram. We needed a picture of Russell Payne's brain under the influence of this drug Deaner. It was our only shot at truly understanding what had happened on June 11.

"You see, I am an attorney in Las Vegas, and I represent a young man in Wyoming charged with killing his parents. He is in custody in jail in Las Vegas, but they are trying to take him back to Wyoming right away. He denies any knowledge relating to the disappearance of his mother and father, but the circumstantial evidence looks real bad. There was a lot of carnage at the home where the deaths probably occurred. He was drinking substantial amounts of vodka, up to a fifth a day, and was taking two prescribed drugs, Deaner and Quaalude."

No response.

"Doctor, what do you think?"

There was a long pause. Finally, Dr. Marinacci said, "Get it set up in Las Vegas. I need a board-certified neurologist or neurosurgeon to assist. I can do it next Saturday. It will take at least half a day."

He didn't talk about how much it would cost. I was afraid to ask.

At the time, Las Vegas had one neurosurgeon. His name was Adrien Verbrugghen, and he was known to be eccentric, temperamental, and expensive.

Dr. Marinacci had begun writing on alcohol-activated electroencephalograms in 1949. He had initially become famous as a result of his studying more than eight hundred cases for the Superior Court of Los Angeles. He had studied murderers and other violent criminals. Often, someone who commits such a crime will claim no recollection of his behavior. Marinacci felt that through his EEG tracings he could support or invalidate such a claim. I felt he could do us no harm. If his tests proved negative, too bad. But if the tests showed some form of improper brain wave spiking, then we'd have a deeper understanding of what had happened.

So on August 3, 1969, Dr. Marinacci flew into McCarran Field in Las Vegas and took a cab directly to Dr. Verbrugghen's office on West Charleston Boulevard, next door to Southern Nevada Memorial Hospital, where Dr. Payne used to operate on broken legs and bad backs.

Payne was due to arrive at Verbrugghen's office at 11 A.M. The jail crew had shackled him hand and foot and turned him over to two deputy sheriffs. As Payne left the Clark County Jail, the flashbulbs popped and the television cameras rolled. In his shackles and with his wild look, with a deputy on either side, Payne looked every part the vicious killer.

When he was brought into the doctor's office, the shackles were removed. Marinacci's assistant began hooking up the equipment. The main machine looked like a telephone switchboard or the dashboard of an airliner. Lots of gauges, lights, and instruments. Near Payne's chair was another instrument box. From this box came the wires to be attached to Payne's head. The brain produces huge amounts of electricity, and this machine measures its voltage. During a grand mal seizure, the brain produces enough electricity to power a 100-watt lightbulb.

The first part of the test on Russell Payne would be a baseline EEG, to be conducted with Payne taking no drugs of any kind. This was so Dr. Marinacci could determine if Payne had normal EEG tracings to begin with. After about twenty-five minutes of this, it was plain to see that Payne's brain produced perfectly normal brain waves.

The tension was quite high. Everyone felt it, even the two deputy sheriffs. The tests were being conducted in a medical office, but one could not forget that the patient's parents were missing and believed to have been murdered. All the evidence pointed to Payne, the guy with the wires sticking out of his head.

For part two of the test, Payne was given 600 mg of Quaalude. An hour later, the doctors added 25 mg of Deaner, and then after a few minutes, another 25 mg. It seemed that almost immediately Verbrugghen and Marinacci began paying closer attention to the wavy lines produced by the machine. Another pill brought Payne up to the dosage of Deaner he had been taking at the time of his parents' disappearance. And now even a layman could tell that the tracings were abnormal. The spiking became persistent and regular.

Dr. Marinacci almost showed some emotion. He turned to Verbrugghen. "I'll be *damned,*" he said.

But they weren't done yet. The doctors needed to see what effect alcohol would have. Payne was given six ounces of Wolfschmidt vodka in gradual increments. The spiking increased.

Dr. Marinacci took the more than three hours of tracings, taking up more than 750 pages, back to his Los Angeles office to analyze. The next day, he called.

"Mr. Reid, I have no doubt and can show empirically that the tracings unquestionably show an epileptic condition in Russell Payne induced by Deaner and accentuated by alcohol, which would produce, and did produce, violence and furor."

Temporal lobe epilepsy was probably first reported in Greek mythology. We remember Hercules for his godlike feats of strength.

Hercules performed twelve great labors, including killing the many-headed serpent and catching the bull of the Cretan king.

What we may not remember is that Hercules had been sentenced by an oracle to serve his cousin, the king of Argos, for twelve years after he had gone insane and slaughtered his wife and children. Euripides described Hercules in *The Madness of Heracles*: "And everyone looks at the man who has been struck dumb and is completely changed, whose reddened eyes roll, from whose beard froth drips. . . . He beats his body and struggles to breathe." And for two thousand years, this mysterious malady of the brain was called Herakliea nosos, the illness of Hercules.

So the world has known this kind of crime for centuries. We just hadn't understood it very well. I read this account of rage and parricide and couldn't help but think of Russell Payne.

NEWPORT BEACH, CALIFORNIA, is a fantastic place. It has great restaurants, great beaches, and near-perfect weather, and it's close to Disneyland, the Angels, and the Dodgers. Newport Beach was the site of my 1969 summer vacation. A beach house for the whole family. Heaven, especially after this case. And Russell Payne wasn't all that was demanding my time. The previous year I had run for a Nevada Assembly seat from Las Vegas and won. So between spending time with our growing brood—by then son Leif had joined Lana and Rory—and immersing myself in this labyrinthine case, I had legislative duties to attend to. So I was a little busy. My family needed the break, and Newport Beach was a welcome change of scenery.

The first three days were uneventful—sun, food, trying to unwind. But on the fourth day, I received a call from my Las Vegas office. The bodies of Dr. and Mrs. Payne had been found.

My vacation was over. I had to return. As long as there were no bodies, many viable theories of the crime could be held. But speculation was now over.

Two men named Campbell, father and son, were hunting not far from the Payne residence when they both smelled a very strong odor. Except for the fact that Mr. Campbell was an undertaker, the smell of putrefying flesh may have gone unnoticed. But that smell is unmistakable to anyone who has ever smelled it before.

The bodies were found three miles as the crow flies south of Dr. and Emmalyn Payne's dream house, and about 175 feet from the nearest road, in an area of dense brush. Upon approaching the smell, the two Campbells first saw the top portion of a skull protruding from the side of a bank of earth.

The special investigator in the case, Robert Ranck, theorized that Payne carried the bodies, one by one, to the garage, where the Payne Land Cruiser was parked. The garage door was down and the rear gate of the Toyota was malfunctioning and could not be lowered, so the bodies were placed on the front passenger seat floorboard. After this, Russell drove south in the Toyota on Fall Creek Road to Mosquito Creek Road, and then almost two more miles to an abandoned dumping area where Russell and his dad had gone on other occasions.

Russell then had driven into the clearing a little over 150 yards, Ranck figured, an area accessible only to four-wheel-drive vehicles. There, he believed that Payne had simply dumped the bodies into the thicket before driving the Toyota vehicle another eight miles, where the car was abandoned and later found by authorities.

This is where Ranck had trouble explaining his theory about Payne's activities. Because after dumping the bodies, Payne would then have had to go cross-country along the Snake River all the way back to his home. Going cross-country through this marshy forest wilderness is nearly impossible to do.

People who knew the country and terrain around the Payne home derided Ranck's theory. No human being, in the time set out by Ranck, could do these things. One forest ranger was heard to say, "Only a crazy man would even attempt it, and then could only make it if he were deranged and using other than human strength." People in a furor, like Payne, can do superhuman things. His trek home from dumping the bodies crossed swampland and dense forest with no roads whatsoever, and was thought by locals who knew the avenue to be impossible.

The bodies were found piled one on top of the other. The corpse of Mrs. Payne was lying on that of the doctor. Both were face-up. The man was completely naked, and the woman was wearing only her wedding ring and a Kotex belt.

Tommy Benson, together with a pathologist from Salt Lake City, conducted the autopsies.

I apologized to my family and suggested that they stay on vacation in Newport while I returned to Las Vegas, but they decided to come back with me. The drive from California to Nevada was quick.

Upon arriving home, I went to the jail to see Payne. I thought if he were confronted with the fact that the bodies had been found, his memory, his attitude might change.

I walked into the jail and met him, he on one side of the wire mesh and I on the other. He had already heard about the bodies on the television set they had available for prisoners. He couldn't say anything. His only attitudinal change was that he seemed more confused—something like a person who is involved in a serious automobile accident and can't remember the facts.

As soon as I left Russell, I went directly to my office to call Dr.

Laverne. He had been paid, and to this point he meant nothing to the case other than that he was a very nice man with an interesting background. "Dr. Laverne, they found the bodies a few miles from the house."

"What did the autopsies show?" he asked.

"You can't believe it, but I hadn't thought of that," I replied, embarrassed.

"If the autopsies show some violence being done to the bodies, it will be in keeping with my theory that he was in a hypothalamic frenzy when they were killed," he said. "If there is no extreme violence, you have trouble, but I can almost guarantee you the bodies will be all broken up. How's Russell?"

Through this whole case, it really did seem to be Dr. Laverne's biggest concern that Russell was okay. His doctor image was always intact as far as I was concerned; Payne was his patient, and the medical/legal aspect of the case only came after Laverne felt Payne was okay.

"He seems almost in a daze when I try to talk about the facts of the case, even though he seems to be very sharp about everything else," I said. "I think he would like to make something up, so people would no longer bother him about something he obviously is personally totally in the dark about.

"Doctor, let's assume he killed his parents, and knows how and why he did it," I said. "Is it possible to suppress everything the way he has?"

"No. He was closely examined by Dr. O'Gorman, did not fail a polygraph, I've reviewed the case, and then we have Marinacci's work on the EEG. No, that's why I'm convinced Dr. Dabrowska is right about her hypothalamic theory. Harry, don't worry. You have done a good job. Get a good pathologist to go up and look at the bodies. I'm going to come out to Las Vegas and run some tests on Russell that will hopefully give us insight as to the killings—it has to be done. Don't worry, counselor."

Dr. Swift was the Salt Lake pathologist the State of Wyoming used. He came well recommended. The State of Wyoming death certificates could now be drawn up. When prepared, they looked so cold, so impersonal.

Emmalyn Payne—female.
Race—White.
Age 50.
Died outside the city limits, not in a hospital.
Born in Maryland.
No surviving spouse.
Usual occupation—news correspondent in the newspaper business.

The immediate cause of death was listed as a gunshot wound in the head, with the interval between onset and death being given as minutes. The certificate stated that "Homicide on June 11, 1969, at an unknown hour by a shot in the head with a .22-caliber gun" was how the injury occurred.

Her husband's death certificate was basically the same.

Two people, now represented only by two small pieces of paper.

I called Thorne Butler, a soft-spoken, very articulate Las Vegas pathologist, to see if he could go to Salt Lake City for me, as the corpses had been transported there. We talked about how busy he was, which finally led to a discussion of what would be a fair price for his services, and to Salt Lake City he did go.

The two bodies, when found, were badly decomposed. Maggots had taken over their flesh; the putrefaction of the bodies was abhorrent to smell.

Dr. Butler was familiar with the case. He knew what we were looking for: What damage had been done to their bodies?

He reported that Martin Payne's body was entirely covered with mud and maggots. It was accounted that the maggots were so intense when the bodies were first found that the body of Dr. Payne appeared to be moving. The only unusual thing revealed in the internal examination and cardiovascular examination, reported Dr. Butler, was the sclerosis, which was severe. Dr. Payne would have soon had a heart attack.

Dr. Butler retrieved the skull from a bag marked "Evidence." He found a circumferential fracture extending from the left temple in various fracture lines across the top of the skull. He found another fracture line going from the left ear into the forehead. Right over the left temple area was a hole that was very probably the result of a bullet. The bullet hole for Mrs. Payne was over her left eye. In short, both Dr. and Mrs. Payne had been shot and then beaten about the head.

Dr. Laverne was right, and so was Dr. Dabowska—these people had been savaged. Russell Payne had been in a rage when he attacked them, in the throes of a drug-induced hypothalamic brain seizure. No one could argue about this. The evidence was clear.

LAVERNE WORKED QUICKLY when he arrived, giving Payne sodium amytal—truth serum. Sodium amytal is administered as though you are giving the person a blood transfusion. It drips into the patient's body drop by drop, very slowly, putting the person into a trance-like condition. When Payne was in his trance, Dr. Laverne began his slow and deliberate questioning. And it was then that Russell Payne described the night he killed his parents. A night of which he had no conscious memory. Payne spoke with his eyes closed, his voice floating, even and low.

> LAVERNE: What was the conversation that went on that
>     evening before you shot them?
> PAYNE: My father said, "What's up, Charlie?"
> LAVERNE: Go ahead, continue.
> PAYNE: I walked over there and my mother didn't
>     say anything.
> LAVERNE: Did she see the gun?
> PAYNE: No.
> LAVERNE: Then what happened?
> PAYNE: The damn thing went off.

"It was *compulsive,*" Payne said. "It was a *driving force.*"

"DO YOU HAVE anything to say before sentence is imposed?" the judge asked Russell Payne.

It is customary for a judge to look into the eyes of a defendant as he pronounces sentence. It is generally as customary for a defendant not to return the judge's gaze. Here, we had the reverse. Payne, chin up, shoulders squared, looked directly at Judge C. Stuart Brown of Wyoming's Third Judicial District Court. Brown refused to look at Payne.

Rex and I had brought Russell Payne back to Jackson Hole to face justice, bringing our satchel of evidence, our theory of the crime, and Dr. Alberto Laverne with us. Finding the evidence we'd gathered to be compelling, the district attorney, a man by the name of Hufsmith, came to believe that Payne hadn't knowingly killed his parents, and agreed to drop charges of premeditated murder in favor of manslaughter. Given the ferocity of public opinion in Wyoming against Payne, this was an extraordinary outcome. Hufsmith did what was right, and he took much political grief.

"Mr. Payne, I am going to impose on you a severe sentence, and I want you to face it like a man and make something of your life. Counsel for the defense has made a very persuasive plea, indicating that the court ought to take into consideration your diminished responsibility by way of extenuation and mitigation, and it has been suggested that the court should exercise some compassion in your behalf, and some leniency. I would say that I do have considerable compassion for you, and I feel real bad about this thing, but I am not going to shirk my duty."

Brown then talked about the dangers of Deaner, and stated explicitly that a harsh sentence for Payne in no way was intended to "acquit the drug." He then sentenced Payne to the maximum term for manslaughter: twenty years.

Back in chambers, the judge apologized, saying that he would speak on Payne's behalf if in a year his EEG was normal. He was afraid that Payne had suffered irreparable brain damage.

These, of course, were not comments he made publicly.

He also said that he would personally commute Russell's sentence at a later date, something that it turned out he had neither the power nor the time to do. Within a year, Judge Brown would be felled by a massive heart attack.

I came out of this case feeling a few years older. The experience had changed me, as a lawyer and as a man. More than ever before, I felt a compulsion to follow the facts, wherever they led, however uncomfortable the truth might be, however long it takes, however much it costs. All of the expert witnesses, time, and travel required to save Russell Payne had been expensive. And because he had not been convicted of murder, Payne was able to inherit his parents' assets. After he paid his legal bills, Payne would end up with a nice piece of real estate in Las Vegas. The rest went to Rex and me.

They put Russell Payne in prison in Rawlins, Wyoming, where the wind blows cold all the time. I'd go visit him there sometimes. It's a terrible place for anything but a prison, so it's a good place to punish people. You'd walk into the lobby, and there would be a picture recalling Rawlins's most famous prisoner, Butch Cassidy, who was the fifth prisoner in the history of the state.

The State of Wyoming took the place down some years ago. It's no longer there. And so neither is Russell Payne, who served six years before he was released to live a peaceable and productive life.

# SEVEN

# THE NUCLEAR OPTION

PEACEABLE AND PRODUCTIVE are not two words I would use to describe Washington in 2005.

I just couldn't believe that Bill Frist was going to do this.

The storm had been gathering all year, and word from conservative columnists and in conservative circles was that Senator Frist of Tennessee, who was the Majority Leader, had decided to pursue a rules change that would kill the filibuster for judicial nominations. And once you opened that Pandora's box, it was just a matter of time before a Senate leader who couldn't get his way on something moved to eliminate the filibuster for regular business as well. And that, simply put, would be the end of the United States Senate.

It is the genius of the founders that they conceived the Senate as a solution to the small state/big state problem. And central to that solution was the protection of the rights of the minority. A filibuster is the minority's way of not allowing the majority to shut off debate, and without robust debate, the Senate is crippled. Such a move would transform the body into an institution that looked just like the House of Representatives, where everything passes with a simple majority. And it would tamper dangerously with the Senate's advise-and-consent function as enshrined in the Constitution. If even the most controversial nominee could simply be rubber-stamped by a simple majority, advise-and-consent would be gutted. Trent Lott of Mississippi knew what he was talking about when he coined a name for what they were doing: the nuclear option.

And that was their point. They knew—Lott knew—if they trifled with the basic framework of the Senate like that, it would be nuclear. They knew that it would be a very radical thing to do. They knew that it would shut the Senate down. United States senators can be a self-regarding bunch sometimes, and I include myself in that description, but there will come a time when we will all be gone, and the institutions that we now serve will be run by men and women not yet living, and those institutions will either function well because we've taken care with them, or they will be in disarray and someone else's problem to solve. Well, because the Republicans couldn't get their way getting some radical judges confirmed to the federal bench, they were threatening to change the Senate so fundamentally that it would never be the same again. In a fit of partisan fury, they were trying to blow up the Senate. Senate rules can only be changed by a two-thirds vote of the Senate, or sixty-seven senators. The Republicans were going to do it illegally with a simple majority, or fifty-one. Vice President Cheney was prepared to overrule the Senate parliamentarian. Future generations be damned.

Given that the filibuster is a perfectly reasonable tool to effect compromise, we had been resorting to the filibuster on a few judges. And that's just the way it was. For 230 years, the U.S. Senate had been known as the world's greatest deliberative body—not always efficient, but ultimately effective.

There had once been a time when the White House would consult with home-state senators, of either party, before sending prospective judges to the Senate for confirmation. If either senator had a serious reservation about the nominee, the nomination wouldn't go forward. The process was called "blue slips." The slips were sent to individual senators. If the slips didn't come back, there was a problem. The Bush White House ignored the blue-slip tradition, among many other traditions, and showed little deference to home-state senators.

We realized that if they were not going to adhere to our blue slips or entertain any advice from us, then they were trying to subvert the minority's ability to perform its advise-and-consent function under the Constitution. It was clear that Bush and Karl Rove were going to try to load all the courts—especially the circuit courts of appeals, because you can't count on Supreme Court vacancies. And most of the decisions are made by circuit courts anyway, so it could be said that they are the most important judicial nominees of all.

We Democrats made a decision that since the White House was ignoring the Constitutional role of the Senate, then we were going to have to delay some of the more extreme nominees. Be cautious and look closely was the byword. One rule we tried to follow was that if all Democrats on the Judiciary Committee voted no on a nominee, then we would say, "Slow down."

The Republicans immediately complained that they had never filibustered Clinton's judges, a claim that simply wasn't true. Frist himself had participated in the filibuster of the nomination of Judge Richard Paez, which at the time had been pending in the Senate for four years. When Senator Schumer had called him on it on the Senate floor, Frist had stammered to try to find a way to explain how their use of the filibuster was legitimate and ours wasn't. And moreover, it was a disingenuous claim. The reason the Republicans didn't deploy the filibuster that often when Clinton was President is that they had a majority in the Senate, and they had simply refused to report more than sixty of President Clinton's judicial nominees out of committee, saving them the trouble of a filibuster. In any case, the U.S. Senate had never reached a crisis point like this before.

In the early part of 2005, I hadn't wanted to believe it was true, and felt confident that we could certainly avoid it. We make deals in the Senate, we compromise. It is essential to the enterprise. I was determined to deal in good faith, and in a fair and open-minded way. "What I would like to do is say there is no nuclear option in this Congress," I said on the floor one day, "and then move forward." Give us a chance to show that we're going to deal with these nominees in good faith and in the ordinary course. And if you don't think we are fair, you can always come back next Congress and try to invoke the nuclear option. Because it would take a miracle for us to retake the Senate next year.

Did I regret saying this? No. Because at the time I believed it, and so did everyone else.

And in any case, we had confirmed 204, or 95 percent, of Bush's judicial nominations. It was almost inconceivable to me that the Republicans would debilitate the Senate over seven judges. But the President's man, Karl Rove, was declaring that nothing short of 100 percent confirmation rate would be acceptable to the White House, as if it were his prerogative to simply eliminate the checks-and-balances function of the Senate. Meanwhile, we were at war, gas prices were spiking, and we were doing nothing about failing pensions, failing schools, and a debt-riven economy. Where was our sense of priorities?

I had been pressing Majority Leader Bill Frist in direct talks for a compromise—one in which Democrats prevented the confirmation of some objectionable judges and confirmed some that we didn't want to confirm, all in the interest of the long-term survival of the Senate. But I had been getting nowhere. Those talks had essentially ceased by the end of February. And then Senator Frist began advertising that he was aggressively rounding up votes to change the Senate rules, and Republican senators, some quite prominent, began to announce publicly that they supported the idea. Pete Domenici of New Mexico. Thad Cochran of Mississippi. Ted Stevens of Alaska. Orrin Hatch of Utah. I was so disappointed that they were willing to throw the Senate overboard to side with a man who, it was clear, was becoming one of the worst Presidents in our history. President Bush tried at any cost to increase the power of the executive branch, and had only disdain for the legislative branch. Throughout his first term, he basically ignored Congress, and could count on getting anything he wanted from the Republicans. But from senators who had been around for a while and had a sense of obligation to the institution, I found this capitulation stunningly shortsighted. It was clear to me that Frist wanted this confrontation, no matter the consequences.

And as the weeks and months passed, it dawned on me that Frist's intransigence was owed in no small part to the fact that he was running for President. Ending the filibuster so that extremist judges could be confirmed with ease had become a rallying cry for the Republican base, especially the religious right. In fact, Senator Frist would be the featured act at "Justice Sunday," a raucous meeting at a church in Louisville on the last Sunday in April that was billed as a rally to "Stop the Filibuster Against People of Faith."

This implied, of course, that the filibuster itself was somehow anti-Christian. I found this critique, which was becoming common in those circles, to be very strange, to say the least. Democratic opposition to a few of President Bush's nominees had nothing whatsoever to do with their private religious beliefs. But that did not stop James Dobson of Focus on the Family of accusing me of "judicial tyranny to people of faith."

"The future of democracy and ordered liberty actually depends on the outcome of this struggle," Dobson declared from the pulpit at Justice Sunday.

So the battle lines were drawn.

All the while, very quietly, a small group of senators had begun to talk about ways to avert the looming disaster.

Earlier in the year, Lamar Alexander, the Republican junior senator from Tennessee, had gone to the floor and given a speech that hadn't gotten much notice in which he had proposed a solution. Since under Senate rules a supermajority of sixty votes is required to end a filibuster, and the makeup of the Senate stood at fifty-five in the Republican caucus and forty-five in the Democratic, Alexander had suggested that if six Republicans would pledge not to vote to change Senate rules and six Democrats would pledge to never filibuster judicial nominees, then we could dodge this bullet. This would come to be known as "the Alexander solution."

Of course, this was an imperfect solution—if the minority, be it Democratic or Republican, pledged to never use the filibuster, then you were de facto killing the filibuster anyway and may as well change the rules. But Alexander's thinking was in the right direction. In fact, I had begun talking quietly to Republican senators one by one, canvassing to see if I could get to the magic number six as well, should Frist press a vote to change the rules. If he wanted to go that way, maybe we could win the vote outright, without having to forge a grand compromise.

I knew we had Lincoln Chafee of Rhode Island. So there was one. I thought we had the two Mainers, Olympia Snowe and Susan Collins. I thought we had a good shot at Mike DeWine of Ohio. We had a shot at Arlen Specter of Pennsylvania. Maybe Chuck Hagel of Nebraska. I knew we had a good shot at John Warner of Virginia. Warner, a former Marine and secretary of the Navy, was a man of high character. When Oliver North ran as a Republican against Senator Chuck Robb in 1994, Warner crossed party lines to campaign all over Virginia against North. I also felt that Bob Bennett of Utah would, at the end of the day, vote with us.

But these counts are very fluid and completely unreliable. It would be hard to get and keep six. We were preparing ourselves for a vote, but a vote would carry great risk.

As it turned out, Alexander's chief of staff was roommates with the chief of staff of the freshman Democratic senator from Arkansas, Mark Pryor. Pryor, whose father before him had served three terms in the Senate, had been worrying over a way to solve this thing. His chief of staff, a gravelly voiced guy from Smackover, Arkansas, named Bob Russell, got a copy of Alexander's speech from his roommate and gave it to Pryor. Alexander's idea of a bipartisan coalition got Pryor thinking, and he sought out the Tennessean and began a quiet conversation about it.

At the same time, Ben Nelson of Nebraska, one of the more conservative Democrats in the Senate, began having a similar conversation with Trent Lott. At some point they became aware of each other's efforts, and one day in late March, Pryor approached Nelson on the floor to compare notes.

Lott and Alexander would quickly drop out of any discussions. Such negotiations without Bill Frist's knowledge proved too awkward, particularly for Alexander, who was a fellow Tennessean. And even though there was antipathy between Lott and Frist over the leadership shake-up in 2002, Lott backed away as well.

But others were eager to talk.

Knowing what was at stake, John McCain and Lindsey Graham began meeting sub rosa with Pryor and Nelson. They would go to a new office each time, so as not to arouse suspicion. These four would form the nucleus of what would become the Gang of Fourteen, the group of seven Republicans and seven Democrats who would eventually bring the Senate back from the brink. Starting early on in their negotiations, Pryor and Nelson came to brief me on their talks, and I gave my quiet sanction to the enterprise. Senator Joe Lieberman came to me and said that he was going to drop out of the talks. I said, "Joe, stay, we might be able to get it done. It's a gamble. But stay and try to work something out."

Each meeting would be dedicated to some aspect of the problem, and there was a lot of back and forth about what would be the specific terminology that could trigger a filibuster. Someone, probably Pryor, suggested "extraordinary circumstances," and that's what the group would eventually settle on. What that meant is that to filibuster a judicial nominee, you'd have to have an articulable reason. And a good reason, not just fluff. Slowly, they were joined by others. Ben Nelson approached Robert Byrd to ask if he would join the effort. No one cares more about the Senate than Byrd, and he agreed, anything to preserve the rules. John Warner was the same way, and it may have been Warner's presence in the negotiations that would serve as the biggest rebuke to Frist. Ultimately, seven Republican senators would step away from their leader, in an unmistakable comment on his recklessness.

Meanwhile, the drumbeat for the nuclear option was intensifying in Washington, and was beginning to crowd out all else. James

Dobson said that the faithful were in their foxholes, with bullets whizzing overhead. In mid-March, Frist had promised to offer a compromise of some sort. A month later, nothing. In mid-April, I was with the President at a White House breakfast and took the opportunity to talk with him about it. "This nuclear option is very bad for the country, Mr. President," I said. "You shouldn't do this."

Bush protested his innocence. "I'm not involved in it at all," he said. "Not my deal." It may not have been the President's deal, but it was Karl Rove's deal.

A couple of days later, Dick Cheney spoke for the White House when he announced that the nuclear option was the way to go, and that he'd be honored to break a tie vote in the Senate when it was time to change the rules. The President had misled me and the Senate.

And that was the second time I called George Bush a liar.

The first time was over the nuclear waste repository located at Yucca Mountain, in my home state of Nevada. I have successfully opposed this facility with every fiber in me since I got to Washington, as it proposes to unsafely encase tons of radioactive waste in a geological feature that is too close to the water table, crossed by fault lines, unstable, and unsound. And Yucca Mountain posed a grave danger to the whole country, given that the waste—70,000 tons of the most poisonous substance known to man—would have to be transported over rail and road to the site from all over America, past our homes, schools, and churches. Not a good idea. President Bush committed to the people of Nevada that he was similarly opposed to Yucca Mountain, and would only allow it based on sound science. Within a few months of his election, and with a hundred scientific studies awaiting completion, Bush reversed himself. When one lies, one is a liar. I called him a liar then, and with his obvious duplicity

on the nuclear option revealed by the Vice President's pronouncement, I called the President a liar again.

I then met again with Mark Pryor and Ben Nelson. I knew that
they were trying to close a deal with the Gang of Fourteen. I was
afraid to tell them to stop, and afraid to go forward. But I patted
them on the back and off they went.

"Make a deal," I told them.

BY THIS TIME, Bill Frist had been in the Senate for a decade. An
affable man and a brilliant heart-lung transplant surgeon, he had
been two years into his second term when Majority Leader Trent
Lott had heralded Senator Strom Thurmond on his one hundredth
birthday in early December 2002 by saying that if Thurmond's
segregationist campaign for the presidency in 1948 had been successful, "we wouldn't have all these problems today." The uproar over
Lott's comments had wounded the Majority Leader, and just before
Christmas the White House had in effect ordered that Frist would
replace Lott and become the new Majority Leader, the first time in
Senate history that the President had chosen a Senate party leader.

As Majority Leader, Frist had almost no legislative experience,
and always seemed to me to be a little off balance and unsure of himself. For someone who came from a career at which he was consummate, this must have been frustrating. When I became Minority
Leader after the 2004 election, I obviously got to watch Frist from
a closer vantage point. My sense of his slight discomfort in the role
only deepened. In negotiations, he sometimes would not be able to
commit to a position until he went back to check with his caucus, as
if he was unsure of his own authority. Now, anyone in a leadership
position who must constantly balance the interests of several dozen

powerful people, as well as the interests of the country, can understand the challenges of such a balancing act. And to a certain extent, I was in sympathy with Frist. But my sympathy had limits. What Frist was doing in driving the nuclear-option train was extremely reckless, and betrayed no concern for the long-term welfare of the institution. There are senators who are institutionalists and there are senators who are not. Frist was not. He might not mind, or fully grasp, the damage that he was about to do just to gain short-term advantage. I reminded him: We are in the minority at the moment, but we won't always be. You will regret this if you do it.

By this time, the Senate was a swirl of activity. More senators were taking to the floor to declare themselves in support of the nuclear option or issue stern denunciations. Senator Byrd gave a very dramatic speech excoriating Frist for closely aligning his drive to the nuclear option with the religious right's drive to pack the judiciary. And he insisted that Frist remain on the floor to hear it. "My wife and I will soon be married, the Lord willing, in about sixteen or seventeen more days, sixty-eight years," Byrd said. "We were both put under the water in that old churchyard pool under the apple orchard in West Virginia, the old Missionary Baptist Church there. Both Erma and I went under the water. So I speak as a born-again Christian. You hear that term thrown around. I have never made a big whoop-de-do about being a born-again Christian, but I speak as a born-again Christian.

"*Hear me,* all you evangelicals out there! *Hear me!*"

Byrd was in his eighth term in the Senate, and before that had served three terms in the House. He has been in Congress about 25 percent of the time we have been a country. So his testimony carried great power.

Negotiations among the Gang of Fourteen continued feverishly.

Not even a panicked Capitol evacuation in early May could stop them. An unidentified plane had violated the airspace over Washington, and the Capitol had to be cleared in a hurry, but McCain, Pryor, and Nelson continued talking nonetheless.

Joe Lieberman of Connecticut came to me again, concerned. Talks had gotten down to specific judges, and the group was trying to hammer out a number that would be acceptable to confirm. Senator Lieberman was worried that our side might have been giving away too much, and that in his view the group was in danger of hatching a deal that would be unacceptable to Democrats. He wanted to drop out. I told him again that he couldn't. The future of the country could well depend on his participation.

"Joe, I need you there," I told him. "Help protect us."

ONCE THE EXISTENCE of the Gang of Fourteen became known, once a ferocious scrutiny became trained on them, the group started to feel an even more determined sense of mission. They realized that they were doing something crucial, and loyalty to party became less important than loyalty to the Senate and to the country, at least for a little while.

And until the day that a deal was struck, the Republican leader's office boasted that no such deal was possible.

As if to underscore this point, and see his game of chicken through to the end, Frist actually scheduled a vote to change Rule XXII of the Standing Rules of the Senate for May 24.

The Democratic senators came to see me and told me that they had completed a deal to stop the nuclear option. They had done it. I told Pryor, Nelson, and Salazar, "Let's hope it works." It did. And on the evening of May 23, 2005, the brave Gang of Fourteen, patriots all—Pryor of Arkansas, McCain of Arizona, Nelson of Nebraska, Graham of South Carolina, Salazar of Colorado, Warner of Virginia, Inouye of Hawaii, Snowe of Maine, Lieberman of Connecticut, Collins of Maine, Landrieu of Louisiana, DeWine of Ohio, Byrd of West Virginia, and Chafee of Rhode Island—signed a Memorandum of Understanding, in which they allowed for the consideration of three of the disputed judges, and tabled a couple more. Personally I found these judges unacceptable, but such is compromise. The deal that was struck was very similar to that which I had proposed to Bill Frist months before.

As Frist and I were just about to discuss the Gang of Fourteen deal before hordes of gathered press, Susan McCue, my chief of staff, pulled me aside and said, "Stop smiling so much. Don't gloat."

I didn't gloat, but I was indeed smiling. I couldn't help it.

IT HAD BEEN an eventful year as we headed into the summer of 2005. The August recess was going to be a welcome break, and I wanted to go home. I needed to see Searchlight, the desert, the mountains.

One night during the recess, Landra and I had had dinner in Boulder City and then drove back home, about thirty-five minutes. I wanted to catch a baseball game and I couldn't get the TV to work right, which happens frequently in Searchlight. I reached for something on the night table, and the next thing I knew I was on the floor. Landra came running to see what had happened. The pillows from the bed had softened my landing, and I was okay. But Landra was asking a lot of questions. As I climbed back into bed, she brought me an aspirin and some water. "I'm fine, nothing hurts," I said.

"Just take it," she insisted. "An aspirin can't hurt you."

I heard her making telephone calls in the next room, so I got out of bed. "Who are you calling at this hour?" I asked.

"Dr. Anwar wants you to come see him tonight."

I talked to Javaid Anwar, a longtime friend. I told him I was fine, and that I'd come see him in the morning. I heard a knock on the back door, and welcomed the Searchlight volunteer ambulance service. I assured them I was just fine and thanked them for coming, and told them I wasn't going anywhere. I was back in bed when there came another visitor, Brian McGinty, the head of my Capitol police detail. "How are you doing, Senator?" he asked. "Your wife's a little worried about you, and she thinks you should see the doctor tonight." I talked to two of my sons, Rory and Key, who had been called by Officer McGinty. My boys said they were coming to Searchlight.

"No," I said, relenting. "I'll just come up to Vegas."

Landra had outmaneuvered me and, reluctantly, I drove to town at 11:30 that night, where I would meet my two devoted friends, Ikram Khan and Javaid Anwar. Dr. Khan is a prominent surgeon and a member of the board of governors of the United States military medical schools, and Dr. Anwar is a well-known internist. We'd all been close friends for thirty years.

What I experienced is called a transient ischemic attack, or more colloquially, a "warning stroke," the doctors told me. It's a fleeting phenomenon, lasting just a few seconds, and it has no lasting effects. "Don't worry about it, sometimes these things just happen," the Sunrise Hospital neurologist said. But back in Washington, Admiral John Eisold, the Capitol physician, told me that to be safe I had better go see one of the foremost neurologists in the world, a doctor by the name of Thomas DeGraba. This was his area of specialty. Dr. DeGraba ran me through a battery of cognitive drills to test my memory, giving me a list of words or telling me a story and asking me to repeat everything back to him. He said, "I don't think things just happen. This had to happen for some reason. I'm going to try to find what it is." He put a heart monitor on me for twenty-four hours—nothing unusual. So he decided to put the monitor on for two weeks, and instructed me that if anything "feels funny" around my heart, I was to push a little button on the monitor and this would be transmitted to a facility in Maryland, which would record what was going on with my heart. After a couple of days, I did feel a few funny sensations—no pain, more that my heartbeat just jumped a little bit. Dr. DeGraba called me the next day and said, "I told you it was something that caused your problem. Things don't just happen. Once in a while, you have an arrhythmic heartbeat, where the beat is irregular." He said anytime that happens, it tends to pool blood at one of the lower parts of the heart, and when you pool blood, it tends to clot. "It just threw a small clot up into your brain," he said. He prescribed me some medicine to take care of it.

THE EXCITEMENT WAS OVER, and it was time to get back to work.

Just before Congress would reconvene after Labor Day, a disaster that many had predicted for decades befell New Orleans. The catastrophic Hurricane Katrina leveled a staggering swath of the Gulf Coast, killing more than a thousand in Louisiana and swamping the Big Easy, making the city uninhabitable in many areas and causing its population to have to disperse far and wide.

As images of misery spread around the world from New Orleans, the federal response was sluggish and incompetent in the extreme.

Many of us never thought we would live to see the day when tens of thousands of our fellow citizens would be left for nearly a week to fend for themselves without food, without water, and stranded on rooftops. But there it was. Under President Clinton, FEMA had been a well-oiled machine. And now this.

Katrina would come to be a defining moment for an administration so hidebound by ideology and so hardwired to distrust the role of government that it didn't understand what its job was in the face of catastrophe. It was also a moment of tragic clarity for the American people on the competence of their government.

As former House Speaker Newt Gingrich said at the time, "If we can't respond faster than this to an event we saw coming across the Gulf for days, then why do we think we're prepared to respond to a nuclear or biological attack?"

Of the disaster, President Bush would later say, "I wasn't satisfied with the federal response," as if the federal response were someone else's responsibility.

THAT FALL, a matter of some urgency for Democrats was getting to the bottom of the failure of our intelligence agencies in the run-up to the Iraq War. We simply had to learn how what we thought had been the case in Iraq had been so wrong. Our future security depended on our ability to learn from our mistakes.

The White House did not share our desire to learn what had happened and why, nor did its Republican enablers in the Congress. They were stonewalling us because they knew—as some of us were beginning to think—that the war was based on trumped-up evidence.

But it was simply objective fact that our intelligence agencies and the executive branch had given Congress information that was not true. Saddam Hussein did not have weapons of mass destruction or the capability to deploy them against American citizens. He certainly did not have the capacity to produce nuclear weapons, and we clearly know he had no connection to the horrific events of September 11, 2001.

Whether you support or oppose the war in Iraq, like or dislike President Bush, believe we should stay in Iraq indefinitely or pull out our troops right now, it was clear we needed to get to the bottom of our intelligence failures in the lead up to the war with Iraq, so that we might not repeat them in the future. This was not about placing blame or having heads roll, it was about ensuring that our most important policy decisions were based on hard facts. We cannot win the war on terrorism fighting blind. We must make sure that the deficiencies in our intelligence-gathering systems are corrected before we are forced to make any other decisions that might needlessly cost American lives and dollars.

The cost of bad intelligence is high. For more than two years, Jay Rockefeller of West Virginia, the top Democrat on the Intelligence Committee, had pressed the committee chairman, Pat Roberts of Kansas, to investigate the misuse of intelligence in advance of the war. An investigation had commenced but had not been completed. It was past time—long past time—for the so-called Phase II intelligence investigation to be completed. At each turn, promises were made and never fulfilled. These broken pledges simply reflected a lack of desire to do any oversight on the Bush administration, period.

It was extremely disheartening to me that the Senate had abdicated its Constitutional responsibility to perform oversight on the executive branch. No matter which party controls the White House, our federal government depends on the sunlight of oversight to ward off the corruption that unchecked power fosters. The founding fathers were very wise to give Congress this check on the executive branch. But the Republican Congress was asleep at the switch.

Senator Rockefeller had grown increasingly frustrated by the intransigence of the Republicans. By the middle of October, he was fed up. I went to Jay and asked him what I could do to help. The American people deserved answers from their government, and this Congress was not going to provide them. That much was plain. Rockefeller called me a few nights later and said, "I don't care what you do, but do something. This is a stall coming directly from the Vice President. Roberts takes his orders from Cheney every day."

The announcement that Special Prosecutor Patrick Fitzgerald would file charges against Vice President Cheney's Chief of Staff Scooter Libby for obstruction of justice in the Valerie Plame affair was the last straw. Scooter Libby was the first sitting White House staff member to be indicted in 130 years. These were serious charges, and the Libby indictment provided a window into how the administration manufactured and manipulated intelligence in order to sell the war in Iraq and attempted to destroy those who dared to challenge its actions.

We now know that within hours of the terrorist attacks on 9/11, senior Bush administration officials recognized that these attacks could be used as a pretext to invade Iraq, which had been a long-established goal of neoconservatives within the administration. In the months and years that followed the terrorist attacks, George Bush's cronies engaged in a pattern of manipulation of the facts and retribution against anyone who got in their way, as they made the case for attacking Iraq.

Playing upon the understandable fears of Americans after September 11, the White House raised the specter that, left unchecked, Saddam Hussein could soon attack America with nuclear weapons.

Obviously their nuclear claims were wholly inaccurate. Claims about Saddam's nuclear capabilities were false from the start, and were known to be false well before the invasion. The invasion of Iraq was the worst foreign policy blunder in our nation's history, but those falsehoods were even more troubling.

This sad story was repeated when the same people attempted to make a case linking Saddam to al Qaeda. Vice President Cheney told the American people, "We know he's out trying once again to produce nuclear weapons and we know he has a long-standing relationship with various terrorist groups, including the al Qaeda organization." Once again, this assertion was completely false and is discredited by the public record.

There was another pattern of behavior from the White House that I found abhorrent. Time and again it had attacked and discredited anyone who dared to raise questions about its preferred course.

For example, when Army Chief of Staff General Eric Shinseki said that several hundred thousand troops would be needed in Iraq, his military career came to an end. When the director of the National Economic Council, Larry Lindsey, suggested before the invasion that the cost of this war would approach $200 billion, his career in the administration came to an end (we are now at $800 billion and counting). When the UN chief weapons inspector, Hans Blix, challenged conclusions about Saddam's WMD capabilities, the administration pulled out his inspectors. When Nobel Prize winner and International Atomic Energy Agency head Mohamed ElBaradei raised questions about the White House's claims of Saddam's nuclear capabilities, the administration attempted to discredit him and remove him from his post. When ambassador Joe Wilson stated in a *New York Times* op-ed that there was no attempt by Saddam to acquire uranium from Niger, the administration, led by the Vice President, launched a vicious and coordinated campaign to demean and discredit him, going so far as to expose the fact that his wife worked as a covert CIA agent.

All the while, there was no Congressional oversight from the Republican Congress whatsoever. And we still had not gotten key questions answered: How did the Bush administration assemble its case for war against Iraq? Who did Bush administration officials listen to and whom did they ignore? How did senior administration officials manipulate or manufacture intelligence presented to the Congress and the American people? What was the role of the White House Iraq Group or WHIG, a group of senior White House officials tasked with marketing the war and taking down its critics?

It was time the Senate did its job and demanded answers.

On the evening of October 31, Dick Durbin of Illinois, Chuck Schumer of New York, and Debbie Stabenow of Michigan were in my office, and we were talking over the situation, when we decided to consider the dramatic step of taking the Senate into closed session to force the issue. Invoking Rule XXI is seldom done, and almost never without consulting the other side first. But in this case, if Bill Frist knew that we planned to force the majority to answer for its refusal to investigate disastrous prewar intelligence, he'd easily be able to prevent us from doing it. It was nighttime, and most of my staff had already left, but we reached Martin Paone in his car on the way home. Marty is the longtime secretary for the Democrats in the Senate, and is encyclopedic about rules and floor strategy. Having never invoked Rule XXI before, I asked him how it was done. Simple, he said. Make a motion and get a second, and the presiding officer is required to clear the gallery and close the session. Marty cautioned that the greatest consideration should be how it might affect my relationship with Bill Frist. Frist, he said, would be likely to regard it as a breach of etiquette.

Maybe. But Bill Frist had threatened the nuclear option. And he'd gone to South Dakota and campaigned against Tom Daschle. And then he had bragged about it afterward. Now *those* were breaches of etiquette. And it was just a fact that Frist and his caucus were more determined to cover for the administration than seek the truth about the needless war in Iraq.

We would invoke Rule XXI. The oversight process in the Senate would no longer be hijacked by the administration. The American people would get answers they deserved on why we got into the war in Iraq. It would take unprecedented action, but it had to be done.

The next morning, I spoke to the members of the Democratic leadership team. These days most political moments are choreographed events, planned and scripted, with people on each side of the aisle knowing exactly what the other is going to do. For this to work, it couldn't be one of those moments. So on the morning of November 1, only a handful of senators and staff knew what the day would bring.

I went about the day normally, including having lunch with the Democratic caucus. As much as it pained me, I simply could not tell them what I was about to do. When lunch ended, I stepped onto the Senate floor and began my speech on the failure of the Senate to investigate President Bush's and Vice President Cheney's intelligence failures. During the speech, I noticed the press gallery and staff sections filling out. Obviously, word was spreading that something was about to happen, because several Republican senators began hurrying to the floor, clustering in the back of the chamber.

Jon Kyl of Arizona tried to get the floor. "Would the senator yield?" he asked, over and over. I ignored him, and continued my speech.

Finally, the speech reached its culmination when I pounded my hand on the podium and said, "I demand on behalf of the American people that we understand why these investigations are not being conducted, and in accordance with Rule XXI, I now move the Senate go into closed session."

Dick Durbin sprang to his feet and seconded the motion. And with that, the sergeant at arms cleared the chamber. I knew the punch had landed. The results of the action speak for themselves. In the closed session, the Senate agreed that the Intelligence Committee would complete the Phase II investigation as soon as possible. Democrats had freed the committee, and a vital process that had been stalled for months was suddenly begun again.

Republicans were incredibly angry, Frist especially.

While the closed session was proceeding, Frist, steam coming out his ears, talked to the press outside. "About ten minutes ago or so, the United States Senate has been hijacked by the Democratic leadership!" he announced. Never, he said, have "I been slapped in the face with such an affront to the leadership of this grand institution!"

Huh. Now he was concerned with the grand institution? After what he had tried to do with the nuclear option?

When we struck our deal to restart the investigation and the Senate resumed regular session, someone told me of Frist's comment. And to be perfectly honest, the fact that he had taken this personally bothered me some. This had nothing to do with Bill Frist. This was about the Senate's Constitutional obligations. The more I considered this comment, the more irksome I found it to be.

As I spoke to the press, a reporter asked me about what Frist had said. I paused before answering.

"It's a slap in the face to the American people that this investigation has been stymied."

My anger began to rise, and I was in danger of giving back to Frist what he had given to me, when Chuck Schumer lightly touched me on the back. I stopped, and addressed my fellow senators in the leadership. "Do you, my colleagues, want to say anything?" I asked.

"You said it all," Schumer answered.

IT HAD BEEN a bitterly divisive year, and 2006 wouldn't be any better. As the midterm election came into focus, it became clear that this would not be a run-of-the-mill election, one in which you want your side to win "just because." This was an election to begin the rollback of the gross excesses of the administration of George W. Bush. This was an election to do nothing less than restore our Constitutional balance of powers.

# EIGHT

# THE BEST DAY, THE WORST DAY, AND THE MOB

I ONLY SPENT ONE TERM in the Nevada Assembly, and when I went up to Carson City they called me a liberal. I don't know why, exactly, as I've never been big on labels. Maybe it was because I was young and a lawyer from Las Vegas and I tried to do things that had never been done in Nevada before. I introduced the first antipollution legislation ever in the state, called for a cooling-off period when buying a handgun, tried to help consumers by having utilities pay interest on hookup deposits. I went after collection agencies, too.

And I helped fashion an abortion law. This was the late sixties, a world before *Roe v. Wade,* and I believed that if individual states didn't do something to define abortion in the law, then the Supreme Court would come in and take it away from us. And ultimately, of course, that's what happened. But at the time I was struggling with a number of other legislators to write a law in the State of Nevada— a law that would be upheld by the court—that under certain conditions would give a woman the right to have an abortion in the first trimester.

Being a legislator is a lot like being a lawyer. Both involve the art of compromise. Back then, those for and those against abortion dealt with each other in a civil manner; there was no name-calling, and no one was deemed more or less moral because of his views on abortion. I don't favor abortion and have never changed my position, but if it was going to be permitted in the state, then establishing standards for the procedure was just a matter of good law to me. Especially with the U.S. Supreme Court breathing down our necks. At this time, in 1969, both sides of the debate agreed that abortion should be handled like any other political issue. Oh, how times have changed. The animosity and mistrust that now surround the issue did not exist back then.

But even then, the bill was very controversial. At that time, there were forty Nevada assemblymen, and the vote was expected to be extremely close. Tensions were running high. We were in the cramped quarters on the old assembly side of the state capitol, and as the vote was being called, we heard a window open and the fire escape go crashing down. *What the hell's that?* Everyone turned to look. A legislator by the name of Brian Hafen, from Mesquite, wanted to avoid voting on the bill at any cost, so he went right out the window. The vote was suspended while the sergeant at arms was ordered to go find him. With the apprehended Hafen returned to the room and voting no, we ended in a 20–20 tie, and with a tie, the legislation fails.

If Nevada had had a decent law like the one we proposed—and if a number of other states had passed similar legislation—it's likely that the Supreme Court would not have gotten involved in the now never-ending abortion debate. Virtually every other country has handled the issue of abortion legislatively—not in the courts, as we in the United States have done.

My basic view on abortion has not changed. But later, in Congress, I would work very hard to maintain the trust of women, those with whom I work, and those advocacy groups on the outside. I would also remain on good terms with groups such as Planned Parenthood and the Feminist Majority because I've always been willing to talk and reason with them and they always know where I stand. With Olympia Snowe of Maine, I worked hard on legislation that compelled insurance companies to pay for prescription contraceptives. If those big insurance companies will pay for a vasectomy, or an abortion, or for a tubal ligation, or for Viagra, it's only logical that they pay for birth control pills. That bill passed and is now federal law. Senator Snowe and I felt that the central problem was unintended pregnancies, as half of those result in abortions. When Senator Hillary Clinton came to the Senate, she became a very strong voice on this subject as well.

But it was the controversial bill that drove Assemblyman Hafen out the window that day that marked my first exposure to the abortion issue.


MY TWO YEARS in the Nevada Assembly were terrific. It was there that Richard Bryan and I became inseparable. He and I were the only two freshmen in the legislature that term. Bryan later became a state senator, an attorney general, a two-term governor, and a two-term Unites States senator. We had taken the Nevada bar exam together in September 1963. Within a year or so, he, as a deputy DA, and I, as a court-appointed attorney, formally met for the first time, in a courtroom. He was prosecuting a young tough by the name of Clayton Sampson for burglary. Sampson had been a star football player at Las Vegas High School, and had been an Army paratrooper. He was charged with breaking into a warehouse, climbing through the roof, and dropping twenty feet to the floor to steal what he could find. But awaiting him when he hit the floor were police officers and a private detective, who shot him in the stomach. The defense I pursued for Sampson was that he had been set up—entrapped. A bartender by the name of John Long had been in cahoots with the cops and had set Clayton up for the crime. I proved it to the jury, and Sampson was acquitted.

Richard Bryan and I didn't see eye-to-eye on the Sampson case, but from then on we would be on the same side of things much more often than not. He and I became known as "the Gold Dust Twins." We were everywhere, and tried to do everything. In my one term in the assembly, I set the record for the number of bills introduced in one session. But on occasion maybe we tried to do too much. Once, Bryan and I introduced what we thought was a blockbuster piece of legislation, a bill dealing with firefighting. It flew through the assembly. We then marched to the senate side of the capitol to testify to the righteousness of our cause. The chairman of the senate committee was Bill Farr of Sparks, who was also the town's fire chief. We were addressing the committee as to the merits of the bill when Chairman Farr interrupted us and said, "This legislation is good. In fact, it's so good, we passed it last year."

Okay, so we were a little embarrassed.


I WAS AT CIRCUS CIRCUS HOTEL with my campaign manager Don Williams and Tom Wilson, a friend and newspaper reporter. Williams worked at the hotel, and we met to talk about my reelection. My first election to the assembly had turned out better than most people thought it would. I had run against nine incumbents, and had broken through and won. But now what should I do? Williams and Wilson were joking around and one of them said, "Why not run for lieutenant governor?" I didn't take it as a joke, and said, "Okay." Within five minutes I had decided I was going to buck the establishment and go for statewide office.

So I decided in 1970 to announce for lieutenant governor. I think the fact that my friend Mike O'Callaghan was running for governor made my decision easier. Lyndon Johnson had appointed Mike to be the regional director of the Office of Emergency Preparedness in 1964, and in 1966, Mike himself had gone for lieutenant governor and lost. In Nevada, the governor and lieutenant governor run separately, not as a team as they do in many states.

Well, nobody favored us to win, and Mike was running against the man who had beaten him in 1966, Ed Fike, who was a popular lieutenant governor. But we won anyway. At thirty, I was the youngest lieutenant governor in the country and the youngest in Nevada history. What an adventure it would be to serve side by side with Big Mike.

As lieutenant governor, I was involved in every decision of state government, and I was with Governor O'Callaghan virtually all the time. And Mike demanded a lot of me. In fact, one of the first and strangest assignments Mike gave me soon after settling into office was to go and find Howard Hughes. He was serious. And if I didn't find him, the reclusive billionaire would lose his Nevada gaming license. First, a little background.

By the 1970s, Vegas was a brand-new game. Corporate ownership and Wall Street capital had begun to replace the mobsters who ran the city's casino industry, and the challenge now was to assure new investors that Vegas was a safe place to do business. It wasn't easy. The city, little more than a stop on the Union-Pacific Railroad at the turn of the century with fewer than a thousand people, had literally been built by the mob—Bugsy Siegel, Moe Dalitz, Gus Greenbaum, Sidney Korshak, Johnny Rosselli, Moe Sedway, Meyer Lansky, to name only a few in the mobster's hall of fame who played a role in putting Las Vegas on the map. Because of their experience in running underworld gambling in other cities, gangsters were well versed in gaming, and they pounced on the opportunity to make easy money. Or steal it by skimming away the profits before they could be counted. The first casino on the Strip, the Pair-O-Dice, opened in the 1930s when the barren stretch of asphalt was known simply as the Los Angeles Highway. It was run by a close friend of Al Capone's and featured craps, roulette, blackjack, and hefty payoffs and kickbacks. The Pair-O-Dice was followed by Bugsy Siegel's notorious Flamingo hotel and casino. Siegel, who oversaw New York's Murder Inc. with Meyer Lansky, hoped to use his connections to the underworld and its control over construction firms to build a lavish casino resort like no other. "What you see here is nothing," he would boast. "In ten years, this'll be the biggest gambling center in the world." Siegel may have accurately predicted the future for Las Vegas, but he was in over his head at the Flamingo. The cost of the resort, originally estimated at $1.5 million, soon exploded to $6 million, and by the time it finally opened after numerous delays, Siegel's mob investors had had enough of his arrogant cowboy ways. He wouldn't live to see his prophecy fulfilled. Six months after opening the Flamingo, Siegel was found murdered, shot twice in the head in his Beverly Hills home.

After the Flamingo fiasco, organized crime didn't back away from Vegas. In fact, the real push would soon follow. In the coming years, its influence would metastasize throughout the gaming industry. When the Thunderbird found itself strapped for cash in 1948, unable to secure loans from legitimate banks who at the time still viewed gambling as a detestable vice, the mob's coffers provided the capital necessary to keep the casino afloat. Over the next decade, the mob invested in or took control of several major casinos—the Desert Inn, the Sands, the Dunes, the Stardust. Illegal bookies and criminals would soon flock to Vegas, in part because there was nowhere else to hide. As the federal government began a crackdown on illegal gambling with Senator Estes Kefauver's Special Committee on Organized Crime, the mob was forced out of nearly every other state in the country. Seeking safe haven, they turned to Nevada, the only state in the country with legalized gambling, and specifically to Las Vegas. By the 1960s, the Strip was teeming with mobsters, and it was an open secret that the city's dominant industry was thoroughly corrupt. That is, until Howard Hughes, the richest and perhaps strangest man in the world, boarded a night train for the desert on Thanksgiving Day in 1966 and changed the city forever.

Hughes didn't come to Vegas intending to buy anything. In his career, he never built anything, anywhere. He only bought. Flush with more than half a billion dollars in cash from his sale of Trans World Airlines, he was initially looking for a way to avoid paying taxes on the windfall by refusing to establish residency in any one state. He booked the entire top floor of the Desert Inn and didn't leave his room for ten days. When checkout time arrived, he wouldn't budge. The casino's management explained that they had promised the rooms to their high rollers (the *big* gamblers) over the New Year's holiday, but Hughes didn't care. He remained holed up in his room, stalling the owners for months. One of his associates had even placed a call to Teamsters boss Jimmy Hoffa asking him to intervene on Hughes's behalf; the Teamsters' state pension fund was one of the hotel's largest investors. Even that tactic didn't work. Running out of options and time, Hughes's accountants learned that if the billionaire invested his profits from the TWA sale in a casino, the money would be taxed at a significantly lower rate. The solutions to both Hughes's housing crisis and his tax bill were now perfectly clear: he would buy the Desert Inn.

Although he adamantly avoided the public eye, Hughes remained a national hero and the subject of extreme fascination, and his purchase of a famous Las Vegas landmark made headlines throughout the country. The state so welcomed the infusion of capital untainted by the mob's dirty fingerprints that laws were loosened to allow corporate ownership of casinos. Governor Paul Laxalt even waived the requirement for Hughes to personally appear before the Nevada Gaming Commission for his casino license. And the reclusive billionaire simply kept on buying. By 1972, he would add the Landmark, the Castaways, the Frontier, the Sands, and the Silver Slipper to his collection—every one a notoriously mob-infiltrated casino until Hughes bought them. The Landmark had been built and never opened. Hughes, from his hideout at the Desert Inn, instructed his agents to buy it because he hated to see it sitting there with its lights out. Soon, Hughes controlled a third of the city's gambling revenues and was the largest private employer in the entire state. He also owned 22,000 acres of raw land on the west side of Las Vegas. After Hughes died, this tract would become one of America's premier planned communities, called Summerlin. But the only improvement he ever made to the land when he was alive was a cheap wire fence to keep people out.

Soon after O'Callaghan was sworn in as governor in 1971, he deemed that no one was above the laws of Nevada, not even Howard Hughes. If Hughes wanted to maintain his state gaming license, he would have to appear before the Gaming Board.

But where was Hughes? By now he had decamped from the Desert Inn and, at last report, had fled the Intercontinental Hotel near Managua for another hotel in England after a powerful earthquake rocked Central America. Getting Hughes to agree to a sit-down seemed nearly impossible. He had not granted an interview in twenty years. He *had not been seen* in twenty years. Mike called me into his office. "You're just going to have to get Howard Hughes for me," he told me. He was dead serious. I had to arrange a meeting with a man who had refused to see *anyone* for two decades. Okay, I would do it!

Finding Hughes in Europe, I realized, meant tracking down his Mormons in America. In the depths of his eccentricities, he had surrounded himself with a cadre of loyal employees known as the "Mormon mafia." Hughes felt that because of their devout faith, they were the only people he could trust, and so they became the only people he allowed near him. The half-dozen Mormons—and one Roman Catholic—would feed him, administer his drugs, cater to his every whim, and carry out his business affairs, working around the clock and then taking short, frequent trips back to their homes in the United States. Bob Maheu, who at one time ran Hughes's Nevada operations, had never seen his boss, and he had never spoken to him either. All business with Hughes was conducted through the Mormon mafia. In all, it took me three months—several trips to Southern California to meet with his one-time chauffeur, William Gay, who oversaw Hughes's operation, another to Cedar City, Utah, to explain to his former barber that the governor was dead set on revoking his gaming license unless Hughes met with him—and weeks of dizzying back-and-forth to iron out all of Hughes's terms and conditions.

Finally, in early 1973, Hughes, through his Mormon handlers, agreed to a one-hour meeting with Mike and the chairman of the Nevada Gaming Control Board, Phil Hannifin, in a hotel room in London on St. Patrick's Day.

I never saw Howard Hughes face-to-face. With the governor out of the country, I stayed behind in Nevada to run the state. (Leonardo DiCaprio's portrayal of Hughes in *The Aviator* was as close as I would ever come to meeting the recluse in person.) When the governor returned to Nevada, he told me that Hughes had looked emaciated, with sunken eyes, free-range fingernails, and a mop of long, stringy hair. Mike and I agreed that we would never speak publicly of his weirdness, and we never did. When he died in 1976, Hughes was an addled corpse with hypodermic needles broken off in his arms.

But both Hannifin and O'Callaghan said that the man who lived in such severe isolation had pulled himself together for the meeting. Hughes spoke hesitantly, unpracticed in conversation after spending so many years alone. But he was lucid, his mind still sharp, and he could speak at length about Nevada and his holdings in Las Vegas. The governor told Hughes that he would be allowed to retain his gaming license.

The hour had passed, and with business finished, Mike wished Howard Hughes good day and good luck.

JUNE 22, 1972, dawned a very good day for me. In fact, one of the best mornings of my life. I was going to Caesars Palace to hang out with Muhammad Ali, who was in Vegas to fight Jerry Quarry. Ali! Not bad for a kid from Searchlight, I was thinking. Risking pride, I have to say that I was feeling pretty good about things. I was thirty-two years old. Wonderful family. Second-highest elective office in the state of Nevada. And now I was going to meet the Greatest of All Time.

Ali was making a comeback. It had been a little more than a year since his stunning loss to Joe Frazier in Madison Square Garden, the spectacularly epic battle that had come to be known as the Fight of the Century. Ali had been hoping to storm back from the defeat, but in his previous two fights he'd gone twenty-seven rounds without scoring a single knockdown. Many fight watchers were starting to ask if, at the age of thirty, the great Muhammad Ali was past his prime. He seemed slower in the ring, his punches and combinations lacking the speed and power necessary to go hit-for-hit with someone like Frazier or a young George Foreman, the 1968 Olympic champion and one of the most ferocious fighters ever. But his mouth was working better than ever.

And now Ali was pitted against Quarry, ranked alternately as the third or fourth contender for the heavyweight crown, in a twelve-rounder. Ali had previously squared off against Quarry in 1970 and had beaten him, but it was hardly convincing. Returning to the ring for the first time after a three-and-a-half-year suspension following his conviction for draft evasion and his impassioned denouncements of the Vietnam War, Ali found himself evenly matched until Quarry, a notorious bleeder, suffered a severe cut over his eye and failed to answer the bell for the fourth round. But Quarry was a quick and powerful counterpuncher, and some felt that if only he could find a way to keep his skin intact, he might be able to wear Ali down and take him.

Not that the Greatest was showing any fear. For several days, he trained at Caesars before a capacity crowd that paid to watch the former champion skip rope, work the heavy bag, and jaw with reporters and spectators. Another fight was scheduled for the same night at the Convention Center, Bob Foster versus Mike Quarry for the light-heavyweight crown, but Ali was the main event. For the first time in boxing history, a world-championship match served as the undercard.

The fights were promoted by Don King, who dubbed the evening "The Soul Brothers versus the Quarry Brothers."

I got there just before 10 to watch Ali work out.

We met in an anteroom and sat on a couch and talked for about ninety minutes. He was very relaxed, cordial. There had been concerns about his conditioning after the Frazier fight, but he looked to be in peak condition now. Someone had told him that I had judged some fights in Vegas and done a little boxing, and he was very indulgent with me. I asked him about his workouts and diet and what his routines were before and after a fight. I was like a kid. I couldn't get enough. "When I have to train, I can't eat what I want," Ali said, "so after a fight, I get all the French fries, cheeseburgers, and milkshakes I want. I'm hungry right now."

After a while, he came to his feet and said, "I've got to go work out now." He explained that he was about to start carrying on—time to go be Muhammad Ali—and that I shouldn't take it too seriously. "I'm fighting some white guy," he said. And true to his word, he promptly kicked the door and went out and started yelling and taunting.

Five days later, for the first time in years, the world would witness the return of Ali in all his awesome power. Although he would toy with Quarry for the first few rounds—shouting, *"Ain't this a easy way to make a livin'?"* to the press row between rounds—he would stalk Quarry in earnest in the sixth with a series of rhythmic jabs and fierce uppercuts. Suddenly, the beautifully fluid hitter, the man who dominated the boxing world in the 1960s with uncommon grace and frightening power, reappeared. As the bell sounded for the next round, Ali charged hard across the ring and trapped Quarry in his own corner. He then unleashed two impossibly vicious right uppercuts that snapped Quarry's skull clear backward and sent his limp body to the ropes. The referee would immediately end the fight.

. . .

WHAT A MORNING!

It would definitely be hard to beat that one.

But now I had work to do. It was close to noon when I got back to my office just off Las Vegas Boulevard. Just inside the door of my office was a little window with a receptionist sitting inside. She looked at me. "Your mother's on the phone," Joni said. So I walked into the first office that was open and picked up the phone.

"Hello?"

I could tell her voice was ragged before she spoke. "Your pop shot himself," my mother said.

You can count on one finger the times in your life you'll hear something so brutal as that.

She was crying and alone in Searchlight.

"Who is with you?" I asked her. "I'm leaving right now, Mother."

I called my brothers Larry and Dale and told them to come quick. It would take my brother Don longer to get home, as he lived in Southern California.

I've driven from Las Vegas to Searchlight more times than I can count. This time I don't much remember. Something automatic seemed to take over.

I got out there, and there lay my dad, still on his bed, his troubles over. Nothing had been touched. The gun and the blood were still there.

The local coroner had come. Gordon Colton was his name. His grandfather, Frederick Colton, had founded the Duplex Mine, which made Searchlight a town. Gordon was a wonderful man, a former Los Angeles Ram football player who had returned home after his playing days. He had consoled my mother until I had a chance to get there. We waited for the officials to come from Las Vegas, and then I did what I could to get my mother out of the house. With her taken care of, my brothers and I waited there until the body of my namesake was transferred to the funeral home in Las Vegas.

As a younger man, my dad had put his initials, H.R., every place in Searchlight. Down in the mines with his carbide light, he would burn HR on timbers, on rock outcroppings, on mine buckets, on everything. Aboveground, he did the same. The cement foundation for a big hoist at one of the mines bore his initials. It was the same at the Searchlight Cemetery, an unusual piece of land dating back to the earliest days of the town, where my father had dug many of the graves into the hard ground, occasionally needing to use a few sticks of dynamite. As we prepared his grave, we found a large rock that he had marked. On it was manfully scratched "HR," with the letters run together. It's as permanent a mark as a man can make for himself on this earth. It won't be washed off by the rain. It won't be faded by the sun. It won't be diminished by time. It says: I was here.

This rock would become his gravestone.

I made it back to Las Vegas in the early evening of June 22, 1972, the day that had started so well. And from simple inertia or some vague sense of duty or for some reason I will never remember, I made it back to my office.

A couple of good friends who were also colleagues, Jan Smith and Harriet Trudell, were there. They'd both worked in various capacities for Governor O'Callaghan and me, and we'd all become bonded over Las Vegas Democratic politics.

I walked in and first saw Jan, who had tears streaming.

"Don't say anything," I said. "Just put your arms around me."

. . .

IT WAS IMPOSSIBLE to comprehend. Impossible to process. And impossible to talk much about. I didn't. I couldn't. It hurt too much. And I felt somewhat ashamed. I would retreat to silence on the subject of my father's suicide for years afterward, until I realized that silence in these matters serves no purpose, and can actually cause great harm.

My dad shot himself, but why? Was it his deteriorating health? He had contracted what's called miner's consumption, but who knew if that condition was at all related to his despair? He was only fifty-seven. He was always reclusive. He was a binge drinker. He'd drink until there was no more money. I can remember him begging me for some of my hard-earned cash when I was just a boy, and he'd be hungover and in withdrawal, like an addict with no more heroin. I now have the language to understand that the alcohol masked a terrible depression. The last year of his life, he had been sober—no more masking his demons with alcohol. My brothers and I still joke that it was being sober that killed him. Admittedly, not much of a joke, but it made us smile. And his sobriety made us all so happy. But not our father.

I set about the task of getting his affairs in order. One thing was to get his insurance papers together for my mother. To file an insurance claim, she found herself in the strange position of having to prove that she had been married to my father. It was then that I found their certificate of marriage, and discovered that they had exchanged vows after both Larry and I already walked the earth. We'd been born out of wedlock! I was really surprised, smiled to myself, and I took the occasion to pick up the phone and call Larry.

"Hey, you little bastard," I said when he answered.

. . .

SLOWLY, LIFE RESUMED. And new life, as always, conquers death. Two months after my father died, Landra gave birth to our fourth baby and third boy, Josh.

And slowly, I began to get my head back into the business of the state.

Also requiring my attention, there was a significant new political opportunity just over the horizon. In 1974, Governor Mike had begun to make plans to run for the United States Senate seat being vacated by retiring senator Alan Bible. On the Republican side, Paul Laxalt, who had served one term as governor, was expected to jump into the race. And that cleared the way for me to run for governor of Nevada. If elected, I would be, at thirty-four, the youngest governor in Nevada history.

And that was very much the plan until just before the filing deadline, when Mike abruptly decided that he didn't want to go to Washington, and that he'd rather run for reelection. I had to quickly decide what to do. Mike said, "Run for reelection, and I'll resign before my term is over, and you'll become governor." Being O'Callaghan's lieutenant governor was hard. I had two full-time jobs, being lieutenant governor and being a lawyer. And Mike would call at all times of the day and night. It was because of him that I learned to use a phone in pitch darkness. Four more years of eighty-hour weeks was not looking good.

So I had my sights set on the Senate. I would run against Governor Laxalt for Senator Bible's open seat.

Nineteen seventy-four was shaping up to be a terrible year for Republicans. By August, of course, President Nixon would resign, and the Watergate class of newly elected Democratic congressmen and senators would be one of the largest in history. How could a Democrat lose in such an atmosphere? Well, I managed to find a way. My hot young pollster, Pat Caddell, told me in early October, "It's impossible for you to lose." I showed him.

My defeat in that overwhelmingly Democratic year can be traced to one crucial mistake that I made.

It is a cardinal rule of the practice of law that you don't ask a question in court to which you don't already know the answer. If the same rule applies to politics, I violated it flagrantly in 1974.

Paul Laxalt had been governor when Howard Hughes materialized in Las Vegas. Laxalt had relaxed the licensing requirements for Hughes, and I suspected that Hughes had in turn feathered Laxalt's nest. I made a real stink about it, insisting that Laxalt's whole family disclose their finances.

To my embarrassment, Laxalt complied. Why yes, he said, my sister the nun who has taken a vow of poverty would be more than happy to inventory her meager finances. It made me look bad, and it taught me another lesson: Go after your opponent as hard as you can. But leave his family out of it.

The margin that November was about 600 votes.

PAUL LAXALT would later joke that if I had gone to Hawaii after the primary and not campaigned at all, I would have been elected to the U.S. Senate that year.

Stung by the defeat, I quickly turned around and announced that I was running for mayor of Las Vegas in the following year's elections. My friends begged me not to. But my pride got in the way. Well, my pride and I got beaten again, and this time it wasn't very close.

From defeat, though, I learned that your enemies can become

your friends. Paul Laxalt and his entire family are today my friends. One of my confidantes is his daughter Michelle. His former staff— Sig Rogich, Wayne Pearson, Ed Allison, and Ace Robison—are now all very close to me. Pearson would later become my pollster. Rogich, who would go on to become an adviser to President Reagan and the leader of his ad-producing Tuesday Team, is now one of my best friends.

After I lost to Laxalt, lots of people told me it was for the better. At the time, it made me wince. But I've since learned they were right.

I WOKE THE DAY after the mayoral election a thirty-five-year-old has-been. I assumed that I was finished with political office.

And then, as had been the case so often in my life, Governor O'Callaghan extended a hand to me. The chairmanship of the Nevada Gaming Commission, the most important appointed position in the state, was soon to be vacant, and Mike wanted to appoint me.

Did I know what I was getting into as chairman of the Gaming Commission? The answer is no. I had no idea whatsoever.

In early 1977, I became head of the five-member body that regulates all gambling in the state. It would be a four-year term. I would be overseeing the industry that generates the vast majority of the revenue in the State of Nevada, and what I did know was that I was determined to do a good job. One of the first things the governor did was schedule a meeting with my predecessor, Pete Echeverria, to harvest Pete's insights into the commission's work. Pete was from Ely and was of Basque descent. He was a former butcher, and one finger was missing to prove it. He'd become one of a handful of Nevada lawyers who were world-class and was famous for his persuasiveness in court. We met at his home, a big, swanky house in Reno. Almost immediately, I noticed that Pete seemed very nervous. As soon as we sat down, he excused himself, got up, and walked over to the window. He spent several minutes looking outside. Eventually, he came back and sat down, but after a short while he was back up again and over by the window. Pete was visibly sweating. I didn't understand what was going on.

"See there?" he explained. "In the parked car? They're watching everything I do, Harry, following me everywhere I go."

I didn't know what to think. People tracking his every move? Who was he trying to impress? I left Pete's house that day thinking that he was paranoid.

But he wasn't paranoid. He was frightened.


BEFORE MY APPOINTMENT with Echeverria, I was completely naïve about the inner workings of Las Vegas casinos. I didn't have a flood of stories to tell about the nights I spent next to a roulette wheel or at the blackjack table. I couldn't recount a single one. I don't gamble, never have.

During my first week as chairman, a client of mine tried to help me learn more. Jerry May, who ran one of the largest public-relations firms in the state, asked me to lunch at the Las Vegas Country Club with a friend who knew the industry well—a great guy, May assured me, and someone I should know for sure. I accepted and thanked him.

The day of the lunch arrived, and in the morning I was catching up with Jay Brown, a longtime friend. I knew Jay from the time that he had worked as an associate at my firm, fresh out of law school, and he was now working for another lawyer in the same building as me.

Since we hadn't seen each other in a couple of weeks, Jay asked me to lunch. I told him that I already had plans.

"Who with?"

"Jerry May and Tony Spilotro."

"Spilotro?" A look of shock jolted Jay's face. "No, man. Tony Spilotro? Don't you know who this guy is?"

"No, Jay. I've never heard of him."

Jay knew practically everyone on the Strip. When Governor O'Callaghan was running for reelection, I recommended Jay be the campaign's finance chair, and he solicited contributions from the places where the money was: the casinos. Jay was by now representing gaming interests, loved to bet—football, horses, really anything—and was a man about town.

"Jeez, Harry, there's no way you can have lunch with Spilotro. No way. The guy's a *gangster*. Totally."

"He's what?"

"A gangster. Organized crime," Jay said firmly. "I'm *telling* you."

I came back to my desk, reached for the phone, and quickly canceled the lunch.

Why would Spilotro want to meet me?

And what had I gotten myself into?


THAT EXCHANGE set the tone for the next four years of my life, an intense, surreal time when it sometimes felt as if I'd wandered into some kind of terrible funhouse. I hadn't had any idea what the job entailed when Mike appointed me, but I would quickly learn that decisions we made and actions we took would mean the difference between Las Vegas fulfilling its potential as the city of the future or slipping back into its criminal past. And I would quickly realize that there was real danger involved in this job. Pete Echeverria had good reasons to be afraid.

Just a few months into the job, I received a call out of the blue from a man named Joe Daly. Daly had once run for the Nevada state assembly, but I had heard that he was now living in Southern California and selling funeral plots. He had earned a reputation throughout the state as a political junkie, a hanger-on. I didn't know him well, and frankly never felt comfortable around him. I had felt him to be untrustworthy. Just a hunch. From his phone call, I realized that this hadn't changed.

Daly told me that he was calling on behalf of two men, Jack Gordon and Sol Sayegh. At the time, Sayegh, an Israeli, owned a very large carpeting store in town, while Gordon was managing the wedding chapel, health spa, and photo-button concession stand at Circus Circus on the Strip. (Gordon would later gain notoriety as La Toya Jackson's husband and manager; after seven years of marriage, Jackson filed for divorce in 1996, accusing Gordon of beating her and forcing her to do things she didn't want to do, including dancing topless.) A few weeks before Daly's call, Gordon and Sayegh had tried to get approval for two gaming devices from the Nevada Gaming Control Board. Licensing for the coin-operated games, Flip-A-Winna and Penny Falls, was denied. The three-member board was concerned that the games were rigged in such a way that their players were bound to lose an inordinate amount of money. And the games were also deemed inappropriate, better suited for carnivals than for Nevada's casinos.

The board's decision could be appealed, however, with a unanimous vote by the Gaming Commission. The commission voted for reversal 4–1, with George Swartz as the sole dissenter.

Under Nevada law, the two games could not be reconsidered for licensing for an entire year, but apparently Gordon, Daly, and Sayegh couldn't wait. On the phone, Daly spoke mysteriously, at times incoherently, and it just didn't sound right to me. His tone of voice made me queasy.

When I got off the phone, I called my friend Jeff Silver, who was a member of the Gaming Control Board. I told him about the call. "Jeff, what should I do?"

The board decided that it was time to call the FBI. It seemed clear that Daly had just offered me a bribe. Incredible.

At around the same time, George Swartz's brother-in-law, County Commissioner Bob Broadbent, received a call from Daly as well. Daly told him that he would make it worth his and Swartz's while if they could reverse the commission's ruling. Broadbent put the phone down, turned to his secretary, and said, "I think someone just tried to bribe me."

The FBI then began intercepting the calls between me and Daly. And I was told to drag out the conversations as much as I could. As expected, Daly called back, again on behalf of Gordon and Sayegh.

DALY: They're sure if you keep looking you'll find a way
    you can get it back on the agenda. As you know,
    we're talking money.
REID: Oh, is that right?
DALY: The machines have got to have money.
REID: Well, what does that mean to me?
DALY: I don't even know what it meant to you in the
    past. I hope to see you run for something again. . . .
REID: As I understand what you're saying, you were
    sent by some people to say if I can figure out a way
    to get this thing on, then there's money in it.

DALY: If that's what you want, they want it. . . . You
   know what it's worth.
REID: No, I really don't.
DALY: I would say something around three.
REID: Three what?
DALY: Three thousand.

The next day, I received a call from Jack Gordon himself. The FBI
recorded every word.

GORDON: Hello. Harry?
REID: Yeah.
GORDON: Jack. Okay to come over now?
REID: No, Jack, I'm pretty busy. I've thought about, uh,
   what's, uh, the last . . . Daly's conversation. I think
   for what . . .
GORDON: Now look, whatever is right, Harry.
REID: Well, uh, what does that mean?
GORDON: Whatever. Whatever it . . . whatever it takes.
REID: Maybe about four times that.
GORDON: That's fine. No problem whatsoever.

And so it was on. Gordon and Sayegh were to come to my office
at Valley Bank Plaza at 5:30 in the afternoon with the twelve thousand dollars. The FBI would videotape everything. And when I gave
them the signal—saying, "Is this the money?"—federal agents would
rush into my office and arrest the two men. It seemed unbelievable
to me at the time that this was really happening.

Gordon and Sayegh arrived at my office right on schedule. I met
them with a female FBI agent who was posing as a member of my

staff. A special camera had been flown in from Detroit. It looked like an attaché case, and its lens covered the whole room. "As I understand, there are two things that are important," I told the men. "One is to get it back on the agenda and the second is to try and pick up another vote. Fair enough?"

The two men agreed and, with that, Gordon left the room. He returned a few minutes later and closed the door. Gordon then reached into his left front pants pocket, pulled out a fat envelope, and handed it to me. It was time to give the signal—"Is this the money?" I said— and now it was up to the federal agents to come in and do their work.

Except they didn't. Nothing happened. No agents. I waited a little longer, but still no FBI. But I could hear them trying to get in, and then I realized it: The FBI couldn't get in. Gordon had locked my office door when he had returned with the money.

I got pretty upset. And a little frightened. I couldn't believe they were trying to do this—and in my own office. I talked and beat around the bush for a few minutes, then I got up, trying to be nonchalant, and unlocked the door so that the FBI could come in and arrest these criminals. The agents rushed in, and then I lost my temper. How could they think they could do this to me? I was so angry that I went at Jack Gordon. "You son of a bitch, you tried to bribe me!" I lunged and got him in a choke hold. I was in a rage. The FBI agents had to pull me off of Gordon. And then it was over.

All three men were charged in federal court with conspiracy, interstate travel in aid of racketeering, and aiding and abetting in connection with an alleged bribe. At trial, Gordon and Daly defended their actions by saying they were simply laying a bribery trap—on me—and somehow neglected to inform federal authorities of their freelance crime-fighting hobby. The jury didn't buy a word of it, and Gordon and Daly were each sent to federal prison.

Sayegh's case was never brought to trial. After his indictment, his six-year-old son, Cary, disappeared while playing outside his school. The Sayeghs received a phone call later the same day demanding a half-million-dollar ransom for their son's safe return and were told to await another call with further instructions. That call never came. The bribery case was delayed, and the charges—with my permission—were eventually dropped. Cary Sayegh, last seen wearing a white T-shirt, brown pants, and brown tennis shoes, was never found. Sadly, to this day the case remains unsolved.

I felt sorry for the Sayegh family. Two years later, Las Vegas newspaper publisher Hank Greenspun called me. The conversation was strange. Hank told me that Sol Sayegh believed that I had arranged to have his boy kidnapped. Although most believed that a low-level crook by the name of Burgess did it, it didn't matter to Sayegh; he was now after me. So Hank arranged for me to be polygraphed about the kidnapping by the famous D.C. lawyer Ed Morgan. Afterward, he showed the test to the distraught father, and that was that.

This was the world that I was charged with policing.

These were a few of the characters I was facing. Organized crime was making one last beach landing in Las Vegas. It's no exaggeration to say that if they weren't repelled, the town would be ruined.

But things were about to get worse.

IF I HAD BEEN ignorant of who Tony Spilotro was when I first took over the Gaming Commission, I wouldn't be for long.

When Anthony Spilotro first arrived in the hot Vegas sun in early 1971, he had brought with him plenty of heat from federal authorities. By his early twenties, Spilotro had been arrested more than a dozen times in his hometown of Chicago. One of his nicknames was

"Icepick," because he had once murdered one of his hapless victims with an icepick to the head. His lawlessness was so pervasive that even during his honeymoon in Belgium, he was caught in possession of burglary tools and thrown out of the country.

Back in Chicago, Spilotro's criminal streak caught the attention of "Mad Sam" DeStefano, a major force in the mob's loan-sharking operations in Chicago and one of the most sadistic, brutal murderers in the history of American organized crime. According to federal investigators, Spilotro became Mad Sam's trusted enforcer, emulating his mentor when carrying out murders for the mob. Once, he put a victim's head in a vise and tightened it until the man's eye popped out of his skull.

In 1971, Spilotro appeared in Las Vegas, opening a gift shop at the Circus Circus casino under an assumed name. Soon, detectives on the Strip were confronted with a series of unsolved crimes, including murder victims who had been viciously tortured and casino employees buried in the desert. Icepick Tony had infiltrated the Metro Police Department. At least one cop was part of his gang.

If Spilotro took a break from his ruthlessness in Vegas, it was only because he was forced to. Arrested and brought back to Chicago to stand trial for the brutal murder of an informant, Spilotro saw to it that the prosecution's witnesses either disappeared or showed up dead. He was acquitted for lack of evidence, returned to Vegas, and got back to work: committing burglaries, fencing stolen goods, and murdering. According to a 1974 *Los Angeles Times* study, there were more gangland-style slayings committed in Las Vegas between the years 1971 and 1974—in other words, when Spilotro was in Vegas— than in the previous twenty-five years.

In 1975, the state Gaming Control Board learned that Spilotro had been working out of the Dunes casino. The board told the casino's owners to get rid of him. Spilotro left, but returned a few weeks later as if nothing had happened. The board now made a more formal request, summoning the Dunes' two owners to testify about Spilotro's continued presence. Both denied knowing anything about Spilotro's past. According to their testimony, they had simply assumed Spilotro was a good-hearted man extending low-interest loans to the casino's patrons. Their answers smacked of either sheer ignorance or blatant gamesmanship, but one thing was clear: Keeping Spilotro away from the gaming industry was critical to its integrity.

The Gaming Commission now moved toward its ultimate punishment: to ban Spilotro from ever setting foot in a casino again by adding his name to Nevada's List of Excluded Persons, more commonly known as the Black Book. Under the law, anyone could be placed in the Black Book: mob bosses, organized-crime associates, convicted felons, tax or gaming cheats, and anyone deemed to have "a notorious and unsavory reputation which would adversely affect public confidence and trust that the gaming industry is free from criminal or corruptive elements." The Black Book's first list, created in 1960, identified eleven men, including the boss of the Chicago Outfit, Sam Giancana. Effectively, it was the kiss of death in Vegas. Spilotro's addition to the Black Book was absolutely clear-cut.

No wonder he'd wanted to have lunch with me.

I learned about Spilotro in several ways—through the press, of course, and through law enforcement. But I had also come to represent an ex-con from Buffalo named Tony Domino, who had even become a friend. He had a big heart, and even though I suspected he had mob ties, there was nothing violent about him.

Domino came to my law office one day and explained that he had lent money to another hoodlum, and as was the practice among these types, his loan was secured by a deed of trust—a mortgage—on the guy's home. The loan was several years past due. "What should I do?" he asked me.

"Foreclose," I told him.

I started the foreclosure process, which takes about 120 days to complete. It was about day 115 when Domino called and said he had to see me. When he got to my office, he said, "Harry, stop everything."

"What are you talking about?" I said. "It's just a few more days, and you'll get your money or the home."

Domino shook his head. He said the guy had called him and said, "Meet me at Marie Callender's," a pie and sandwich spot.

"So I went there, sat down at his booth, and I realized another Tony was at the table," Domino said. "It was Tony Spilotro."

"Domino, you're not going to collect that debt," Spilotro said. "Do you understand?"

"I understand," Tony Domino said.

The debt was never collected.

The order to add Spilotro's name to the Black Book and seal his fate became final in 1978. As the new commission chairman, I was very gratified to put my signature to it.

IN NOVEMBER 1978, Joe Agosto, the entertainment director of the Tropicana Hotel and Casino, flew to Kansas City and met privately in a basement with Nick Civella. Civella had been identified more than twenty years before by the U.S. Senate Committee on Organized Crime as the boss of the Kansas City crime family. He and his brother Carl were in charge of drug trafficking, labor racketeering, prostitution, and sports betting, and controlled a large share of the company's mob business. Because Nick attended the ill-fated Apalachin Summit in 1957, when mob bosses convened in upstate New York to carve up the country for their illegal activities, investigators knew that Civella's interests extended far beyond Kansas City.

Kansas City? Mob? I had no idea. FBI agents listened in as Agosto explained in detail his actual responsibilities at the Tropicana Hotel. It was clear that he was running the place for the Mafia, overseeing a skimming operation that funneled at least $40,000 per month back to his underbosses in Kansas City.

The Agosto tapes came to light the following year, when a federal court in Kansas City released a 1,100-page FBI affidavit that included transcripts of the bugged meeting. But there were further allegations on the tapes. Speaking elliptically and using code names, Agosto told his bosses that he had a high-ranking gaming official—a "Mister Clean" or a "Mister Cleanface"—in his pay. "I gotta Cleanface in my pocket" is exactly how Agosto put it. In his conversations, he referred to virtually every Nevada politician. Bob Rose, the lieutenant governor, for example, was called "Flower" on the tapes. Agosto had nicknames for everybody.

The tapes put the state's entire gaming industry under a dark cloud of suspicion. Worse still, the FBI suspected that the Mister Cleanface that Agosto was referring to was me.

On the day the FBI affidavits were unsealed in Kansas City, I received a phone call in my office late in the afternoon. I did not recognize the caller's voice. "You're going out of your way to prosecute people," the voice said. "Remember the federal judge who got shot in the head. So you'd better be careful and have your cars checked before you start them. . . . You're going out on a table." The caller quickly hung up, and the line went dead.

The police deemed the call a very serious threat and immediately assigned protection for me. They also kept an eye on Landra and the kids. My family. Toddler Josh and baby Key now made five altogether. For a moment after I got off the phone, it felt like everything just stopped. It is one thing to put yourself in a threatening situation; to expose your wife and children to danger is quite another. I had never felt afraid, but I had to admit, this was scary. As the risks of this job dawned on me, I had tried to shield Landra from it. But it was impossible to keep things from her. She knows me far too well. We sat down that night and had a long talk. Did I really need this job? It took lots of time and paid only $500 a month. And now my integrity was being questioned. Maybe I should just quit.

I then went to Mike O'Callaghan's home, and laid out the whole deal to him. "Listen, and listen close," he told me. "You quit this job, and you'll regret it the rest of your life." Mike knew me better than anyone else, except Landra.

And so that was the last of that. I knew that I would have to see this through, no matter how hard it would get or how long it would take.

The following day, police officers saw my children off to school. From then on, police cars were around all the time. And my friend Gary Bates took up where the police left off, going on my morning run with me. Bates was also from Henderson, a few years younger than I was, and it turned out that Mike O'Callaghan had taught him to box, too. He showed up one day at the Boys Club, a short, pudgy kid with two black eyes whose mother had dropped him off, saying, "Gary needs to learn how to box." I had fights in college, but Gary had grown into a big man and become a professional boxer. A heavyweight, he fought all the good ones of the time. We came from similar backgrounds.

"Harry, I know your life was as screwed up as mine," he once told me. "Our lives are the same. This is a thread. That's raw, pure. I'm with you. I'm with you to the end."

And if I could help Gary, I would, too. As it happened, I had to help him out often when I was working as a lawyer.

By that time, he was living in Las Vegas and working at the casinos. One time I remember, he called me from the county jail after he'd been locked up for shooting the windows out of a car. I went down to see what was going on. "I didn't shoot nothing, Harry," he said. "I'm driving, and there's a guy who's giving me a hard time, so I roll down my window, reach under the seat, and throw a tire iron at him. I threw it so hard that it went in the window where the driver was, the guy ducked, and the tire iron goes clear over to the other window and breaks it. I know I'm in a lot of trouble, Harry, but I didn't shoot nothing."

Now, with my life threatened, I could do worse than have Gary Bates accompany me on my morning runs.

AFTER THE COMMISSION busted Spilotro to the Black Book, he moved on, setting up a jewelry shop called the Gold Rush that operated as a base for his continued illegal activities. It was located on Sahara Avenue, just off the Strip. FBI wiretaps revealed that Spilotro was maintaining regular contact with mobsters throughout the country and amassing a large cache of stolen goods and jewelry. During a search, investigators found handguns, $6,000 in cash, and a private investigator's report on Frank "Lefty" Rosenthal.

Spilotro was dangerous, but I found Rosenthal even more frightening. The two were a real study in contrasts. Spilotro was short, about 5´5˝, and he had piercing black eyes that all who saw them said were scary. He dressed modestly, usually slacks and a sport shirt. Rosenthal was tall and thin, and dressed expensively and immaculately. But his eyes were the same as Spilotro's.

While Spilotro had killed people, his pal Rosenthal inspired raw fear during his reign in Vegas. Both hailed from the Chicago streets, where for years Rosenthal ran one of the city's leading underground bookmaking operations until his name appeared on the Chicago Crime Commission's list of known gamblers. Rosenthal fled for

Miami. Called to testify in the United States Senate Judiciary Committee's investigation into organized crime and gambling, Rosenthal invoked the Fifth Amendment against self-incrimination thirty-five times, refusing even to say whether he was left-handed. When he returned to Miami, he was arrested by the FBI. The following year, he was indicted for attempting to bribe a college basketball player; he pleaded no contest, which in the law is saying, Okay, I'm guilty; I'm not going to make you prove it. After being questioned about a series of bombings involving local gamblers, Rosenthal had had enough: he left for Las Vegas and soon began working as an executive at the Stardust casino.

If you crossed Rosenthal, bad things tended to happen to you. In fact, Gary Bates tells the story of his friend, Johnny Hicks. Johnny's father Marion was one of the original mobbed-up Las Vegas investors, involved in several Strip properties, including the Thunderbird. Johnny was spoiled, and at age fifteen, he had a brand-new red Corvette convertible. He played hard, and he used a lot of cocaine. Bates and Hicks were pals and even had an apartment together.

Bates once had a girlfriend named Linda Christian, who was a showgirl at the Tropicana in the Folies Bergère show. She dressed backstage right next to another showgirl by the name of Geri McGee. Linda and Geri were chip hustlers—gambling chips—and they both made big money. They had regular clients and were well practiced at getting them to part with lots of chips. Once, Geri gave Johnny Hicks $65,000 in cash to invest in the stock market. Geri was under the misimpression that that was where he made his money. In fact, he never worked. Hicks invested the $65,000 in cocaine. He was a user, never a seller. For ten days, he treated the Strip to dope—whores, pimps, dealers, bosses, showgirls, everyone. Hicks had so much cocaine he didn't know what to do with it. Geri was a tad upset at Hicks. She was dating Lefty Rosenthal by this time, and they would soon be married. Hicks and Rosenthal got into a fistfight. And on Friday, January 13, 1977, it is said, Hicks slapped Rosenthal at the Tropicana. It would be about the last thing he ever did.

The next day, the *Las Vegas Sun* led with the blaring headline "Burst of Gunfire Kills Strip Gaming Heir." Hicks was shot five times in the head in the hallway of the apartment he shared with Bates.

No one was ever arrested or charged in Hicks's murder, and even though lots of people suspected Lefty, including his wife, Geri, he has always denied any involvement.

THE STARDUST, owned by Allen Glick and the Argent Corporation, was raising the suspicions of the Control Board. Within four years, Glick, a California lawyer with a Yul Brynner head of hair, had gained control of four Vegas casinos, borrowing more than $150 million from the Teamsters' state pension fund, which at the time was the largest privately controlled fund in the world. Glick's loan made him the fund's largest debtor. In the past, borrowers from the pension fund had been jailed on charges ranging from fraud to kickbacks. Allen Dorfman, appointed by Jimmy Hoffa to oversee the fund's management, was himself convicted in the early 1970s of accepting $55,000 in loan kickbacks and was sentenced to nine months in federal prison.

All of us, the Nevada gaming authorities and the feds, wanted to find out who was actually running the Argent properties, which included the Hacienda and the Stardust hotels. Why Glick? Was it because of his management skills? It appeared he had none. Or was it because he had connections?

· · ·

BY THIS TIME, I had built a small office building of my own at 328 South Fourth Street. And we were getting used to having to evacuate the offices because the bomb threats were becoming routine.

On one day like many during this time, one of the secretaries ran into my office as I was reviewing a file at my desk. "We have to clear the building, Mr. Reid. There's been another threat."

In all, I'd lost count of how many bomb scares we had received, but this was the second one in less than a month. We all filed out into the street and waited for the bomb squads to arrive. No cell phones then, so I went in search of a phone to call Landra.


"I KNOW THE SOB is connected, Harry, but we have no proof. I just don't have any proof."

Phil Hannifin, head of the Gaming Control Board, was briefing me on Allen Glick. The Control Board had previously ordered Glick to submit to a polygraph test and questioned him about his connections to the bad guys on the Teamsters' board, or his dealings with mob guys. He passed the test with ease. "He must have ice water in his veins," Hannifin said. "We all know he's a liar, but we can't prove it."

Before he was granted a gaming license, Glick was put through a rigorous background check. He came back Boy Scout clean: raised in middle-class Pittsburgh, attended Ohio State University and Western Reserve law school, Army captain, awarded a Bronze Star in Vietnam. But after he returned from the service, Glick's business dealings in Southern California appeared extraordinary. He was quickly and mysteriously given a 45 percent interest in a real estate firm, which led one board member to wonder, "Where did Santa Claus come from?"

Even though in Nevada a gaming license is considered a privilege, not a right, you still need some facts before you deny a license. Glick's finances seemed to be okay. His background was favorable. But things just didn't look right. It was the old cops' admonition, "JDLR." Still, Glick was granted an unlimited gaming license.

WITH LEFTY ROSENTHAL, the commission had all the proof it needed not only to prevent him from obtaining a gaming license but also to keep him as far away from a casino as possible. The man had been caught trying to fix basketball games, a textbook example of the "notorious and unsavory reputation" that the Black Book called for. But we also had a fight on our hands.

Before my term as chairman, the commission had determined that Lefty, who claimed merely to be the "food-and-beverage director" at the Stardust, was in fact a highly placed executive at the casino, and so was required to file for a gaming card. Lefty, who knew he wouldn't be granted one, maintained that he simply looked after the food and drink, and that the gambling regulators should leave him alone. He continued working at the casino, within easy reach of the house gambling winnings. But his lie was blatant and apparent, and his swagger was about to end. The Gaming Commission ordered him to leave all Argent properties immediately. Rosenthal appealed and challenged the constitutionality of the decision, taking the case to the Nevada Supreme Court, which quickly upheld Nevada's gaming laws and the commission's decision.

Undaunted, Rosenthal recast himself yet again as the Stardust's "entertainment director," a position that also did not require a gaming card. To further the ruse, he started his own talk show, which was broadcast on local television, a bizarre spectacle that featured guests like Frank Sinatra and O.J. Simpson, showgirls, Rosenthal's weekly sports picks, and his inscrutable harangues against the commission and Control Board. All the while, he was still overseeing the casino, flouting the law as he strutted past the Stardust's gaming tables in his loud suits.

And then Lefty got into the newspaper business. At the time, Las Vegas had three dailies. There was the *Las Vegas Review-Journal,* owned by Don Reynolds, who was known to his enemies and employees alike as "Mr. Piggy." Reynolds owned dozens of newspapers from Hawaii to Oklahoma to Washington State, as well as radio and television stations. He would direct the *Review-Journal* to print all the programming for his local NBC station in boldface type, and to print the listings for CBS and ABC in a light, hard-to-read type. He eventually lost his NBC station for various unethical practices. When he lost the license for the station, he blamed it on his son. So Mr. Piggy was a nice guy. (When Reynolds died in 1993, he left a huge estate. His foundation, run by his longtime employee Fred Smith, has been as generous as Reynolds was miserly.)

During my 1986 Senate race, Reynolds asked me to meet him at his home in Lake Tahoe. After a short visit with him and Smith, he said, "I hate labor unions. When I first bought the *Review-Journal,* the paper was on strike. The strikers would lay down in the road leading to the newspaper. Our drivers couldn't get through, so I drove a truck over a couple of them. It cost me a few bucks, but it was worth it."

The rivalry between Reynolds and Hank Greenspun of the *Las Vegas Sun* was bitter and enduring. Greenspun is a Nevada legend. He took on Joe McCarthy and won. He took on powerful Nevada sena-

tor Pat McCarran and won. He took on the powerful Strip hotel owners and won. He was everything Don Reynolds was not. But then all
of a sudden, out of nowhere, a weekly newspaper, the *North Las Vegas
Valley Times*, became a daily. It had a publisher who for years had worked
for the *Review-Journal* but had resigned because Don Reynolds had ordered his editorial board to endorse Howard Cannon for the United
States Senate. The new *Valley Times* editorials were biting and well
written. But slowly, strangely, the editorials morphed into advertise-
ments for the nefarious Lefty Rosenthal. Why? We wouldn't find out
until later, but Lefty had actually paid for the newspaper to go daily.
The *Valley Times* had become the mob's newspaper.

Well, we had had enough. Enough of his TV show and enough of
his editorials. It was time to put Lefty Rosenthal away for good and
into the Black Book. We ordered him to appear before the commission to formally announce his enrollment in the Nevada Book of
Excluded Persons. With such a tattoo, a person cannot set foot in a
casino, any casino, at any time. And the Black Book is forever.

As chairman, I conducted the meetings as they should be
conducted—not as ceremony but as business. This was no time or
place for pageantry, and no time for the Lefty Rosenthal show.

But not according to Lefty. He was anticipating a chance to turn
the commission's proceedings into a surreal carnival. He showed up
wearing a shockingly bright yellow suit matched with a yellow
porkpie hat. When he started in with a long diatribe, I cut him off
and moved for a vote. The commission ruled that Rosenthal's name
be added to the Black Book. Rosenthal went ballistic. Except inside
a boxing ring, I had never seen so much spit fly. After the meeting,
as I was walking to my car, Lefty showed up with a horde of news-
men and cameras. *"After all I've done for you!"* He was screaming, and
I couldn't make out much. He barked about previously meeting me.

I still am not sure why I felt compelled to stop and engage Lefty. I guess I just don't like to run from fights, but before the cameras, I explained that as lieutenant governor, I had lunch at the Stardust once, and Rosenthal was on the premises at the time, but what did that matter? Did he honestly think he could convince anyone that he and I had been conspiring for years based upon a tuna melt?

After his tirade, I got in my car. Lefty remained, screaming foul invective. But the Lefty Rosenthal show was over in Nevada.

THE DEATH THREATS seemed to come almost cyclically. Whenever my picture ran in one of the local newspapers, I could expect another series of bizarre letters or phone calls. The police questioned me after every incident, but they never arrested anyone. Maybe their list of suspects was too long. I kept my own list, which included only one name: Jack Gordon.

I had never received a single death threat before the bribery sting. After Gordon's arrest, the phone calls and threats started coming in droves. If this had been a serious, professional killer, I would have been dead by this time. But these threats were maddening, and it seemed that they could only be fueled by the same kind of madness.

I knew that Jack Gordon was crazy. Literally. He had begun to see a psychiatrist, a good friend of mine, a prominent Las Vegas doctor who, in an extraordinary act of candor, came to my home one day to talk about Gordon. He was violating doctor-patient confidentiality, no doubt about it, but he believed that it was more important for me to know what kind of a mind I was dealing with.

"Jack Gordon is a dangerous man," the psychiatrist warned me, "and he has a deep hatred for you. He will kill you if he can figure out a way to do it."

. . .

MEANWHILE, BECAUSE OF the "Cleanface" allegations, my life was being turned inside out and upside down.

In order to determine whether or not I was "mobbed up"—even now, nearly thirty years later, writing those words seems otherworldly to me—the Nevada Gaming Control Board hired two retired Texas Rangers to oversee an investigation that turned out to be the most thorough examination of any public official in Nevada history. First, they sought to find a paper trail and hired Elmer Fox & Co., a national accounting firm, to comb through all personal and professional transactions valued at more than $250 over the prior two years. Payments my law firm received, any expenses, where I bought my office and home furniture, how Landra paid for the groceries, any change in our total net worth, every business transaction, even my children's savings accounts were closely examined, dollar for dollar. At my request, I took and passed a polygraph test in which I was asked about financial payoffs, Joe Agosto, and my commission votes concerning the Tropicana. I had also learned that once Agosto's claim was heard on tape, the FBI was granted a court order to tap any phone calls I placed to certain Tropicana employees and representatives. After nearly three months of surveillance, the agents found that there were no calls to intercept.

The Control Board investigators conducted extensive interviews and took sworn statements from me and from more than a dozen other people. Since Agosto claimed to have channeled money to me directly—up to $10,000 a week—as well as through Jay Brown and his law partner Oscar Goodman, I had to explain and account for any personal contacts I had had with the three men over the years.

Did I know Joe Agosto? Of course I did. In Las Vegas at the time, it seemed everyone knew everyone. And I had represented his wife in their divorce. The divorce was not contested, and it was resolved rather quickly, because Agosto was reluctant to go to court. Once, after I was appointed to the Gaming Commission, Agosto came to my office with an attorney and told me that he was going to sue the commission because the commission had been mistreating him, and that I was personally out to get him.

My old friend Ron McAllister had conducted much of Joe Agosto's background check for the Gaming Board. I learned that the real Joe Agosto had been murdered in Sicily in 1953, and that the man who had tried to ruin me was actually named Vincenzo Pianetti. Pianetti had stolen Joe Agosto's identity and used it as his own. Pianetti/Agosto was a con man in Sicily. He had an easy, persuasive air about him. After coming to America, he had business interests across the West. But failure followed him wherever he went. He had owned a restaurant near Tacoma, Washington, called The Black Hand. It burned under very suspicious circumstances. In the 1950s, he had built a shopping center in West Las Vegas. It failed. How then did Agosto become the man at the luxurious Tropicana Hotel and Casino on the Strip?

He made his way in by buying the struggling Folies Bergère show from the owners in France. Through the topless showgirls, Agosto wound up with it all. Never up front, always behind the scenes. If the real owners needed infusions of cash, they went to Joe Agosto.

Del Gustafson was a premier banker from Minneapolis. He was well connected politically, and in fact had been a confidant of Vice President Hubert Humphrey's. But Gustafson came under the Agosto spell. He invested and became the front for more legitimate investors. Before it was over, Gustafson had lost his reputation and his arm in an "accident" at his lakeside cabin. He also lost his freedom, and spent years in prison for skimming and other fraudulent behavior at the Tropicana.

Mitzi Stauffer Briggs was heiress to the Stauffer Chemical fortune. Agosto found her at her swank home in the fashionable suburb of Hillsborough, just south of San Francisco, and persuaded her to go to Las Vegas with her fortune and invest it in the Tropicana. Well, she came to Vegas, and she never left. Relieved of most of her fortune, she is now working as a hostess at a cheap café in town. During his investigation, Ron McAllister interviewed her. She had asked him if he knew who she had had breakfast with that morning. "I can't guess," he said.

"The Virgin Mary," she answered.

Did I know Oscar Goodman? I did. After I went into private practice, Oscar Goodman's law office was one floor above mine in the National Bank Building, and we worked together on a few cases in which we represented codefendants. Through the years, we became friends.

After I became chairman of the Gaming Commission, Goodman had a great deal of problems related to various gaming clients, and I met with him frequently to discuss these issues. You see, Oscar had functionally become the mob's mouthpiece, representing Tony Spilotro, Lefty Rosenthal, and many others. Today, he's the mayor of Las Vegas—the "happiest mayor in the Universe."

Oscar has told the story of how he became the mob's lawyer to a select few. When he first came to Las Vegas to practice law, he left his smart and attractive wife, Carolyn, behind in Philadelphia while he found a home for them. Oscar worked for a slave driver, a very talented lawyer named Morton Galane. Galane had graduated from George Washington University law school as a patent lawyer, but came to Las Vegas and became a renowned trial lawyer, taking complex cases and often winning. In his first case to make history, he represented a Las Vegas orchestra leader by the name of Benny Short, who took on the Strip in an antitrust lawsuit. Galane relished taking on the big guys.

During his first few months in town, Oscar would work late and then take five dollars and go to the Hacienda Hotel on his way home to play 21. With his gift of gab, he soon became acquainted with the pit bosses. When one of the guys at the Hacienda was arrested and accused of having mob ties, one of the pit bosses asked Oscar if he'd take the case. Oscar had never taken a criminal case before. Not one. But he fumbled around and won the case. And this was Oscar's introduction to the Mafia. He became the champion not only for the Las Vegas connected but for all organized crime in America. His record of success has become legendary. And it all started with five-dollar bets on a game of chance.

Did I know Jay Brown? the investigators wanted to know. Jay was an old and dear friend, and our stories trace back to a time when I was in law school. Originally from Brooklyn, Jay was in school at USC when he and a friend drove up to Las Vegas for the night during spring break. They stayed out at the casinos till dawn and then decided to be tourists and drove out to the Hoover Dam for some sightseeing. Catching a nap in the passenger's seat on the drive back to Vegas, Jay didn't notice that his friend had fallen asleep, too, and their car veered off the road, crashing into a light pole at full speed. Both men were rushed to the nearest hospital, St. Rose de Lima in Henderson. Jay was admitted with contusions and lacerations and a jaw broken in three places. He would need more than one hundred stitches. His friend's injuries were far more serious. At the moment of impact, the steering wheel had slammed into his friend's chest cavity with such a force that it practically crushed every internal organ. The doctors could do nothing for him but administer painkillers and wait for him to die. Tending to the young man, one of the nurses noticed a mezuzah on his chest. What does one do for a dying Jew in Henderson, Nevada? The hospital personnel traced his parents to New York City. When they reached Mr. Brown, he asked, "Are there any Jewish families in Henderson?" The hospital gave him Landra's father's name, Earl Gould, and a phone number. Doc visited Jay in the hospital until the Browns arrived, and when they got to town, Doc and Ruth Gould put them up in their house while Jay recovered.

I was away at law school in Washington with Landra when my father-in-law wrote to us about his new friends, the Browns. The experience had touched him deeply. For three weeks, Jay lay in the hospital recovering from his injuries, and the Goulds visited him nearly every day. He would recover, graduate from USC on time, go to law school, and return to Vegas to clerk for Federal Judge Roger Foley for a year, and then he was hired by my law firm as an associate. I had not met him in person before then, but we became very good friends. In those years, he and his wife, Sharyn, would often socialize with Landra and me. Later, our children would all play together. Our two youngest children, Key and David, were born within a few days of each other at Sunrise Hospital in Las Vegas. They have been inseparable friends since. In 1974, Governor O'Callaghan was looking to hire a new finance chair, someone he could trust completely, and I recommended Jay for the job. He did stellar work, and it afforded him the opportunity to make contacts up and down the Strip. A year after the election, Jay left my law firm to work with Oscar Goodman. He expanded his clientele to include casino owners and executives, and he also frequently represented their employees in matters before the Gaming Commission. As chairman, I made sure to keep that aspect of our relationship strictly professional, as I did with all of my friends. But the Browns and Reids spent a lot of time together, and we still do. Just because I was gaming commissioner did not mean that I had to dissolve my friendships.

In Las Vegas, true friendship is all the more cherished. I remember one hearing where the Midnight Idol, Wayne Newton, was trying to get the Gaming Commission's approval to buy the Aladdin Hotel, and he was responding to allegations that he had ties to organized crime. (The charges had been reported by Brian Ross, then at NBC, and they were completely false; a jury would later award Newton $23 million in his libel suit against the network.) At this hearing, however, Newton was really getting grilled, and one commissioner demanded that he distance himself from one figure or another. "I won't," Newton said. "He's my friend. And, frankly, if I need to sacrifice my friends, I'm not sure I even want this license."

I didn't know Wayne Newton—other than as a fixture in Las Vegas for decades, performing since he was fifteen years old, and as a staunch Republican. But I had heard enough to conclude that he was being unfairly maligned. And, in truth, I felt the same way about my friends as he did about his. I stood up and told Newton that he had my vote, and he could count on any influence I might have with the other commissioners. Newton got his license.

In the years since that commission meeting, Wayne Newton and I have become true friends. I'd do anything for him, and he'd do anything for me. Which is not to say that he's changed his political stripes; he's still a conservative Republican. In fact, not long ago, Wayne appeared in negative ads against North Dakota's Democratic senators—Kent Conrad and Byron Dorgan—for not supporting a Constitutional amendment to ban flag burning. When Dorgan heard that Wayne was going to perform at a fundraising event for me in

Washington, D.C., he came to me with a message for Wayne. "Tell Wayne Newton to go eff himself," Dorgan said. I dutifully delivered Dorgan's message to Wayne, who got a hearty laugh out of it.

WORKING ON A FULL-TIME basis, the Cleanface investigators spent more than one thousand man-hours over five months reviewing every vote I cast as commissioner and interviewing my colleagues, clients, and friends to prepare a 77-page report for the Gaming Control Board chairman, Richard Bunker, who had replaced Hannifin. An outside accounting firm submitted all files related to my corporate and personal financial matters. Every rock they saw, they picked up and turned it over, twice. In February 1980, Bunker held an hour-long press conference to announce that the investigation had completely cleared me of any wrongdoing. But the ordeal had taken its toll. Terrible claims had been released by federal agents without a shred of substantiating evidence that created, in Bunker's words, "an aura of distrust." To me, the whole period was the worst time in my family's life.

WE ENDED UP running Glick out of town.

In 1978, after federal investigators determined that the Stardust was being skimmed of more than $2 million a year, we ordered Glick to sell all his Vegas holdings. Somehow, he was never prosecuted. Instead, he served as a witness for the government. Whether he was knowingly a front man for the mob or the most naïve businessman in the history of Nevada, I don't know. But I do have my suspicions, and they're pretty good.

Lefty stayed behind in Vegas until 1982, when his car was

bombed. Lucky for him the driver-side door was still open, and the blast threw him clear of the inferno. Shortly thereafter, his wife, Geri, died under suspicious circumstances in Southern California. Lefty now lives in Florida and fashions himself a gambling expert.

After his name was added to the Black Book and he was banned from ever setting foot in a casino again, Tony Spilotro sold drugs, slept with Lefty's wife, and started the notorious Hole in the Wall Gang, which was named for Spilotro's preferred method of robbery: in order to avoid a store's alarm system, Spilotro would simply blast his way through a wall with explosives. His brazen lawlessness, it turns out, was too much even for the mob, and he was beaten to death by the boys near Chicago in 1986 and then buried in an Indiana cornfield.

In 1995, the lives of all of these characters would be mythologized by Martin Scorsese in the movie *Casino,* which was all in good fun unless you're a stickler for the truth. I know from experience that the reality was completely different. I refused to see the movie, because the review I read said that Rosenthal had been turned into a good guy. Lefty Rosenthal, a good guy? That's no movie for me.

Steve Wynn also knew that reality was very different from the movies. And he should know. Wynn practically invented modern Las Vegas. More than anyone else, he has been at the center of the historic transformation of the town from seedy, mob-influenced back rooms to its current world-class status and its corporate boardrooms and 10-K annual reports. He transformed the Strip with lavish properties like the Mirage, Treasure Island, the Bellagio, and most recently, the Wynn Las Vegas on the site of the old Desert Inn. At the time, though, he was trying to run a legitimate business in the midst of all the thievery. And in Wynn's experience, as in mine, the mobsters weren't romantic figures:

"Spilotro, Lefty Rosenthal, and all those beauties had somehow gotten a grip on the Stardust, and they were there only to steal the money. I didn't understand how those imbeciles thought they could get away with it.

"I remember when the slot manager at the Stardust disappeared. Jay Vandersomething—never heard from since. We were talking about it up and down the Strip: What happened to the slot boss at that joint? People with children and a wife don't just vanish without saying anything unless they've been the victim of foul play. And the word on the street was that Spilotro had him done in, either because he did something or wouldn't do something, that he stole money or didn't want to steal, or maybe he threatened to go to the cops. We're sitting at a Nevada resort association meeting, and it's in all the papers: MISSING, FBI LOOKING. We're all cringing. What's next out of these subnormals? Shit, we'll get set back twenty years. We were borrowing money from banks, had Wall Street relationships—I was in business with Merrill Lynch—and now *this* happens? We could lose all our credibility at the hands of these morons."

Wynn has seen *Casino*. In fact, the few seconds of footage of the demolition of the Sands that is shown in the movie was shot by Wynn himself; he asked Scorsese to donate $25,000 to the United Way in return for the rights to use it. He also introduced Joe Pesci to Tony Spilotro's longtime attorney, Oscar Goodman, when Pesci was conducting research into his role. Oscar went on to serve as a technical adviser for the movie and even played himself in a brief cameo. As the movie was wrapping up, Oscar invited Wynn and his wife, Elaine, over to his house for dinner with the stars of *Casino*. "I had already read the script, because I wanted to see what the movie was about before I let them use my footage.of the Sands," Wynn says. But he felt that some of the characters in the movie didn't exactly jibe with his own recollections, and he wasn't going to be shy about letting the other dinner guests know it.

"At dinner, I was sitting across the table from Sharon Stone, Marty Scorsese was next to her, then Nick Pileggi, over here was Pesci and De Niro—De Niro was next to Sharon Stone on the other side. Elaine and I were on this side with Carolyn Goodman and Oscar. Marty Scorsese turns to me and says, "Did you read the script? What'd you think?"

"Well, I'll tell you the truth," Wynn said. "You made Rosenthal out to be something he isn't. He didn't know the first thing about gaming. But in this movie, he's a genius. He's got eyes in the back of his head, like in the movies where the casino guy is mean and cruel but smart, always omniscient. That's the stereotype of the casino manager—except Rosenthal was a moron. He had a head like a pigeon."

"Lefty Rosenthal was so dumb," Wynn told Scorsese, "that he couldn't spell 'it' if you spotted him the 't.'"

"Now I'm laughing, because they're all laughing," Wynn says. "And I'm talking to Marty Scorsese, who had asked the question, and I said, 'Who wrote that?'

"Nick Pileggi, the writer, says, 'Don't look at me,' and he points to Scorsese, who's sitting next to him. Scorsese goes like this, not me. He points at Sharon Stone, and she's already pointing at De Niro, because it turns out that De Niro wanted the part rewritten so he'd look smart. And says Bobby De Niro, '*Okay,* so I took a little license.'"

IN ADDITION to Steve Wynn, there were others back then who transformed Las Vegas, and I would be remiss if I didn't mention a couple.

I was born in Nevada. I can remember seeing people play the penny and nickel slots in Searchlight. Oh, how it has changed. The dollar slots came about because of one man: Si Redd.

Redd was from Mississippi, and I could never get enough of his stories. He bet on college games in Mississippi and around the country, mostly football. He would work every advantage, including sending somebody to the stadium on game day to see how wet the field was. He'd pay team managers a little something to get the skinny on how serious the players' injuries really were.

Well, in Vegas, no one thought Redd's dollar slot would ever work. Machines couldn't handle the big coins, and gamblers would never go for such a high-stakes slot. Redd disagreed. He told the first casino owner he pitched, "I'll build the arcade, I'll pay for the new machines, I'll bankroll the whole operation, and pay for the help. I'll keep forty percent, and you keep sixty percent." A deal was made, and dollar slots and Redd went everywhere. His company is now International Gaming Technologies, a multibillion-dollar company. Si Redd, the gambler from Mississippi, came to Las Vegas and changed the city forever.

Another innovator: Kirk Kerkorian, the son of Armenian immigrants, who came to Vegas in the late 1960s from Fresno, California. Bill Singleton, a partner at my first law firm, represented him. Kerkorian flew airplanes during World War II, and upon his return from the war started a small charter airline called Trans International. Because I had already started my political career, Singleton asked me if I knew Darwin Lamb, who was at the time chairman of the Clark County Commission. The Lamb family was powerful in Nevada. I did know him, and arranged a meeting between Singleton and Lamb on Kirk's behalf.

Bill got right to the point. "Kirk wants to pay five million cash for a piece of property near the Strip," he said. "And he doesn't want any licensing problems, because he wants to build the first hotel and casino off the Strip."

"If he's got five million cash, he should give the commissioners some consideration," Lamb replied. "They all have campaigns and other obligations."

"Kirk doesn't do business that way," Singleton snapped back.

We left the meeting.

When I got back to my office, Darwin Lamb called and said, "You misunderstood. It would be good to build a gambling establishment off the Strip."

Thus the International Hotel went up. It's now the Las Vegas Hilton. This was the start of something very good for Las Vegas. Kerkorian brought high finance to Las Vegas, and has been building and buying there for forty years now. MGM, Western Airlines, Chrysler, General Motors, and so many more ventures have made Kirk one of America's legendary businessmen.

He's now worth billions, but with the same down-to-earth attitude he had the first day I met him all those years ago. You'll find him paying for his dinners on the Strip, and when indulging in his favorite pastime, professional boxing, he buys his own ticket, at his own hotel. And he doesn't sit ringside, but several rows up. He doesn't want to attract attention. The "comp" is king in Las Vegas, but that's not Kirk Kerkorian.

One more visionary: It is legend that Circus Circus and Caesars Palace were the brainchild of a man named Jay Sarno. Sarno was sometimes crude, and a pathological gambler. I liked him, and he liked me, and it wasn't unusual for me to drop by his house for breakfast. I regret a few things I have done in the past, none more so than when Jay died. I had just been elected to Congress. Because of Jay's irascibility, he didn't have a lot of friends. His nineteen-year-old son called me and said that his father would have liked for me to speak at his funeral. I told the young man that I couldn't, because I was too busy.

If I have regretted my decision once, I have regretted it a thousand times. Who did I think I was to turn down such a request from a nineteen-year-old boy? I hope he reads this, and accepts my apology.

Las Vegas was built by characters like these. Benny Binion. Andy Tompkins. Sam Boyd. Mike Ensign. Jackie Gaughan. Each is a seismic figure. Each is worth his own book.


WITH GANGSTERS, investigations, extortions, smear campaigns, and constant death threats, there was never a time for me to catch my breath during the commission years, let alone relax. During the years of the late 1970s, Las Vegas had come to the dreaded realization that organized crime had remained very active there—indeed, outrageously active—and we took on the mob and helped rid Las Vegas of the influence of organized crime. There hadn't been much at stake, just the future of fabulous, famous Las Vegas and the economy of an entire state. At the same time, I'd learned that there were those who would stop at nothing to try to compromise a man's morals, or ruin his reputation, or even try to kill him. Or kill his family. What my wife and children endured during my time on the Gaming Commission has stayed with me through all these years and through all the places I've lived since. Whenever I hear people talk about how rough-and-tumble things can get in Washington, I remind myself of these years in Las Vegas. I will never forget them. Nor will my family.

My term was coming to an end. To my surprise, Governor Bob List had asked me to stay on as chairman to finish my four-year term. I was surprised by the offer, but flattered. Bob List was a dyed-in-the-wool Republican. He and I had often been on opposite sides, and we have remained political opposites, but personal friends. His request took political courage and showed class.

Appointees in Nevada almost always share the party affiliation of those who appoint them. I was honored that governors from two different parties had shown confidence in my service, but when the term ended, I was looking forward to a return to normal life with Landra and the kids.

But when you've made enemies, normal life can be hard to come by. We had two cars, one of them an Oldsmobile station wagon, which was good with five kids. I usually drove the other car to the office. It was late one afternoon that Landra called. She rarely called me at work, and this call was immediately something very different. Her voice was taut. "Whatever you do," she said, "don't start the car."

"Why?" I asked.

She had taken the station wagon to drive our son to a scout meeting. Our daughter, Lana, had been complaining for a few days that the station wagon was not running right, but she was a teenager, what did she know? In any case, we hadn't yet gotten around to taking it in for a check-up.

On the way home, Landra noticed that the engine was starting to lurch, then misfire. She didn't think too much of it, but then as she pulled into the driveway, she was suddenly struck by the memory of a dinner conversation from a few weeks before.

We were at a restaurant with George Swartz and his wife when he told us that he had recently noticed that his car was running strangely. He pulled into his driveway, shut off the engine, and went to check under the hood. It was there that he saw a coaxial cable at the battery, which had been wound back to the gas tank and rigged with a spark plug. A crudely constructed bomb—one spark in the fuel tank and the car explodes into a deadly inferno. But George was lucky. Whoever rigged his car hadn't grounded the wire properly, and the bomb failed to detonate. The police didn't know what to make of it, and neither did the Swartzes. It could have been someone just trying to scare them. It could have been anybody.

Back in our driveway, Landra remembered what George had told us. She turned off the engine and lifted the hood. A wire had been wound from the spark plug and then trailed off to somewhere out of sight. Then she opened the gas tank. The same wire. She ran straight into the house and called me. *Don't start your car!*

I don't think I can describe fully how terrifying the next few minutes were. My son was at a scout meeting. Was he safe? Where was Lana? I didn't even want to consider the fact that she had been behind the wheel of that car for days. The police were sent to gather our children and escort them home safely, and the bomb squad arrived to examine the station wagon. Apparently, the gas tank hadn't detonated because the tip of the spark plug had broken off, but it didn't matter. I came home that night to a family that had been living in terror for years, and it seemed now like it might be a permanent condition.

I will never forget the sight of Key, our youngest son, staring out onto the driveway from the bay window in the dining room. He just stood there, mesmerized by the flashing lights and all the craziness. And afraid. He wasn't yet six years old, but kids take everything in, and they understand.

A day or two after all of this went down and everyone suspected Jack Gordon was the culprit, my friend Gary Bates called and said he needed to see me, and I had to be alone. He came by and picked me up in his car. He had the radio on quite loud, because he didn't want anyone to be able to eavesdrop in case there was a bug. The threats enraged him, and he had an idea. "I've decided I'll kill Gordon," he told me. "I know how and where. And no one would ever suspect me. Gordon has far too many enemies. And I'm not one of them. Give me the word, and the bastard's gone in forty-eight hours."

Wow, I thought, this is loyalty. "No, Gary. Thanks, but forget about it," I said. "And let's hope nothing happens to him, because I would blame it on you."

My good friend had just told me that he would kill for me. And the thing is, he would have.

Thereafter, we would start our cars by remote control. Outside our home, a patrol car was stationed on lookout every night. In those weeks, I began carrying a gun with me wherever I went. I was told to never be caught defenseless. I even trained in evasive driving maneuvers, so that I might better throw off a pursuer. Carrying a gun became a habit, and I even dropped my revolver into my briefcase later for the trip to Washington. I had set my sights on Nevada's new Congressional seat, the first one granted to the state in 120 years, and I won election to the United States House of Representatives. The gun came with me.

# NINE

## THE PAST MEETS
## THE PRESENT

"Yes, the old Democrat, he is so old-fashioned that he
thinks politics is one of the honored professions."
—WILL ROGERS

"May your trails be crooked, winding, lonesome, dangerous,
leading to the most amazing view."
—EDWARD ABBEY

SO THIS IS WHERE, as the title of this chapter indicates, the stories come together. Where, as the gifted writer Elie Wiesel put it,
all the rivers run to the sea. It is mighty hard to do justice to something like a life in something like a book, but I have done my best
to put down what I thought most belonged here, and what I have
left out would fill several books more. But we're not done with this
one yet.

I didn't know it at the time, but my arrival in Washington was the
culmination of all else that I had done in my life, and brought me to
what I have come to think of as my life's work, work that is ongoing.
I don't mean that to sound immodest, because I am humbled by the
privilege daily. And to see each day as I travel to work the dome of

the United States Capitol, our nation's beacon of liberty, never fails to quicken my heart just a little.

And here I also don't mean to be comprehensive of my Congressional career, because it's probable that neither of us has the patience for that. And to be perfectly honest, an exhaustive nuts-and-bolts account of my time in the House and Senate has not been my purpose here. But I will say that since getting to Washington, I have had the privilege to participate and sometimes lead on a broad range of issues that matter to Nevada and to our country.

I have cared deeply about wilderness preservation, first in Nevada and then throughout the country, and have fought to preserve public lands and parks. I have worked to create Great Basin National Park, Nevada's only national park, and the Red Rock conservation area. My landmark legislation, called the Negotiated Settlement, stabilized Pyramid Lake, settled a hundred-year water war between California and Nevada, and preserved a vital part of the great American flyway, the Stillwater Marsh.

As a result of my annual Lake Tahoe Summit (which began ten years ago, with President Clinton, Vice President Gore, and seven cabinet secretaries in attendance), America's only alpine glacial lake is being saved. Walker Lake is on the road to recovery. In the whole world, there are only twenty-one desert terminus lakes. Only two are in the United States, and they are in Nevada—Pyramid Lake and Walker Lake. They were doomed until I focused attention on them. My legislation has also resulted in the creation of sixty-eight designated wilderness areas, 3.3 million acres in all.

I believe that Nevada can be the Saudi Arabia of geothermal energy, and other states of the West the Saudi Arabia of solar and wind energy, and I have worked hard to advance the cause of American energy independence by promoting the renewable energy sources of the future. How much clearer can it be that our country must achieve energy independence?

I have been involved in scores of bills that are now laws that affect more than just Nevada. My favorite was the legislation that I introduced with my maiden speech in the U.S. Senate. This bill led to the enactment of the Taxpayer Bill of Rights, which put the American taxpayers on a more equal footing with the tax collector, the IRS. Another law I passed affecting hundreds of thousands of people was the Source Tax, which prevented the unfair taxation of retirees.

As mentioned before, I took on the entire federal government and the energy industry to make sure that Yucca Mountain nuclear waste repository in Nevada never opens, because it is unsafe for my state and for America.

I have promoted women's health. When I came to Washington, research into illnesses that women face was virtually unknown, so I worked with Barbara Mikulski of Maryland to gain funding to establish the Office of Research on Women's Health at the National Institutes of Health.

I passed a law to ban female genital mutilation in America, and focused greater attention on the practice with the aim of eradicating it throughout the world.

To preserve our American heritage, I helped create the American Folklife Center at the Library of Congress.

Along the way, I have had some tough elections. I've even had to run against God Almighty himself. (This was actually the legal name of my primary challenger in 1992. I defeated him). And I have learned something about grace in defeat. In 1998, I had the electoral scare of my life when John Ensign came within a few hundred votes of beating me after a bruising campaign. A recount was dragging on until one evening in early December when Landra and I were out to dinner, and my phone rang. It was Ensign. "Senator, I want you to know I'm not going to continue the recount. You won. Congratulations." Ensign could have, out of spite, continued the expensive recount, filed lawsuits, and filed a contest before the U.S. Senate. But Ensign was far too decent.

And that was it. Tom Daschle had told everybody before the election that I was going to be the Democratic whip. And in the throes of a recount, that future hung in the balance. And then John Ensign called. Well, two years later, Ensign was elected to the other Senate seat from Nevada, succeeding Richard Bryan, and he and I have forged a very good relationship for our state. John Ensign is my friend. He and I, in spite of our different political philosophies, have set a tone and pattern of bipartisanship never seen before in Nevada and rarely seen in the U.S. Senate.

In March 2004, we lost Mike O'Callaghan when he suffered a heart attack at mass, which he attended daily. And on that day I lost my mentor, my sounding board, and the best friend a man could ever have. More than anyone I have known, he was exemplary in his honesty, his charity, his character, and his friendship. After I got to Washington, I'd talk to Mike at least once a week. He would say, "Just don't call during *Jeopardy.*" I knew I'd get the unvarnished truth as he saw it, and he didn't care if he hurt my feelings. Sometimes he'd say, "What the fuck are you doing?" Mike could have a foul mouth. "Are you crazy?" he'd sometimes say. He always told me how he felt, and I could trust him. He was my guy. He loved Israel, and he hated wiretaps and lie detectors with a passion, because he didn't feel that those measures should be the prerogatives of the states. And he supported a Constitutional amendment to ban flag burning. Out of love and regard for Mike, so have I, even though this is hardly one of the most pressing problems we face as a country. But then, I will never be able to pay adequate tribute to Governor O'Callaghan.

Nor will I ever be able to pay adequate tribute to my wife, Landra. She made it easy for me to be a father by being such a wonderful mother. And through our time in Washington, our five children grew to adulthood, and have graced us with sixteen grandchildren. All, I believe, inherited Landra's best traits and suffer not too much from my worst traits. All are proud of their Jewish heritage, and when they were growing up, we would celebrate both the Jewish and Christian holidays. All went to Brigham Young University. Lana became a teacher, starting at an inner-city school in Denver before moving to a job in the suburbs of Washington, D.C., before devoting herself full-time to raising her family. She has been a model oldest sibling and daughter, and is the kindest person I have ever known.

All four boys went to law school. Rory was an interesting kid. He played football and was very popular in high school, but he loved to stay home. When his friends would drop by and ask if Rory could go out, Rory would often say, "Tell them I can't go." He just liked to hang out with his family. He has made a life of public service for himself, and is now the elected chairman of the Clark County Commission. I have never had a better campaign worker than Rory. In 1998, my campaign was in disarray, and, even though he had an important full-time position as a corporate executive, he dropped everything to work on the campaign. Most of us believe Rory was the difference between winning and losing.

Leif is our most academically gifted. All five children were very bright. Leif, though, was truly precocious. His sister and brothers acknowledge Leif's brainpower and in fact often joke with him about it. He is the family encyclopedia. He thought nothing of joining in adult conversations when he was just a kid, and of assuming that he

knew more than we did. Often he was right. He is now an outstanding trial lawyer in Reno.

When Josh was in high school he had long hair, and sometimes
had it purple, sometimes blue, and sometimes streaked with both.
And when I say long, I mean really long. I didn't always like it, but
I never said anything to him, because that's the way he liked it, and
he wasn't hurting a soul. To complete the look, he'd dress himself at
the army surplus store. Josh is the comedian in the family. In the
early 1980s we had just moved to Washington and Landra and I had
some people over to our new home one evening for dinner. Just to
make conversation, I said, "Josh, what do you want to be when you
grow up?"

Without missing a beat, he said, "A proctologist."

I said, "What's your second choice?"

"Lawn maintenance," he said.

He was ten years old.

During the Gaming Commission days of threats and bombs, Josh
frightened the daylights out of me. One day, he wanted to be with his
dad. And so he secretly climbed into the backseat of my car, still in
his pajamas just before I left for work. I was on high alert those days
anyway, and as I was driving I sensed something was not right.
Someone else was in the car. In the rearview mirror, I saw a wisp of
brown, curly hair, and had a few seconds of terror before I realized
that those curls were just Josh and not one of the bad guys.

It was times like those that I wondered, Would Josh make it
through high school, to college? Or would he run a record store? Or
be a stand-up comedian? He did make it to college, and got his bach-
elor's at BYU, his master's at Yale, and his law degree from Arizona.

Josh is now an environmental lawyer in Utah and is a member of
the State Board of Regents.

Key, our youngest, was named for Key Pittman, who was a Nevada senator for twenty-seven years. Pittman, at the beginning of World War II, was a confidant to President Roosevelt, and was chairman of the Senate Foreign Relations Committee. From the time he was three years old, it was obvious that our son Key was a gifted athlete. He could do it all, and outplayed kids much older and bigger than he. At the University of Virginia, he started and played on three consecutive NCAA Division I national championship soccer teams, under the tutelage of coach Bruce Arena, and was teammates with great ball players, including the greatest player in the history of American soccer, Claudio Reyna. Key is now a lawyer and corporate executive in Las Vegas.

I recount these stories of our children because all of this happened while I was in politics. Rarely did I miss the family dinner, and I would always try to make it to the kids' games, and we'd always go to church together. But it was Landra who made a home for us and enabled our five children to fulfill their dreams and make lives for themselves, all while I continued to go to work, first in the House and then, after the election of 1986, in the Senate—work that became increasingly important to me and, I hope, to the country.

And sometimes the intersection of the personal and the political can be staggering.

In 1996, somewhat to my surprise, I began to work in the field of mental health and suicide prevention. In February of that year, Bill Cohen of Maine, who was chairman of the Aging Committee, convened a hearing in a wood-paneled committee room of the Dirksen Senate Office Building on the problem of depression among the elderly. Cohen believed that many older people were becoming stranded in nursing homes because they descended into depression that went untreated. This was inhumane—and from the government's perspective, very costly. Untreated mental disorders were costing us $30 billion a year in long-term care. With treatment, Cohen believed, 80 percent of those patients could lead reasonably healthy lives.

The star witness at the hearing was the legendary journalist Mike Wallace, the toughest of the tough at *60 Minutes,* who had come to talk about the depression that had nearly killed him.

"I was ashamed to acknowledge what was going on," he began.

It had started for him during the 1984 libel trial brought by General William Westmoreland against CBS for a story that Wallace had produced, and it continued to get worse even after the lawsuit was disposed of in Wallace's favor.

The depression had mounted a full assault on Wallace, and it had affected him physically. He would feel tingling and pain in his arms. He couldn't eat, couldn't sleep, couldn't think clearly, in fact would become completely disoriented. And over time, the depression became who he was, and nothing else mattered to him anymore. He could not bring himself to care about the things that had once been most important to him and that had defined him to the world.

Finally, as is typical in severe depression, Wallace began to think of killing himself.

He had been sleeping irregularly and taking sleeping pills and was behaving very strangely, and his wife Mary had become so concerned that at last she got her husband to check himself into the hospital. It was then that he was told for the first time that he had clinical depression, and that help was on the way. It would take time and effort to find the right medication, and he would need to spend time talking with a counselor, but he was going to be okay. "Anything. Anything," he said. "I'll do anything to get rid of this."

Wallace told the committee that he had been ashamed, that he had told himself, Come on, snap out of it! and that he had tried to hide his condition from everyone in his life. But then the time came when he simply could not hide it anymore. Treatment works, he told us, and he was living proof. Treatment saves lives and families.

Wallace's story hit me like a fist.

As he concluded his statement, I told Chairman Cohen that I had something I wanted to say. I set aside my prepared statement, and said, "Mr. Wallace, if you are brave enough to come before us today and tell the American people the remarkable story of your battle with depression, then I should tell the American people about my pop. My pop shot himself."

In the twenty-four years since my father's suicide, I had remained virtually silent on the subject, mentioning it to very few people. My colleagues didn't know. My legislative aide at the time on aging issues, Jerry Reed—who, in helping me prepare for the hearing had contacted the National Institute of Mental Health and the Centers for Disease Control to get the latest data on aging and depression, only to find that Nevada leads the nation in older adult suicide—didn't know either. Telling the story of my father's depression and death was liberating. I then turned back to Senator Cohen and requested that the committee sharpen its focus to further investigate senior suicide. He agreed without hesitation.

After that, I began to hear from Americans coast-to-coast who had suicide in their families, and not just senior suicide either. Remember, about 32,000 Americans kill themselves each year. From the profoundly moving testimony of these people, I became aware of the scale of the national problem. And it became clear to me that as a country, we needed to recognize that suicide was a national problem, and merited a national solution, and that any such solution required political will and a national strategy.

These hearings were just the beginning.

On May 6, 1997, I introduced Senate Resolution 84, which was a call to action on this killer, with cosponsors Mary Landrieu and John Breaux of Louisiana, Paul Coverdell of Georgia, Patty Murray of Washington, and Paul Wellstone of Minnesota. The resolution passed unanimously that day.

At that time, David Satcher was being confirmed as surgeon general. I asked, and he agreed, to make sure that suicide was regarded as a major public health problem during his tenure.

The next year, we convened a conference in Reno with hundreds of survivors and clinicians to conduct a review of the latest research and devise a national strategy. Out of the Reno Conference came the National Suicide Prevention Strategy, which was adopted in 2001. The strategy was meant to be a model and a blueprint for the states. Since then, all fifty states have adopted their own strategies, aided by the National Suicide Prevention Resource Center, which addresses the specific needs of each state.

In Washington, the best thing that we can do is solve problems that impede the greatness of America, and to make sure that the American people have the tools to fulfill their greatest potential. It is the unfettered potential of our countrymen and -women that renews us generation to generation. And as legislators with temporary stewardship over the leadership of the country, we must always give preference to future generations over our own. That is the story of America at its best. And as legislators, we must balance the needs of our states with the nation's needs, and public interests with private interests, and at the same time reconcile our sometimes very different ideas of government. It is a very important balance to strike, and a delicate one, and in my view it is a privilege to try to do so. As Will Rogers said at the top of this chapter, "Yes, the old Democrat, he is so old-fashioned that he thinks politics is one of the honored professions."

. . .

I HAVE SERVED with four presidents. Ronald Reagan was in the White House when I arrived in the Congress, and although I disagreed on some of his initiatives, I thought he was a good man. One of the biggest mistakes I made during that time was taking Mike O'Callaghan with me on a trip with a Congressional delegation to Central America. I was opposed to our funding the Contra war in Nicaragua (especially since, by then, it was illegal to fund the war), but Mike came away from the experience an ardent supporter of the Contras, and I never heard the end of it. After that trip, he traveled to Central America at least twenty times, each time taking money and supplies for widows, orphans, and amputees, as well as toys, bats, and gloves for the children. Around that time I was summoned to the White House to meet with President Reagan. This was my first visit to the Oval Office. President Reagan and Vice President Bush were there. With me were three other Democratic congressmen. Representative Paul Kanjorski of Pennsylvania said, "Mr. President, I am afraid you're going to invade Nicaragua."

President Reagan quickly answered, "I'm not going to invade Nicaragua, but I want those sons of bitches going to bed every night thinking that I'm going to." That was Reagan: brief and to the point.

I served with President George H.W. Bush, whom, as I said earlier, I found to be eminently decent, and as different as night and day from his oldest son.

Bill Clinton was like Rocky Balboa. He would be flat on his back, but simply would not stay down. At his lowest, he was at his best. History will mark his presidency as one of the best ever.

Alone among the presidents I have served with, George W. Bush will rank among the worst presidents—if not the worst—in the history of our country. He has been bad for America and for the world. And he will leave severe, long-term damage in his wake.

In addition to getting us entangled in a needless war, in the wrong country, under false pretenses, and in addition to giving up the fight against the true culprits of 9/11 to get us into that war, and in addition to compromising our moral standing in the world, the Bush administration's blithe disregard for the Constitution and for the balance of powers written therein has led us to have a government that sanctions torture and spies on its own people without cause. In perhaps the most troubling development of all, his government has devised a theory of executive power that is so thoroughly unconstitutional and so un-American that it may take years after Bush and Cheney are finally gone to fully expunge its effects from our national affairs. Here I speak of the so-called "unitary executive" theory espoused by this White House, which holds, essentially, in the immortal words of Richard Nixon, that if the President does it, that means it's not illegal.

President Bush has most directly signaled his literal disregard for the law by his use of presidential signing statements, hundreds of them, in which he has announced which features of laws duly passed by Congress—to which the rest of us are subject—he intends to ignore. It has been 320 years since King William of Orange, in a relatively bloodless affair now called the Glorious Revolution, agreed to govern with the assent of Parliament and submit the English monarchy to the laws it passed. And with that, the divine right of kings was dead. Or so we thought, until the new King George came along.

For that watershed moment in the history of constitutional democracy seems to have been missed by George W. Bush and Dick Cheney. They have done more than enough damage. And that is why we cannot be rid of them soon enough. As a country, we have faced greater threats to our survival with our ingeniously designed tripartite system of government intact. We beat the Nazis without junking our Constitution. We can, we will, and we must defeat the threat of Islamic terrorism without jettisoning our principles and turning them into mere memories.

THE DAY AFTER the 2006 election dawned gray and misty in Washington. The night before had gone late, with the Senate contests out West leaving us hanging until just before first light. At a suite at the Capitol Hill Hyatt, an election night had unfolded that was much different from the devastation of just two years before. It had long been anticipated that the Democrats would take back the House, and that Nancy Pelosi would become the first woman to be Speaker. I was very happy about this, because I found Pelosi to be an exemplary leader—tough, smart, and compassionate.

But while we thought we'd pick up seats in the Senate, few believed it possible that we'd take back the majority. Senator Schumer, who was head of the Democratic Senate Campaign Committee, and I thought it possible, but a long shot. In fact, we would have to run the table to take the Senate, and that's exactly what happened. With the exception of Harold Ford's close loss in a racially tinged election in Tennessee, and Jim Pederson's very close election in Arizona, Democrats won every close race in the country. It wasn't until I kissed the television as the networks called the Missouri race for Claire McCaskill that I thought we might just pull it off. But still, at 3 A.M., Chuck Schumer was hunched over a computer across the room, studying county-by-county results from the contest in Montana between Republican Conrad Burns and our candidate, rancher Jon Tester. A couple of counties were still out, and the race was extremely close. Schumer had run our campaign effort brilliantly, and we weren't going to sleep until we saw it through to the end.

"Anybody ever been to Gallatin County?" Schumer asked the room, staring at the screen. "Any Democrats in Gallatin County?"

Tester would win by sunup. And of course, it would be Jim Webb's great victory in Virginia, which would become final two days later, that sealed the result.

A few days after the election—the election that President Bush described as a "thumping" for Republicans—I met with the President at the White House. In spite of his word after the 2004 election that he wanted to work with the Congress, he had done no such thing. It is a myth that Bush has ever possessed the skills required for working in a bipartisan manner. In Washington, he'd never had to before the 2007 Congress, because the Republican Congress had always been a ready rubber stamp. And so now, in defeat, the President was in the unfamiliar position of straining for comity. Unpracticed at humility, Bush's appeal was not very convincing. "You're from the West. I'm from the West," he said to me. "We're both just two dudes from the West."

I hoped his overture was genuine this time. I would have stopped at nothing to meet him in the middle if he had followed through. But I'd seen this before and was dubious that he was sincere. And in any case, our life experiences as "two dudes from the West" could not have been more different. I never went to Kennebunkport as a kid. I never went anywhere. And I've got no blue blood in my veins, just some desert sand. So as he and I sat there in the Oval Office, I said little in return. I hadn't done as well as I had for Nevada in the House and Senate for more than two decades by being false, and I wasn't going to start now. Even if it meant a somewhat awkward moment with the President of the United States.

TEN

# THE FUTURE

"Fight the good fight . . ."

—1 TIMOTHY 6:12

NOT LONG AGO, my oldest granddaughter, Ryan, who was sixteen at the time, wrote this letter to Landra and me:

> Dear Grammy and Poppy,
>     I am currently working on a values project for personal progress in young women's class. I've completed all of my projects except faith and so I decided to ask close family members to write about an experience that helped shape their testimony about faith. It would be great if you could help me out! You can either write a letter back or email it to me. Have a great day!
> Love you guys,
> Ryan Reid

I wrote this back to Ryan in reply:

Dear Ryan,

From the time I was a little boy I wondered, why does the sun stay hot? Why doesn't it cool each day, each year?

I remember my father pointing in the starry Searchlight sky to the beautiful Milky Way. In my young mind I marveled at this spectacle. And I thought how many hundreds of stars made up the Milky Way.

Ryan, I even remember the first time you looked into the Searchlight sky and saw all the stars. Oh, did you stare with wonder.

I have since learned the Milky Way has not hundreds of stars in it, but rather, about 300 billion stars. I have additionally understood there are about 100 billion other galaxies in our universe, beyond our view.

We could fly to the moon by today's ordinary jet speed in twenty days, but to the sun it would take twenty-one years.

So, when as a young man I was taught the Gospel, I was convinced of God and soon developed a testimony of Jesus Christ.

It was through an understanding of the Plan of Salvation that I understood there was more to life than just me.

As Paul taught in the New Testament, "Now faith is the substance and or assurance of things hoped for, the evidence or demonstration of things not seen. Mortals must live by faith."

I have knowledge of God's existence and an understanding of His character. I believe faith can be nurtured—faith can be renewed by living the Golden Rule, study, including scriptures, and constant prayer.

As I proceed in life I agree with the old Jewish belief that in the struggle with evil, only faith matters.

My outlook on life—my faith—is best summarized by an inscription found in a Cologne, Germany, cellar where Jews hid from the Nazis which reads, "I believe in the sun even when it is not shining. I believe in love even when not feeling it. I believe in God even when He is silent."

That is what I wrote to my granddaughter not long ago, and it is what I believe. I do not talk much about religion in public, because that's not something I feel very comfortable doing, but I do live by a deep and abiding faith in God.

And I have what I can only describe as a comparable faith—a deep and abiding faith—in my country. Even when we go through dark periods, and our best may not seem much in evidence, I believe in America. Even though progress may at times seem hard to discern, we do tend to improve over time. From our standard of living to our life expectancy to our levels of education, we improve. We are as adaptable to change and as self-correcting as any society ever to have existed. But America doesn't just make itself. America requires work. And each of us remakes our country every day.

And we now find ourselves immersed in the greatest act of self-renewal that we have. It is through elections that we begin again. In a single day, we can change our national priorities and direction utterly, and overnight we can show a new face to the world.

I believe that the 2006 elections were a tremendous step forward. But one election is not enough to restore our country's equilibrium. That much is clear. In addition to taking back the White House in 2008, Democrats need to increase our numbers in the Senate as well, because in 2007, the Democrats in the Senate were in the sometimes strange position of being in the majority without having much of a functional majority at all. And it's hard to effect change without numbers.

Yes, technically, we held the advantage over the Republicans, 51 to 49, when you count Bernie Sanders of Vermont and Joe Lieberman of Connecticut, both independents who caucus with the Democrats. But on the issues related to the war in Iraq, Senator Lieberman did not side with the Democrats. I have nothing but the highest regard for Joe; we just disagree on this important issue. On other issues, he's always with me. And Tim Johnson of South Dakota was not able to serve for most of the year because he was recovering from the cerebral hemorrhage that he had suffered just before Christmas 2006. The call I received from Senator Johnson's chief of staff from the ambulance as it raced to the hospital was one I will not soon forget. For several days, we weren't sure Tim would survive. We had just won the majority in the Senate by the slimmest possible margin, and though I tried not to think of Tim's illness in terms of how it might upset that fragile state of affairs, of course I did. It seemed as if the entire country held its breath, and then, when it became apparent that Tim was out of the woods, we all breathed a sigh of relief. Because of the expert care he instantly received at George Washington University Medical Center, and because of the dedication of his family, Tim Johnson was able to return to the Senate last fall and is now running hard for reelection.

And then, of course, there is the top of the ticket. I am a loyal Democrat, and I very much want and expect to see a Democrat elected President. We have never had a better cast of candidates than in 2008—Biden, Clinton, Dodd, Edwards, Obama, Richardson, and Kucinich. And now, as I write this, it's down to Clinton and Obama, both of whom are extraordinary. I will work tirelessly to make sure that one of them reaches the White House.

But when I say with candor that whoever is elected President—from either party—will be an improvement over the last seven years, I mean it.

January 2009, the twenty-first century truly begins.

# ACKNOWLEDGMENTS

This effort began with the hard work and dogged research of Ari Rabin-Havt, and would have been impossible without Janice Shelton and Robin McCain in Washington, Marge Van Hoove, who runs my office in Las Vegas, and Mary Conelly, who does the same out of Reno.

My life would not be as rich, nor my memories as vivid, without all my friends from Basic High School in Henderson, Nevada.

And most especially, I would be nothing without the love of my wife, Landra, our five extraordinary children, Lana, Rory, Leif, Josh, and Key, and all of our beautiful grandchildren.

Mark Warren would like to thank:

First, my longtime friend and fellow Texan Paul Begala, without whom I never would have met Harry Reid. Next, Susan McCue, who trusted me with this story. Next, all of the extraordinary men and women who work or have worked for Senator Reid and kindly made time for me—Gary Myrick, Marty Paone, Richard Verma, Ron Weich, Jon Summers, David Meadvin, Jimmy Ryan, Jim Manley, Rey Martinez, Jerry Reed, Evan Wallach, Ari Rabin-Havt, Janice Shelton, Marge Van Hoove, Robin McCain, Darcell Savage, and Sarah Ferguson. Thank you to Senator Dick Durbin, and to former Senator Tom Daschle for your time and insight. Thank you Jim Messina from Senator Max Baucus's office, and Bob Russell from Senator Mark Pryor's. Thanks to Sandy Jolley, Harriet Trudell, Steve Wynn, Wayne Newton, Larry Reid, J. J. Balk, Gary Bates, and Don Wilson for opening your doors to me, and for your great Nevada hospitality.

Andrew Chaikivsky helped me to organize and research and edit this book. Without Andrew, it's hard to see how we would have finished at all. John Kenney gave this book crucial editing at crucial times. David Granger and Peter Griffin of *Esquire* are a couple of the finest guys I know, and were infinitely patient and supportive. As was the captain of this enterprise, editor Neil Nyren of Putnam. Heather Schroder of ICM believed in this book without hesitation. Thanks to Bill Bradley, Chris Furst, and Corey Sobel for transcribing. And to Jessie Wender for the expert photo research, and digital imaging guru Steve Fusco for working wonders with the oldest pictures.

My parents, James and Faye Warren, helped me constantly, and from the start. I could not have finished this project without my wonderful in-laws, Dieter and Christa Weigmann, who let me take over their house in Princeton and kept me fed and sane.

And most of all, I am grateful to my lovely wife, Jessica, and to my children, Zeke and Oona, for their boundless patience, good humor, and for their love.

Then and only then will we as a country truly set about the business of America again. Then and only then will we be able to pay attention to the myriad issues that have gone neglected thus far in this century. Then and only then will we pay serious attention to global climate change and pursue a foreign policy that will forge strong alliances, defeat the threat of Islamic terrorism, and make us safer at home and in the world. Then and only then will we restore independence to our Department of Justice. Then and only then will we return to fiscal sanity, rebuild the American infrastructure, and invest in our people once again.

Your family and my family are counting on it. From my oldest granddaughter, Ryan, whose letter you just read, to my youngest grandson, who is not yet three years old. His name? Harry Reid.